PROPAGANDA WARS

HOW THE GLOBAL ELITE CONTROL WHAT YOU SEE, THINK, AND FEEL

GLENN BECK

WITH JUSTIN HASKINS

CONTRIBUTOR
DONALD KENDAL

Forefront BOOKS

MERCURY INK

CONTENTS

ACKNOWLEDGMENTS

THE ONE NAME THAT MUST BE MENTIONED, ALONG WITH MY wife and children, the one who is truly responsible for any of the good I may have done in my life, is my most trusted friend and counselor. He saved my career, my family, and my life. He keeps me humble, awake, and gives me the encouragement needed to stand up and do the right thing, even in the darkest of times. All that I am and all that I have ever accomplished in my life, I owe to Him.

Thank you, Jesus Christ.

1

WELCOME TO CLOWN WORLD

Dr. DeLessio-Parson inhaled a deep breath of air, closed her eyes, and then briefly meditated on the importance of the moment. DeLessio-Parson, a respected sociologist, was about to walk into a lion's den, and she knew it. But if history has taught brave academics like her anything, it's that when life presents opportunities to speak your truth to power, you take them.[1]

The television studio's white lights shined brightly. A nervous sweat started to develop over her brow. Then, the silence broke.

"We're almost ready for you," a studio technician announced from behind a large camera. "Just a few minutes more."[2]

DeLessio-Parson adjusted the uncomfortable earpiece, handed to her just moments earlier. As she jammed it further into her ear, she could hear nothing but a slow, steady buzz. Then, abruptly, the voice of a television producer called out through the earpiece.

"Dr. DeLessio-Parson, thanks again for joining us," the producer said. "We're excited for you to be here. Could you please count to ten for us? We need to check your audio levels."

The young academic sighed and began to count. With each number, her thoughts raced faster. Soon, hundreds of thousands of people across the United States would hear her prophetic message. Not long thereafter, perhaps millions would know her name—and maybe, just maybe, see the world for what it *really* is.

Suddenly, the technician signaled that the interview was starting, and the voice of the television host rang out from DeLessio-Parson's earpiece. One of the most important periods of the young academic's career had commenced.

Within one minute of the interview starting, it was clear the conversation would be a hostile one. The host, a white, cisgender male, made the mistake of referring to DeLessio-Parson by her first name, Anne. But she wasn't going to let that mistake slide, not on *her* big night.

"Remember, it's *Dr.* DeLessio-Parson," she calmly noted. "Please don't ever refer to me by Anne, but I appreciate it."[3]

The host smiled and immediately apologized—DeLessio-Parson's first victory of the night, she thought.

The host then attempted to get the interview back on track. DeLessio-Parson politely answered his questions, waiting for the perfect moment to unveil her best argument for this important debate.

Her opportunity finally came.

DeLessio-Parson—sorry, *Dr.* DeLessio-Parson—paused momentarily and then masterfully explained why so many Americans misunderstand the interview's primary topic. Contrary to the patriarchal, cruel claims made by uneducated talk radio hosts like me and ignorant rubes in Flyover Country, the fact of the matter is, *math is racist.*

Wait—what? No, that can't be right. I thought Dr. DeLessio-Parson was the hero of this introductory story. She is a doctor, after all—well, not a real doctor who went to medical school. She's just one of those ivory-tower elites with a lot of degrees hanging on her wall. But still, highly educated people gave her all those framed pieces of paper, so that must mean something, right?

I have faith in the members of my research team, and they really wanted me to use their notes for this part of the book, so let's press on. I am sure this is going somewhere. Where was I? Oh, yes, *math is racist*. But why, you might be wondering, is it racist?

After rambling for what seemed like an eternity, DeLessio-Parson was pressed to provide a clear answer. She paused, smiled, and then capitalized on the moment she had long been waiting for.

"Critical race theory is a framework for understanding the world that helps us understand that this entire country is racist, right?" DeLessio-Parson said matter-of-factly. "We have a white supremacist caste, racial caste system in the United States."[4]

Wait—sorry. We need to pause again. Am I reading this right? There must be something heroic in here. Let's move further down in the notes. It looks like Dr. DeLessio-Parson was also asked if all white people in America are racist, to which she replied, "Yeah. I am too, sometimes. It happens. We were socialized, right?"[5]

Later in the interview, she adds that although it's true that humans in ancient times learned about math by adding sticks together and that this form of mathematics is *not* an example of racism—and no, I'm not making this part of the interview up—math did become racist later on, once humans began to use "math and numbers and statistics in all sorts of ways, from counting black and brown bodies as they made them property and brought them over to these lands, to much more recently, as scholars have said that white people were more intelligent than people of color. That's called scientific racism, the use of statistics and tools to construct the idea. It's like something deep in our brains. It's hard to recognize and that's why it requires time."[6]

No, Dr. DeLessio-Parson. It doesn't require *time* to think that slave traders treating human bodies as property two hundred years ago is proof that math is racist. It requires a lobotomy, or at the very least, a lifetime of propaganda in schools run by left-wing radicals. (Frankly, I'm not sure which experience is worse.) I really have to hand it to the host of that interview, Jesse Watters. I think my head would have exploded long before making it to the commercial break.

Activist academics like DeLessio-Parson have been around for a long time, but their ideas used to be confined to the hallowed halls of left-wing universities and drug-infested outdoor concerts and events, like Woodstock and Burning Man. But today, Marxists like Anne DeLessio-Parson have become prominent enough that they are given opportunities to spew Marxist ideas about, well, just about everything, straight into your living room, using the magic of modern technology.

We shouldn't get too bent out of shape about a single academic drinking too much of the Kool-Aid, though. It's not like this whole math-is-racist thing is catching on in academia. Or is it? After a thorough review—one that took all of ten minutes of online search-ing—I was able to find dozens upon dozens of stories, academic studies, and opinion articles by successful educators, researchers, and journalists claiming that math is racist or in some way perpet-uates racism.

For example, a 2021 article by Rachel Crowell in the *Scientific American* makes the not-so-scientific claim that mathematics has a "white, patriarchal past" and that "mathematicians want to think their field is a meritocracy, but bias, harassment and exclusion persist." Crowell further alleges that mathematics is full of "racism, sexism and other forms of systematic oppression."[7]

What is the primary evidence for these claims? The racial and gender demographics of doctorates in the field. Because only a small percentage of doctorates are awarded to African Americans each year, for example, Crowell reasons that it must be true that African Americans are the victims of racist policies developed by white people in higher-ed institutions. Of course, she fails to provide even a shred of evidence that such policies exist. It's almost as though she's never heard that one of the rules of scientific inquiry is to remember that correlation does not imply causation.

If Crowell's argument is true and the only reason African Americans are underrepresented in PhD mathematics programs is because of the white patriarchy, then why are Asians, including Indian and Chinese scholars, overrepresented in the same field? The only reasonable answer that fits with Crowell's perspective is that white mathematicians favor Asians, at least when it comes to math.

Don't make that argument to Yale University professor Theodore Kim, though. He published an article in 2021 in the *Washington Post* titled "Racism in our curriculums isn't limited to history. It's in math, too." In the piece, Kim laments that discussions over race are difficult in the field of math because it's "perceived, incorrectly, as a neutral space outside the reach of structural racism."[8]

Kim then goes on to claim that math continues to suffer from anti-Asian racism, perpetrated again by (you guessed it!) white people. So, which is it? Do white people favor Asians in mathematics, or are they trying to suppress their achievements? Critical race theorists generally agree that the answer is, it doesn't matter much, so long as the white racial caste superstructure is dismantled. How, exactly, do educators plan to do that?

In a 2019 article in the *International Journal of Critical Pedagogy*, education scholars at Vanderbilt University, Lake Forest College, and the Choctaw Nation sought to provide an answer to that question. They, like the other academics previously mentioned, agreed that racism is a massive problem in mathematics. Citing additional scholars, they wrote, "The cultures, languages, and identities of students of color are regularly devalued in schools. Howard and Navarro (2016) assert 'that many students of color are expected to learn in schools where content, instruction, school culture, and assessment are often racially hostile, exclusive, and serve as impediments for school success.""[9]

Fixing these problems won't be easy, they argue. Scholarly published works and conferences seeking to enhance solidarity against the white man have been successful, but more work is needed. "Building on these efforts, we aim to identify the specific ways that White supremacy operates in each of these groups and to strategically engage in research to transform mathematics education spaces for marginalized students of color," the scholars wrote. "In this paper, our overarching goal is an expansive solidarity effort in mathematics education that will contribute to a collective resistance against the oppression of students of color, towards a culturally affirmative education."[10]

Other anti-racism activists are focusing their efforts on your children, which, you must admit, makes a lot more sense. I mean, if you think you're going to solve the math-is-racist crisis in ivory-tower math departments alone, then clearly you don't understand how best to tear down the white patriarchy. It is always best to start with young, impressionable children, and once you have them hooked, it's all downhill from there.

Heroic anti-racism activists in Seattle are one such group committed to using school math classes to increase racial equity. In 2019, public school officials developed "ethnic-studies frameworks" for grades K–12, covering a variety of academic subjects, including math. Among the questions asked of students and educators as part of the math frameworks were, "Where does Power and Oppression show up in our math experiences?" and "How is math manipulated to allow inequality and oppression to persist?"[11]

As discussed in an article by the *Seattle Times* about the frameworks, Tracy Castro-Gill, the ethnic-studies program manager for Seattle Public Schools, says the frameworks don't claim "math is inherently racist," but rather, "It's how math is used as a tool for oppression."[12]

The *Times* reported, "One example teachers might mention in an ethnic studies math class, [Castro-Gill] said, is how black voters in the South were given literacy and numeracy tests before they could cast their ballot. Another might be a lesson on ratios that discusses gaps in incarceration rates and how the weight of a type of drug determines the length of a sentence."

The *Times* further noted, "Classes might also talk about how different cultures have practiced math, such as how Aztecs used a base-20 number system, as opposed to the base-10 system Americans use."[13]

You might be wondering why American children, who are already struggling with math compared to their peers in many other developed nations,[14] would need to know how an ancient civilization—which no longer exists—counted. But if you are wondering that, it's likely only because you've been indoctrinated by the very same white patriarchy that the Seattle Public Schools are trying to push back against. The Aztecs deserve to be celebrated as part of an effort to enhance inclusivity, we're told. Sure, they may have been a notoriously violent, slaveholding society that sacrificed humans to false gods by ripping people's beating hearts straight from their chests while they were still alive,[15] but there's still a lot of moral lessons about destroying the white racial caste system that children can learn from them.

Seattle isn't the only school district embedding social justice ideology into their math curriculums, either. States like California, Oregon, and Vermont, as well as numerous local school districts across the country, including some big ones in red and purple states, have embraced a similar approach.[16]

I know it's a little bizarre that states like Oregon and Vermont and cities such as Seattle, Washington, where most people are white, are leading the charge to teach children that math should be used to dismantle white supremacism. How do these white people teaching that white people are supremacists know that they aren't themselves the white supremacists? After all, they were indoctrinated by the same racial caste system that they claim has made all white people blind to their deeply embedded privilege.

And how, precisely, is a white math teacher in Seattle or Portland, Oregon, supposed to handle the inevitable confrontations that will arise between him and the minority children in his classroom? If white people are as bad as these math teachers and school officials claim they are, then why should minority children listen to them? Just think how confusing it would be for a female African American fifth grader to hear that she is the victim of systemic oppression led by white people, taught to her by a white guy with blue hair who thinks it's vital that she learn to count in a twenty-base number system, just like the murderous Aztecs did.

Well, I'm sure all these concerns have been thought of by the elites dreaming up these curriculum changes. We need to trust the experts, right?—experts like Crystal Watson, an eighth-grade teacher in Cincinnati. In one article discussing the issue of racism in math, she was highlighted for her interesting lesson plans.[17] Yeah, let's go with *interesting*. According to the report, in one exercise she asked the students "to imagine designing affordable housing for Black and Hispanic families like theirs in Cincinnati who have been priced out of their neighborhoods.

"But when she had them add a hallway down the middle of their floor plans, with apartments on either side, some struggled with the idea of reflection—flipping a figure to create a mirror image," the report noted.

"At that point, she pulled students aside individually to explain the difference and offered tips for remembering," the reporter wrote. "Her strategy—connecting math to socio-economic issues in the community and letting students proceed even if they haven't mastered the skills—is captured in a workbook that gives teachers steps for 'dismantling racism' in math instruction."

The workbook is the product of a nonprofit education organization called Education Trust–West. Education Trust–West says its workbook, which also teaches that math instructors who focus on finding the correct answer to a problem are promoting "white supremacy culture," is part of the group's math equity project. As of 2021, the workbook had been adopted as part of exciting teacher training programs in districts in California, Georgia, and Ohio.

Where are projects like Education Trust–West getting the massive amount of funding needed to promote their innovative ideas? There's a long list of billionaire activists and charitable organizations promoting these new concepts, including the Bill and Melinda Gates Foundation, a major donor of Education Trust–West.[18] I don't know about you, but when I think of the best person to help dismantle white privilege, the first name that comes to mind is Bill Gates, one of the richest, and perhaps whitest, people on the planet. By the way, I wonder if Microsoft has adopted this whole finding-the-right-answer-is-a-form-of-white-supremacy thing. If it hasn't, I'm sure someone over at Microsoft's Diversity, Equity, and Inclusion Office is working on it at this very moment.

At the start of the chapter, I had my doubts that DeLessio-Parson really is a modern-day hero. To be honest, my first impression of her was closer to egotistical lunatic than it was hero of the modern age. But now I think I understand what my handsome research team (they made me write the "handsome" part) had in mind.

In the America we used to live in, people like DeLessio-Parson would have been laughed out of the room. But in today's America, she's a highly qualified PhD. And in the minds of many, she really is heroic, and so are all the social justice warriors in Seattle's schools, the anti-racism champions at the Bill and Melinda Gates Foundation, and even the writers of that crackpot teacher's guide that claims finding the right answer is a form of white supremacy. We don't live in a country that makes sense anymore, so why should our heroes?

The America we used to know is long gone, and gang, I hate to break it to you, but it isn't coming back anytime soon. Someday, yes, I believe it will. But not tomorrow, next week, next year, or even this decade. Whether we like it or not, *that* country—the greatest, wealthiest, freest, and most powerful nation in the history of human civilization—has become nothing short of a bizarre circus. And we're all trapped inside of this carnival of horrors for the foreseeable future. So, with that wonderful image in mind, allow me to be the first person to welcome you to your new home, Clown World, where almost nothing outside of our local communities makes sense and nearly everything appears at first glance to be a joke—and a cruel one at that.

Masters of the Circus

Very few of us want to live in Clown World. In fact, I would argue that this is one of Clown World's defining features. But we're all stuck here nonetheless, and that won't change until we fully understand and accept just how screwed up America has become. And nothing will ever improve if we keep resting our hopes of recovery in the hands of our political elites. That's an old idea, one that doesn't work in Clown World, because our politicians are one of the biggest reasons we have ended up in this mess.

In the America of the past, many politicians were known for being self-serving and, yes, more than just a little dishonest. But in Clown World, our political, social, and educational leaders have taken things to whole new heights. The vast majority are completely corrupt, totally incompetent, absolute fools, or some combination of the three.

Our presidents run trillion-dollar deficits while bragging about how fiscally responsible they are.[19]

Geriatric political leaders on both sides of the aisle regularly struggle to remember basic facts about their own lives. Some can barely function as adult human beings. At one campaign event in 2020, for instance, Joe Biden confused his wife with his sister, both of whom were standing next to him.[20]

On another occasion, just moments after his White House press secretary defended his mental abilities, Biden mixed up two members of his own cabinet.[21]

At a White House kids' event in 2023, Biden forgot how many grandchildren he has, and then painfully struggled to answer an extremely difficult question asked by a child in the audience: Where do your grandchildren live? At the same event—boy, those kids are tougher on the president than the White House press pool— another child asked the president to identify the last country he had visited. Biden couldn't remember that it was Ireland, and that the trip had taken place just two weeks earlier.[22]

Biden may have spent the past four years as the most *powerful* guy in Washington experiencing serious mental decline, but he's hardly the only one. At a small press event in August 2023, former Senate Minority Leader Mitch McConnell (R-KY) appeared completely incapable of speech after being asked if he planned to run for reelection; he just awkwardly and silently stared at the reporters in the room until an aide pulled him away.[23] It was the *second time* in just a handful of weeks that McConnell, one of the most important political figures in America over the past twenty years, was caught struggling to communicate.

Speaking of struggling, have you seen Pennsylvania senator John Fetterman (D-PA)? During the 2022 campaign, Fetterman, age fifty-five, suffered a stroke.[24] Upon his return to the campaign trail, it was obvious that Fetterman had lost the ability to communicate coherently. Democrats made him their candidate anyway, and then voters inexplicably elected him.

Just months into beginning his first term, Fetterman returned to the hospital again, this time for clinical depression. After returning to work, Fetterman refused to conform to the dress code of the Senate, instead choosing to wear gym shorts and a hoodie. To avoid getting into trouble with the Senate chamber's sergeant-at-arms for violating Senate rules, Fetterman often voted from doorways. So, Chuck Schumer, the Senate Majority Leader, changed the Senate's dress code to accommodate Fetterman's sloppy appearance. But just a week later, following outrage from senators on both sides of the aisle, the Senate voted to change the dress code back.[25]

Does anything about this story inspire even the slightest bit of confidence in our leaders? Don't get me wrong. I am extremely sympathetic to those who suffer from health problems, including mental health illnesses. I've seen firsthand how incredibly difficult that can be, and on more than one occasion. But maybe, just maybe, if you're having a hard time speaking, recovering from a serious stroke, *and* suffering from clinical depression, you shouldn't be holding one of the highest positions of power in the world today.

Of course, it could be worse, and in Clown World, it almost always is. Fetterman might be having an extremely difficult time doing his job, but at least he's not sleeping with enemy spies.

In December 2020, Axios reported that California Democratic congressman Eric Swalwell had previously grown close with a Chinese woman named Fang Fang, also known as Christine Fang.[26] Fang met Swalwell in 2012 through contacts with the California Democratic Party.[27] Fang had become a successful fundraiser for California Democrats after years of building connections with left-wing groups in the California Bay Area, beginning with on-campus organizations. Fang started her political journey in America posing as an innocent college student.[28]

Although there are still discrepancies about the timing of their relationship, it appears that when Fang first met Swalwell, he was just a city councilman in Dublin, California. However, Fang chose well. Swalwell's political influence soon skyrocketed. He won his party's nomination for a California congressional seat and, seemingly with fundraising help from Fang, was subsequently elected in the general election. Fang stuck around. She fundraised for Swalwell's campaign again in 2014, and even successfully had a low-level staff person placed in Swalwell's congressional office.

For years, nothing seemed off about Fang's role within the California Democratic Party. But then, in 2015, intelligence officials notified Swalwell that Fang wasn't who she appeared to be. It turns out Fang Fang was part of a much larger Chinese intelligence operation that sought to use young, attractive women to garner information from influential figures in U.S. politics.

Upon learning Fang's true identity, Swalwell reportedly cut off all ties to her and fully cooperated with intelligence authorities. But by then, the damage had been done. In mid-2015, Fang was feeling the heat from U.S. intelligence officials, so she unexpectedly left the United States, taking who knows how many secrets with her, and it seems as though she hasn't returned since.

For years, the public didn't know about the relationship between Fang Fang and Swalwell, and when the story finally broke in December 2020, few in the mainstream media questioned the nature of Swalwell's relationship with the Chinese spy. But reports from the intelligence community soon leaked out that Swalwell's connection to Fang involved more than meet-and-greets with big donors.

Shortly after Axios published its initial story about Fang, Tucker Carlson, who was working for Fox News at the time, reported, "U.S. intelligence officials believe that Fang had a sexual relationship with Eric Swalwell. When 'Tucker Carlson Tonight' asked Swalwell's office about that Tuesday, his staff replied by saying they couldn't comment because such information might be 'classified.' They did not elaborate or explain what they meant by that."[29]

In subsequent press interviews with Swalwell, the congressman, who was at the time serving on the House Intelligence Committee, refused to answer critics who wondered whether he had once had a sexual relationship with Fang.[30] His silence fueled intense speculation that eventually led to his removal from the Intelligence Committee and a congressional investigation.

Axios's report did not include information about the possible sexual relationship between Swalwell and Fang, but it is clear that the two knew each other well, regularly interacted, and were seen together at events on numerous occasions. Intelligence officials also acknowledged that Fang had at least three sexual or romantic relationships with public officials while living in the United States, including with two mayors in the Midwest.[31] The identities of all three officials have been kept secret from the public, and it remains possible that Swalwell is the third unnamed official identified by intelligence officers.

Now, you might be thinking it's hard to imagine that anything could be more embarrassing for a sitting member of Congress than to wake up one morning and learn the entire country suspects you've been sleeping with an enemy spy. But in our new, bizarre Clown World America, you must dream bigger, because there is now no end to the heights of absurdity that we can expect from our fearless leaders in Washington.

Take socialist congresswoman Ilhan Omar (D-MN), for example. While it's true that she's not guilty of being caught up in a Chinese spy operation, there is significant evidence that she might have married her brother.[32] Yes, *her brother*. It's possible she hatched the scheme to help him with an immigration problem, but the truth is, there are so many strange questions surrounding

Omar's past that we still don't know the full truth, and probably never will.

At the very least, we know Omar was caught lying on her taxes, falsely claiming she was legally married to one man when she only had a "faith marriage" with him and had remained legally married to a completely different man. Campaign finance officials in Minnesota also said Omar is guilty of misusing campaign funds.[33]

In June 2019, the Associated Press (AP) reported, "The [Minnesota] campaign finance board investigated and found [Omar] didn't use the funds to pay for a divorce lawyer as alleged, but other irregularities were found. The board's final report said 'there was an issue with her tax returns that needed to be corrected' and that some campaign funds went to an accounting firm."[34]

The AP further reported, "State officials ruled last week that Omar must repay her campaign committee nearly $3,500, including $1,500 for payments made to the accounting firm for services related to joint tax returns for 2014 and 2015. Omar must also pay a $500 penalty to the state."[35]

A president who can't tell the difference between his own cabinet members, or even his wife and his sister; a Senate leader who suffers from debilitating health problems; a congressman who likely had sexual relations with a Chinese spy; a senator who struggles to communicate and suffers from clinical depression; and a congress-woman who cheats on her taxes and marries her brother—this is what modern American leadership looks like.

There is one potential bright spot, though—the deep state. Wow. I'm not sure that sentence has ever been uttered in the history of human civilization, but take a moment to hear me out. Aren't the nation's bureaucratic elite secretly running things behind the scenes? They might be mini-tyrants who are nearly impossible to remove from their positions, but they can't be as dysfunctional as members of Congress, can they?

One afternoon, that disturbing thought crossed my mind, and for the briefest of moments, I thought, yeah, maybe there is one, just one, good thing about America's administrative state: no matter how absurd our members of Congress are, the bureaucrats are running things, and say what you want about them, but they are professionals. Then I heard the story of Sam Brinton, one of the Biden administration's top "professionals" in the management of nuclear waste.

Brinton first made headlines as living proof of the Biden administration's commitment to celebrating every color of the diversity rainbow. Brinton reportedly uses "they/them" pronouns and refuses to identify as either male or female, making him—sorry; I meant "them"—a darling of the mainstream press.[36] They like to wear—or maybe the proper grammatical structure would be "They likes to wear"? Because there's still only one of "they," so "likes" would be correct, wouldn't it? But if I say, "They likes to wear," I sound like a complete idiot, and for more reasons than one, so yeah, this experiment is over. Time to go back to reality.

In addition to identifying as a non-binary "they/them," Brinton, a bald biological man, likes to wear dresses, lipstick, and fabulous jewelry—but only on special occasions. So, naturally, the Biden administration thought he would be a great fit for the position of deputy assistant secretary for spent fuel and waste disposition at the Department of Energy's (DOE) Office of Nuclear Energy. That was, of course, until he was caught stealing luggage at airports.

In December 2022, the New York Post reported Brinton had been fired from the DOE "after being charged with stealing a woman's suitcase from a Minneapolis airport in September and another woman's bag from a Las Vegas airport in July."

The Post further reported, "Brinton, who was appointed to his former position in June, was caught on surveillance cameras making off with a $320 bag from Las Vegas' Harry Reid International

Airport's baggage claim area—a bag that contained more than $3,500 worth of jewelry, clothing and makeup, according to police."[37]

Brinton isn't the only gender-confused member of the Biden administration to earn significant criticism from the press. Rachel Levine, a transgender woman who serves as the assistant secretary of the Department of Health and Human Services, received significant backlash in December 2022 after calling on Big Tech companies to censor "misinformation" on their platforms. More specifically, Levine, who was also recently made a four-star admiral in the U.S. Public Health Service Commissioned Corps, thinks "gender-affirming care," such as castrating children, should be spared from any criticism on social media platforms.[38]

You see, according to Admiral Levine, to protect children, it's not enough that we must allow them to be castrated, pumped full of hormones, and/or told repeatedly that their biological sex is not tied to their real identity. We also must stop anyone concerned about these practices from talking about it online.

Another bizarre bout of Clown World sprang up in 2022, when the Army opened an investigation into at least two officers who allegedly posted pictures of themselves wearing their uniforms with ... let's call it *improper headgear*. Oh, and by *improper headgear*, I mean BDSM dog masks. Now, does that mean our Army is being run by a bunch of degenerate furries? Fortunately, I am not familiar enough with the societal subculture of canine sex kinks to answer that question, but in Clown World, you can't rule anything out.

I wish I could say that the borders of our Clown World only extend to the realms of math education and the corrupt federal government, but there's virtually no part of American life that has yet to descend into lunacy.

For example, in April 2023, beverage giant Bud Light, a beer brand most popular among football-watching adult men, decided it would be a fun idea to hire an obnoxious transgender social media influencer named Dylan Mulvaney to be the new face of their product.[39] Because, you know, nothing says football fanatic quite like a guy claiming to be a woman selling skincare products on Instagram.

To say the move was a dumpster fire would be going easy on the ad executives at Bud Light. Sales immediately plummeted in the wake of the widespread public backlash that followed commercials featuring Mulvaney. In the month following the hire, sales for Bud Light dropped by a whopping 23 percent compared to the same period one year earlier. The decline was so intense that Bud Light ceased being America's best-selling beer. Again, all within just a few months' time.[40]

In the months that followed, the situation grew even more dire. In fact, Mulvaney helped drag the entire U.S. beer industry down. A *New York Post* report in December 2023 noted that sales for the industry, not just for Bud Light, declined to their lowest level in more than two decades. According to the *Post*, sales dropped in large part because of "the backlash and boycotts against Anheuser-Busch-owned Bud Light" stemming from the Mulvaney ads.[41]

Incredibly, that isn't the craziest part of the story. Rather than simply recognize that American beer drinkers don't want to be bombarded with LGBTQ messaging, mainstream media rallied to Mulvaney's defense and then demanded more trans inclusion in television commercials and online ads. Many treated the failed spokesperson as though he were a champion of LGBTQ rights, all for getting fired for being the world's worst salesperson.

One popular magazine based in the United Kingdom, *Attitude*, even went so far as to name Mulvaney its "Woman of the Year."[42] Putting aside the problematic issue that Mulvaney doesn't have any of the primary qualifiers of such a designation—including a vagina or female genes—there's the ridiculous notion that according to *Attitude*, not a single other woman on the planet was more deserving of being Woman of the Year. That might be the most insulting part of the whole Dylan Mulvaney saga. You're telling me there isn't a female activist in Africa, brain surgeon in South America, or high-profile cancer researcher in the United States who is more qualified than Mulvaney?

Even if it's true that *Attitude* was hellbent on choosing someone from the LGBTQ community, there had to be someone, anyone, who was more deserving. They couldn't find a lesbian volunteer firefighter? How about a gay human rights attorney? Perhaps a well-qualified queer woman who works at a soup kitchen on the weekend? Heck, I think I'd give the award to Sam Brinton, that luggage-stealing nutjob who was fired by the Biden administration before I'd ever award Dylan Mulvaney. Brinton might be a criminal, but at least the government didn't lose 23 percent of its revenue during his time in the Department of Energy. (Although, now that I think about it, I'm not sure someone who is non-binary can qualify as a woman under today's completely fictional rules, so I guess we're going to have to wait and see how he identifies in the future before pulling the trigger on that one.)

Although identity politics isn't the only reason America is now trapped in Clown World, it's undeniably a major component. Tens of millions of people in the West today, not just in the United States, are so hopelessly addicted to grouping themselves and others into nonsensical categories and then drawing conclusions based on those made-up characteristics that they will literally do *anything* in the name of defending their broken ideology.

Take the Queers for Palestine movement, for example. Following the horrific assaults on innocent Jewish civilians on October 7, 2023, perpetrated by Hamas, a terrorist organization and the ruling authority of Gaza, thousands of activists around the world took to the streets to express their solidarity with the Jewish victims, right? No. Instead, they backed the people of Gaza.[43] Among the many groups on the left that have protested against Israel and its retaliatory strikes against Gazan terrorists is the aforementioned Queers for Palestine.

Although reasonable people can disagree about how Israel should have responded to the attacks and the treatment of the people of Gaza before the attacks, it's not even remotely reasonable to defend the idea that Hamas and its constituents should be rewarded for their human rights violations with the creation of a new state. Nor is it reasonable to claim that Israel has no right to fight back against terrorist governments that are willing to rape, kidnap, and kill innocent men, women, and children. And yet, that's exactly what many in the Queers for Palestine movement have done, all despite the fact that under the leadership of Hamas, there is no tolerance for the members of the LGBTQ movement.[44] In fact, under Hamas, their lives are in grave danger.

In the America we used to know, Queers for Palestine would, at best, be labeled bat-crap-crazy. Today, in Clown World, they are treated like selfless champions of human rights.

Speaking of human rights, in American history, few, if any, causes evoke the vision of defending human rights more than the civil rights movement of the mid-twentieth century. Until important changes were made during this influential period, African Americans and other groups had never been treated as equal members of society. That's why the civil rights activists of this era are widely considered today to be important heroes in the annals of American history, and rightfully so. Their sacrifice and commitment to nonviolent forms of protest should serve as a model for future generations.

Unfortunately, however, many people today have a completely warped sense of civil rights and equality, one that has led to strange, destructive, and downright clownish behavior.

For example, in Boston, Massachusetts, in 2020, city officials removed a famous statue depicting Abraham Lincoln and a freed slave from a park near Boston Common. The statue was first erected in 1879. The intent behind the creation of the statue, which is a copy of an identical statue in Washington, DC, was to celebrate the end of slavery in the United States, and the man, Lincoln, who gave his life in the pursuit of that goal. The statue's sculptor, Thomas Ball, was a supporter of emancipation and a resident of Boston.[45]

For more than a century, no one questioned the statue or its purpose—until, that is, the good people of Boston entered our new, *enlightened* era. Then, after more than a hundred years of virtually no one having a problem with the statue, it suddenly became an extremely offensive example of white supremacy. It needed to be removed immediately, activists and city officials agreed, all to promote racial justice.

Only in Clown World can delusional city officials get away with tearing down a statue celebrating the emancipation of black slaves as a way to improve racial harmony.

But as kooky as Boston's Clown World social justice warriors are, they've still got nothing on the whackos in San Francisco. In 2023, a San Franciso city commission proposed that taxpayers should give onetime, lump-sum payments of $5 million to the city's black residents.[46] If the proposal is passed into law—something that has yet to occur at the time of publication of this book—it would be, by far, the most lucrative reparations program ever enacted in American history.

Although forcing current generations of Americans to pay for the racial injustices of the past is crazy enough, the devilish details in the San Francisco proposal make it even more outrageous.

According to a report by CNN:

> To be eligible for reparations, San Francisco residents must be 18 years or older, have been identifying as Black or African American on public documents for at least 10 years, and meet two of eight additional criteria, including having been born or

migrating to the city between 1940 and 1996 as well as showing proof of at least 13 years of residency; Having been incarcerated "by the failed War on Drugs" or being the direct descendant of someone who was; Being a descendant of someone who was enslaved through US chattel slavery before 1865; Having been displaced between 1954 and 1973 or being a descendant of someone who did; Being part of a marginalized group who experienced lending discrimination in the city between 1937 and 1968 or in "formerly redlined" communities within the city between 1968 and 2008, according to the committee's plan.[47]

A cursory look at these rules should raise serious questions from even the staunchest of supporters of reparations, because although the guidelines are meant to help African Americans who have been mistreated in the past by San Francisco officials, they would almost certainly harm many of the city's black residents in the process. And many of the city's African Americans wouldn't be eligible for the program at all.

Consider, for instance, that under the terms of the proposal, an African American woman who moved to San Francisco in 2010, has never been imprisoned, isn't a direct descendant of someone who has been incarcerated for drugs, and whose family has never been displaced could be forced to help pay $5 million in reparations to thousands of other black people in the city. Meanwhile, she would get nothing, even if she were a direct descendent of slaves.

Similarly, many other residents in the city who are descendants of non-black slaves or non-black victims of intense discrimination, such as many Chinese and Japanese residents, would also be required to contribute to the reparations program, all because they don't have the "right" racial composition.

And what about city residents who recently emigrated to the United States for the first time? They would be required to pay

additional taxes for a lucrative reparations program despite having
in no way contributed to the problems of slavery, segregation,
redlining, or any other racist policy that plagued America in the
past. Some of these individuals could even be refugees of war or
decedents of slavery in other nations. Why should they have to pay
for this reparations program?

With these concerns in mind, it's clear that San Francisco's
proposal for racial reparations are, well, *racist*. Only in Clown World
could such a completely absurd policy proposal ever be given serious
consideration. And while it may seem as though policy plans calling
for some black people to pay reparations to other black people is an
abnormally outrageous example of hypocrisy to highlight, the truth
is, in Clown World, outrageous hypocrisy is par for the course.

Take the Biden administration, for example. Old Joe routinely
promised that defending "democracy" is one of his administration's
highest priorities. In one speech delivered in January 2024, he even
went so far as to say, "The defense, protection, and preservation of
American democracy will remain, as it has been, the central cause
of my presidency."[48]

That sounds nice, of course, but at the very moment those words
spewed from Joe's mouth, Democrats were in the midst of waging
an unprecedented legal war against Biden's chief political rival,
President Trump. (And at the time of the writing of this chapter,
the Biden administration and its allies are still actively attempting,
and failing, to put Trump in prison.) Democrat-appointed justices
on the Supreme Court of Colorado, with the support of political
officials in Colorado, even attempted to keep Trump off their state's
2024 ballot before ever being convicted of a crime.[49] Polls also show
that most Democratic voters support these attempts to get Trump
at any cost.[50]

You see, in Clown World, the only way to "defend democracy" is
to stop democracy.

Don't be fooled into thinking the tremendous hypocrisy in Clown World is limited to attacks on Trump, either. No one is safe in Clown World, not even the most helpless among us. That's why the media celebrated the launch of Vice President Kamala Harris's "Reproductive Freedoms Tour" in December 2023.[51] In the old America, human reproduction involved reproducing humans. But in Clown World, "reproductive freedoms" aren't about protecting the human reproductive process, as reasonable people might expect, but are designed to stop reproduction altogether, in many cases by killing unborn children. And all of this is done in the name of "health care."

Even if a baby trapped in Clown World is lucky enough to survive to adolescence, he or she isn't out of the woods. That kid will spend his or her entire childhood being bombarded with contradictory, strange, and harmful messaging, not to mention the cascade of lies from supposed "experts" in the media, politics, government, Hollywood, and, most important, academia. In previous generations, when America still made sense, children were generally protected from such an intense onslaught. Today, it's a normal part of life for nearly all young people.

In the old America, kids watched children's movies about timeless truths, featuring cute talking lions and cartoon toys who come to life.

In Clown World, allegedly family-friendly moviemakers, like Disney, obsess over filling LGBTQ quotas and fighting *against* legislative efforts to keep public school teachers from instructing six-year-olds about gender identity and sexual orientation.[52]

In the old America, teachers and parents read stories to children.

In Clown World, Drag Queen Story Hour is all the rage.

In the old America, police officers were presented to kids as the "good guys" responsible for stopping criminals from hurting children.

In Clown World, police officers *are* the "criminals."

In the old America, a child could either be a boy or a girl, but not both.

In Clown World, not only can a child be both boy and girl, but a child can be neither boy nor girl, or one of dozens of other gender identities, including a demiboy, a novigender, an omnigender, a pangender, a polygender, or, my personal favorite, a stone butch.[53]

In old America, fifty-year-old men who deliberately took all their clothes off in front of children or adults in girls or women's locker rooms were arrested and ostracized.

In Clown World, anyone who tries to stop a self-identifying woman with a penis from showing that penis to biological women and children in a girl's locker room can be arrested and is often labeled a fanatical religious zealot.

Is it really a surprise, then, that Clown World kids are suffering increasingly higher rates of mental health ailments and are more likely to commit suicide? In the ten-year period from 2008 to 2018, the suicide rate among American adolescents doubled, according to a 2023 scholarly study published in the *Annals of Pediatrics and Child Health*.[54]

The most clownish quality of Clown World is that despite our being awash in ludicrous stories, we are told by the media and other institutions that this is all normal.

A president who forgets what day it is? Oh, that's just a stutter.

They/thems who steal luggage are in control of our country's nuclear waste? Diversity is our strength; didn't you hear?

Math is racist? Stop being defiant toward progress, you bigot.

With virtually every example of our descent into Clown World, the mainstream media, Hollywood, and Big Tech companies have lined up to argue that it is those of us who are not trying to blow up every single part of society and culture that are in the wrong. We are the ones who must change our viewpoints to better align with "woke" ideology. It doesn't matter to them that every one of these ideas was considered insane just a decade or two ago.

I could go on and on and on with more stories and studies like the ones referenced above. My research team and I have compiled literally hundreds of specific examples in just the past few years that decisively prove that Americans have entered Clown World. But as tempting as it is to see how close I can get my readers to having a full-blown mental breakdown before getting to the end of the first chapter, I'll spare you the emotional distress and the therapy bills and move on to the real purpose of this book: helping you understand how we can get America out of this mess.

The Truth Shall Set You Free

A country as big, powerful, and storied as the United States doesn't descend into the abyss of Clown World overnight. It takes time and millions of people performing billions of actions over many years, and that's exactly what the Far Left has managed to accomplish. And much of it has occurred in my lifetime. If it weren't all so diabolical and soul crushing, I would be really impressed.

In a similar manner, I think it's fair to say that fixing this colossal catastrophe in which we now find ourselves isn't going to be easy or swiftly accomplished. Pro-liberty Americans need to stop worrying primarily about political failures and victories and start devoting most of their sweat and treasure to winning our nation back over the long run. I'm not pointing the finger at others. I am just as guilty of getting caught up in today's never-ending clickbait battles as anyone else on the right. But as it has often been said, those who don't learn from the past are doomed to repeat it. If we don't change course—and soon—the conservative and libertarian movements in America will remain trapped in an endless cycle of failure and disappointment, no matter what happens on Election Day 2024,

2026, or 2028. It was in my own personal attempt to reevaluate how we can all do better that the idea for this book was born.

On a small scale, there are numerous reasons why any one issue develops into an out-of-control problem, and then later a crisis. So, for those of us living amid many crises, it's easy to get lost in the details and to silo various issues into their own separate spheres, completely detached from one other. This is how we often talk about the problems and solutions of our day. The concerns related to the federal government's addiction to debt and that debt's connection to inflation is typically discussed and evaluated apart from, say, the rise of far-left ideology in K–12 schools, disputes about gender identity, Joe Biden's dangerous foreign policies, and a million other unique problems. But the more you study each of these and dozens of other key issues, the more similar they seem. And if you start to think deeply about the emerging crises coming our way over the next decade or longer—many of which I discussed in my most recent book, *Dark Future*, such as artificial intelligence, central bank digital currencies, and deepfakes—the more obvious it becomes that, really, there is just one root cause behind all these problems. And once you see it, you won't be able to unsee it.

Wake Up

Unlike many other countries around the world, the United States has always been a country brimming with diverse thought. The reason we have a federalist system of government today, where states maintain a significant amount of control in day-to-day life, is that the citizens of those states at the time of America's founding couldn't agree on a whole bunch of important matters, including religion, the organization of government, slavery, taxes, and a seemingly endless list of other concerns. America was from the start a big-tent country.

That's not to say that the Americans of the founding era didn't share foundational values; they most certainly did, and many of those values remain with us, at least on some level, because they have been enshrined in the Bill of Rights. These values include freedom of speech, religious liberty, the right to self-defense, protections from unwarranted government searches and seizures, rights related to criminal prosecutions, and many others. Even these core liberties, however, can be traced back to one overarching value: *an understanding of and commitment to exploring, determining, debating, and protecting the truth.*

For example, the First Amendment guarantees people's right to speak freely, assemble, and protest, all so that Americans can debate what is true, argue for what is true, and pursue what is true.

The right to worship God freely is more important than every other protection in the Bill of Rights and the one that's most clearly tied to the importance of truth, because if people aren't allowed to pursue a greater understanding of the highest, most foundational truths, then what is the point of all the other rights? All religions are, at their core, an attempt to understand eternal truths. That doesn't mean all religions have it right, of course. That would be impossible, because religions teach different, often contradictory ideas about God. But the pursuit of truth is common to all religions, and even to atheism.

The Second Amendment guarantees that the people can defend themselves against a tyrannical government. It is needed precisely because governments around the world have a long track record of abusing eternal truths and undermining human rights, which really are nothing more than widely agreed-upon truth claims about human nature. Self-defense is the last line in the sand against a government that refuses to respect the existence of foundational truths about humanity.

The Third Amendment, the prohibition against quartering soldiers in people's homes, is similarly a guard against authoritarianism and the use of force to limit essential rights.

The purpose of the rights contained in the Fourth Amendment, including protections against unreasonable government searches, as well as the criminal justice protections in the Fifth Amendment, were not meant to help keep criminals out of jail but rather to ensure that the federal government wouldn't become tyrannical. These protections also attempted to keep the federal government from wrongfully imprisoning innocent Americans. A wrongful imprisonment is always contrary to the truth because no innocent person ever deserves to be deprived of his life or property if he or she has acted within the law.

To varying degrees, every other chief component of the Bill of Rights was also crafted to guard the truth or the pursuit of the truth, and the same can be said of numerous amendments to the Constitution that were put in place after the Bill of Rights went into effect.

At this point, it is vital that you keep in mind that the Constitution and the founding of the United States did not and indeed could not guarantee the protection and promotion of all that is true. This is obvious because the First Amendment, the part of the Constitution most often associated with the pursuit and discussion of truth, also protects people from being forced to believe and confess all that is true. In some cases, it even protects people who are actively promoting lies. This isn't because the Bill of Rights is ambivalent about truth but instead because the truth is not always agreed-upon or fully understood. As strange as it may sound at first, one of the best ways to promote the truth is to guarantee that people have the freedom to be wrong, which is to say, contrary to truth. Why? Because it is only through a struggle to discover the truth, which often includes failure and falsehoods, that human beings can learn what is true.

Scientific inquiry, for example, is built on the idea that discovering what is real and true about the natural world can only come through many failed attempts at understanding. Often, scientists learn what is true by first believing hypotheses that are false. Contrary to popular opinion today in Clown World, human progress is never stunted by people believing the wrong things; progress only grinds to a halt when humans are stopped from *pursuing* the right things. If the end goal is truth, and all people are allowed to pursue it without force or coercion, humans have proven time and time again that they will grow in their understanding. There will be bumps and bruises along the way, to be sure, but the truth, when it is honestly pursued, always wins out.

Sometimes, conservatives wrongly argue that the source of all the insanity we see in Clown World is a widespread belief in that which is false. But that really couldn't be further from reality. The biggest problem is the combination of widespread belief in that which is false coupled with coercive and tyrannical attempts to restrict the freedom to pursue truth, no matter where it takes us.

Ironically, the Far Left likes to pretend that conservatives are the ones always imposing their values on others, but that's simply not correct. Expressing an opinion about what is believed to be true, such as a traditional understanding of gender, is not the same as imposing that belief on others. You may be really shocked to hear this (though you shouldn't be), but I don't think there is anything wrong with people questioning long-held ideas about sexual orientation, the meaning of marriage, or even gender. As I've been saying for more than a decade, in the words of Thomas Jefferson, "Question with boldness even the existence of a god; because, if there be one, he must more approve the homage of reason, than that of blindfolded fear."[55] So, question away. Just don't try to force me to agree with you. And if we don't agree, don't attempt to coerce me for disagreeing or punish me for pursuing the truth in my own way.

Of course, in Clown World, that's inevitable. Coercion is a defining characteristic of modern America. It's not enough today for elites to promote their ideas; they must force everyone else to pledge allegiance to them, and if they don't—well, then those dissenters must be destroyed, in whatever way is politically feasible and advantageous. It is this force, coercion, and violence that have rotted away our societal support beams. And now the crushing weight of elites' pervasive lies and confusion are becoming too much for our country to bear. America is buckling under this intense pressure, and it could soon collapse in a most spectacular fashion.

The danger is even greater than most realize. Sometimes, conservatives act as though the worst possible outcome is that America will become like Venezuela, China, Russia, or some other modern authoritarian state. I wish that were the case. The reality is far worse.

In *Dark Future*, I outlined what was at stake—namely, the possible rise of a highly powerful, never-before-seen technocratic hellscape. In this future, which will be dominated by automation, as well as artificial intelligence, government-controlled digital currencies, bio-tracking devices, and other new technologies—all of which are being designed by Davos elites as we speak—human beings would have few, if any, rights, and virtually no property or privacy. Of course, you will be told, as Davos elites are saying now, that you would be better off in such a world.

Take, for example, the World Economic Forum's now infamous article from 2016, written by European politician Ida Auken: "Welcome to 2030. I Own Nothing, Have No Privacy, and Life Has Never Been Better." Auken not only imagines a future Western civilization where people don't own or even want to own most forms of property; she also suggests that governments could monitor your every thought, even your dreams.

"Once in a while, I get annoyed about the fact that I have no real privacy," Auken wrote, from the perspective of herself in the future. "No where I can go and not be registered. I know that, somewhere, everything I do, think and dream of is recorded. I just hope nobody will use it against me."[56]

And yet, as Auken repeatedly notes in her article, even without basic human privacy rights, most people will be totally satisfied with their lives. Why? Because you'll have everything you need, thanks to your benevolent leaders in government and massive corporations.

This disturbing vision for the future, and so much more, is what elites regularly talk about with one another. And it's the future that we have in store for us if we don't change course soon. If you don't believe me, you can see the evidence for yourself in my book *Dark Future*, which includes hundreds of sources and more than one thousand citations.

Only if this nation returns to its former firm and constant pursuit of the truth in all things can we survive the dark future ahead. The trillion-dollar question is, How do we do that? Further, how can we know what is true, and how do we shine a light on those who would obscure the truth from the people to amass greater power for themselves?

The Plan

There are three primary challenges facing us in the months and years ahead. The first is that we need to pull back the curtain on what I like to call the Propaganda Industrial Complex, a vast network of key organizations, government agencies, international institutions, media outlets, and corporations that work together to systematically gain more power, wealth, and influence over society. If we are going to turn the country around, we need more Americans to understand who these people and organizations are, how they operate, and what their end goals are for the United States. The only way we can do that is to unleash an unprecedented wave of journalistic efforts meant to shine a bright spotlight on the Propaganda Industrial Complex. That, more than anything else, is what these entities fear most. But here's the big problem: there aren't enough good journalists and honest media outlets in Clown World to cover the ins and outs of the Propaganda Industrial Complex, or even just the evening news. That's where you come in—yes, *you*, the reader of this book.

In chapter 2, I will provide you with the blueprint the Propaganda Industrial Complex is using to transform our world, and then in chapter 3, I will reveal, for the first time ever, many of the strategies that I've used over the past two decades to uncover the truth and fight back against the Propagada Industrial Complex. These are the same tactics I used to break some of the most important stories in modern American history, including the dangerous Great Reset movement, the truth behind the COVID-19 origin story, the radical socialist and progressive figures behind the rise of Barack Obama, revelations about key details of the Biden crime family, and the destabilization of the financial system in the run-up to the 2008 crash, among many others.

As hard as it may be for you to believe, there is a method to my madness, and you need to know it, because soon, I'm going to call for the biggest grassroots journalism project in history, and *I want you to be a part of it.*

If we can get enough people searching for and uncovering the truth about the ruling class and its plans to seize control over virtually every aspect of your life, we may be able to derail elites' plans for a Great Reset of the global economy and a new Great Narrative for the future of humanity. (If you read my past two books, *The Great Reset* and *Dark Future*, you know what I'm talking about. If you didn't, get your hands on those two classics and prepare to have your mind blown.)

Now, I know what you're thinking: *Me? A journalist? Yeah, right, Glenn. That's not happening. I've got a job, kids, bills to pay, and the car just started to make this weird clanking sound. It's sort of like 'ah-lank, cah-lank, cuh-lunk.' And then there's* ...

Yes, I get it. Life is chaotic. Conservatives are and have been for many years too busy working, saving, and raising kids to become activists. But I promise that I won't ask you for more than you can handle. And let's be honest here: if you really believe America is worth saving, then it's going to take sacrifice. Conservatives and libertarians cannot afford to sit on the sidelines while the United States teeters on the edge of catastrophe. Gang, we're the last line of defense. We're the watchers on the wall. If we don't get the job done, or people like us, anyway, America won't make it. There are no reinforcements coming. We must fight this battle to win, no matter the cost.

The second great challenge we face is that even those of us who are committed to protecting individual rights and do pay close attention to what's happening around the world are falling victim to propaganda campaigns and misinformation. There are many reasons for this, but the biggest is that technology is making it harder than ever to know what's true and what isn't. And that problem is going to get a billion times worse in the coming years, as I'll explain in chapters 4–6.

We need to stop our warped world from becoming even more bent out of shape, but the only way we can successfully do that is if most Americans learn how to determine what is true and what isn't. That sounds simple, of course, but it's not. Americans are inundated daily with huge inflows of misinformation and propaganda, and they can't rely on the methods of the past to draw good conclusions. Because of technological innovations and increased collusion among most of society's institutions, the old ways don't work anymore.

Mainstream media sources regularly withhold important facts from their audiences. In countless cases, they outright lie, because for many in the press, the ends always justify means.

Government agencies, including those once thought to be trustworthy by some in the conservative movement, like the Department of Justice and the intelligence community, have repeatedly proven that they will put politics above their sworn duties. This isn't true of many in the rank and file, of course, but leadership is a completely different story.

Today, most politicians on both sides of the aisle seem more interested in expanding their own power or protecting their privileged positions in office than they do serving the men and women who pay their salaries and voted them into office.

Big Tech companies have a long track record of manipulating what their users do and see on their platforms, giving people a completely distorted view of the real world.

Increasingly, more of our churches would rather bow to woke mobs than kneel before King Jesus. Kneeling is hard work, you know.

And forget about Hollywood, academia, public K–12 schools, and the music industry. They lost all common sense a *long* time ago.

To whom do we turn when it seems as though every single influential institution in America cannot be trusted? The answer is, each other. We, the American people, are the solution. We must become each other's most trusted sources. We all must learn how to decipher what is reliable information, what reports might be true but need further verification, and which stories are likely flat-out wrong. In chapter 3, I'm going to provide you with the tools needed to do just that, by giving you a guide for sorting out fact from fiction.

By the time you get through chapter 3, you will have the foundational skills needed to do two incredibly important things: (1) understand how to recognize the truth and (2) discover the truth about elites' efforts to undermine your freedom, both now and in future decades.

The remaining chapters will give you important knowledge about the biggest stories of our day and offer insights into vital issues that will likely come up within the next decade, with a special emphasis on those topics most susceptible to being influenced by misinformation spread by powerful elites. In each of these chapters, we'll use the guide provided in chapter 3 to help us find our way through the extremely difficult issues discussed.

In chapter 4 you'll see how new and emerging technologies are changing the global landscape, controlling and manipulating the flow of information, and making it harder than ever to know the difference between reality and propaganda. Many readers of this book will think they are prepared for what's coming their way, but I assure you, most are not. The technologies now in development, as well as many that have recently been released, are going to make it extremely difficult for people to know the truth. Americans need to be ready, and after reading this chapter, you will be.

In chapter 5 I will show you some truly unbelievable evidence about the use of misinformation and propaganda in recent elections, as well as how emerging technologies, especially artificial intelligence and deepfakes, have been and will be used to further erode trust in elections across the world—unless, that is, we stop them.

In chapter 6 I'll discuss how the United Nations, influential policy organizations, environmental alarmists, and others are planning to use various crises to amass more power and control over individuals' lives. By the time you finish reading that chapter, you'll be prepared for the next big government power grab and ready to help your friends, family, and neighbors avoid the same traps they fell into when COVID-19 first hit.

Finally, in chapter 7 I'll outline a series of foundational ideas that would help turn the tide against elites, both foreign and domestic, especially when coupled with the grassroots efforts outlined in chapters 2 and 3. These ideas won't be focused on what should be done in Washington, DC, or even in state capitols. Most of what will be discussed is related to the essential nature of truth and its importance. To really save our country, we need to do more than pass laws; we must transform the way we think about everything.

The Fight Has Just Begun

Every day, hundreds of millions of Americans are being lied to. Each time they use their phones, watch the news on television, browse social media, listen to political candidates, attend a college, watch a movie, or use internet search engines, a highly sophisticated network of activists, global elites, government officials, powerful financial interests, and crony corporations manipulate their thoughts and feelings. You may think you've managed to escape their reach, but the truth is, none of us have, at least not completely. This powerful cabal has designed a system of disinformation that is so advanced almost no one can avoid it.

That's why in today's twisted, corrupted version of America, nearly everything is open for debate, from well-established facts about history, elections, and current events to basic truths about biology and the existence of good and evil. In their efforts to rebuild the world in their image, elites are deliberately untethering society from reality. Truth, like gender, has become a social construct that means whatever elites want it to mean to accomplish their purposes. As a result, most of us no longer live in the country we grew up in. We've all been exiled to Clown World, and in the process, the fabric of our communities, churches, and families is being destroyed. Elites know this, but they would rather burn the West to the ground and be kings and queens of the ashes than let regular folks make decisions for themselves.

I don't know about you, but I have had it. No longer will I shrug my shoulders in frustration as the America I love collapses into dust. No longer will I shake my head in disgust, or whisper defeatist slogans like, "There's nothing we can do," and "I'm just one person." The time for sitting down and shutting up is over. The battle to take our country back begins today.

2

THE PROPAGANDA
INDUSTRIAL COMPLEX

O N A CRISP OCTOBER EVENING IN NEW YORK CITY, A GROUP
of highly influential leaders from the public and private sectors
gathered at the historic Pierre Hotel for an important invitation-
only meeting called Event 201.[57]

According to the meeting's official website, "Event 201 was
a 3.5-hour pandemic tabletop exercise that simulated a series
of dramatic, scenario-based facilitated discussions, confronting
difficult, true-to-life dilemmas associated with response to a hypothetical, but scientifically plausible, pandemic." In national security
circles they call such an "exercise" a war game.

Fifteen global leaders were invited to participate as "players" in
Event 201, including academics, nonprofit and business leaders,
pharmaceutical representatives, and officials from the United
Nations and the U.S. Centers for Disease Control and Prevention.
The simulated pandemic was designed to highlight "unresolved
real-world policy and economic issues that could be solved with
sufficient political will, financial investment, and attention."

The players' experience consisted of "pre-recorded news broadcasts, live 'staff' briefings, and moderated discussions on specific topics." Despite the importance of the participants and the topic, only 130 people were allowed to attend Event 201.

The Johns Hopkins Center for Health Security organized Event 201 in partnership with the World Economic Forum (WEF) and the Bill and Melinda Gates Foundation, key organizations in the global "Great Reset" movement.

Following the event's conclusion, the Johns Hopkins Center for Health Security, the WEF, and the Gates Foundation jointly proposed a series of recommendations, all of which were designed to fill "important gaps in pandemic preparedness," with a special emphasis on public-private partnerships.

Included in the seven key recommendations was a call for "governments, international organizations, and businesses" to "plan now for how essential corporate capabilities will be utilized during a large-scale pandemic." This is necessary, they argued, because "during a severe pandemic, public sector efforts to control the outbreak are likely to become overwhelmed.

"But industry assets, if swiftly and appropriately deployed," they went on to say, "could help to save lives and reduce economic losses."

Other recommendations included a public-private collaboration to "enhance internationally held stockpiles of medical countermeasures (MCMs) to enable rapid and equitable distribution during a severe pandemic," as well as "more resources and support for the development and surge manufacturing of vaccines, therapeutics, and diagnostics."

Additionally, "global business leaders" were told that they "should play a far more dynamic role as advocates with a stake in stronger pandemic preparedness," and international organizations were instructed to "identify critical nodes of the banking system and global and national economies that are too essential to fail."

Of course, what would a gathering of control-hungry public-private partners be without demands to control information? The seventh and final recommendation issued declared, "Governments and the private sector should assign a greater priority to developing methods to combat mis- and disinformation prior to the next pandemic response."

To accomplish this exceptionally difficult task, here's what the Event 201 organizations determined:

> Governments will need to partner with traditional and social media companies to research and develop nimble approaches to countering misinformation. This will require developing the ability to flood media with fast, accurate, and consistent information. Public health authorities should work with private employers and trusted community leaders such as faith leaders, to promulgate factual information to employees and citizens. Trusted, influential private-sector employers should create the capacity to readily and reliably augment public messaging, manage rumors and misinformation, and amplify credible information to support emergency public communications. National public health agencies should work in close collaboration with WHO to create the capability to rapidly develop and release consistent health messages. For their part, media companies should commit to ensuring that authoritative messages are prioritized and that false messages are suppressed including though the use of technology.

In the wake of the COVID-19 global pandemic, all of this probably sounds unimpressive to you. After two years of lockdowns, vaccine mandates, countless emergency declarations, and endless hypocrisy, are you really surprised to hear that elites at powerful institutions are planning for the next big global health pandemic? If you're a regular member of my audience, then I seriously doubt it.

But here's the craziest part of the story. Event 201 is not about the *next* global pandemic. It's about the most recent one. Incredibly, Event 201 occurred on October 18, 2019, just months before most people in America had ever heard the word *coronavirus*.

In 2020, when coronavirus lockdowns were in full swing, conspiracy theories about Event 201 circulated across the internet. Initially, I, too, was concerned that perhaps Event 201 was more than just a coincidence. I mean, what are the odds that some of the most important people in the world had decided to play pandemic just months before the biggest global pandemic in decades broke out? Did the World Economic Forum and the Bill and Melinda Gates Foundation have a reason to suspect that scientists were playing fast and loose with dangerous and experimental viruses? Did they have special intelligence about early inklings of a new pandemic in China? What did they know that we didn't?

For months those questions plagued me, but the more research my team and I have conducted about the coronavirus, the pandemic response, and globalists' pandemic call for "a great reset of capitalism," the more convinced that I've become that Event 201 was *not* a secret meeting of elites who possessed special knowledge about the next pandemic. And although there are really good reasons to say aspects of Event 201 were nefarious, it certainly was not a meeting at which elites planned the secret development or release of the novel coronavirus, as some conspiracy theorists have suggested.

However, that doesn't mean Event 201 is nothing more than a strange coincidence or an interesting historical curiosity. As I'll show throughout the rest of this chapter, Event 201 and many meetings like it are incredibly important, and it is vital that we understand why they exist and the extent of their impact.

The truth is, in many respects, Event 201's importance surpasses any one crisis, even a crisis as big as the COVID-19 pandemic. Why? Because it helps to shine a light on a much larger, longer-lasting threat to your freedom—the Propaganda Industrial Complex, introduced in chapter 1.

The Blueprint

Over the course of my long career in radio, I have seen my fair share of breaking news events—everything from the September 11 terrorist attacks in 2001 to the financial crisis in 2008 and, of course, the Wuhan lab experiment gone wrong in 2020— Oh. Sorry. Did I say "Wuhan lab experiment"? I meant bat-soup virus. I wouldn't want anyone to get the wrong impression.

In each of these and many other crises, the response from institutions has consistently followed a similar four-part playbook, which I'll briefly outline:

Part One: It's the End of the World as We Know It

First, nearly all institutions—including those in academia, government, news media, and Hollywood—collectively assert that the crisis is dire and worthy of endless attention and fearmongering from so-called journalists at prestigious television and newspaper outlets. Wild doom-and-gloom predictions run rampant, and tens of millions of people, if not hundreds of millions, suddenly become acutely aware of the crisis issue, which they have little or no understanding of. Only America's "expert" class can be trusted to provide an accurate assessment of the dangers related to the crisis.

Part Two: The Strong Man

Just when it seems as though the crisis, whatever it may be, is poised to ruin life on earth, a white knight group of politicians or, better yet, international multilateral institutions ride into town to save the day. How? By imposing or proposing a vast new, complex system of government programs and policies. One-thousand-page bills suddenly appear out of the blue that promise to put the Western world back on firm ground. And all these masters of the universe ask in return is that we, the people, sacrifice our freedom in exchange for a little security. What's the worst that could happen?

Part Three: The Trusted Sidekicks

Once government has established a plan of action, many of the world's biggest corporations and financial institutions eagerly come to its aid. They express their undying devotion to politicians' quest to save the planet and then usually promise to work hand in hand with government in brand-spanking-new public-private partnerships. "There's no need to blame us for the world's problems," they say. "We're responsible. We're trustworthy. We're on your side."

Part Four: The Crackdown

Inevitably, deplorable dissenters emerge from America's heartland and other rural and suburban areas, catalyzing the activation of the new public-private partnerships and fierce backlash from government and legacy media outlets like the *New York Times*, the *Washington Post*, network television, and CNN. Anyone pushing back against the government-approved narrative is labeled a dangerous "extremist," a "science-denier," or, more recently, an "insurrectionist."

In this fourth phase, reputations are ruined. Lives are thrown into disarray. Family members and friends turn on one another. And the greater the level of dissent, the harsher the crackdown becomes. It sounds rough, I know, but try for a moment to walk for a mile in the thousand-dollar Gucci penny loafers of the ruling class. They want what's best for you. Sometimes, well-meaning rednecks, clinging to their guns and religion, need to be put in their place before true progress can be made. Or, in the words of the highly respected *New York Times* reporter Walter Duranty, who won a Pulitzer Prize in the 1930s for his glowingly positive reports about the Soviet Union, "To put it brutally—you can't make an omelet without breaking eggs."[58] (By the way, Duranty is best known today as the monster who deliberately covered up Soviet atrocities and human rights violations against Ukrainians.[59])

In these epic struggles, sometimes the elites gain the upper hand. In other cases, their plans fall flat. But regardless of who ends up on top, the strategy remains the same.

Preparation Makes Perfect

The most incredible and arguably important part of this never-ending cycle of conflict is that in each case, those seeking more wealth and power appear to have a full-fledged plan ready to go the moment a crisis strikes. Seemingly overnight, coordinated talking points have been distributed, massive government projects have been proposed, down-to-the-minute details have been collected and shared, and media outlets and government agencies located all over the world have come to a common mind. It doesn't seem to matter how swiftly the crisis emerges or how complicated the related issues are. The crisis response always operates as though nearly every major institution in the world were part of a well-oiled machine—methodical, consistent, and precise.

If it seems to you as though all the relevant institutions involved have spent years preparing for these crises, it's because *they have.* How could they possibly know which crises to prepare for or how best to design systems to deal with them? They don't. So, they spend mountains of time and money prepping for as many potential catastrophes as possible, from cyberattacks and pandemics to rising sea levels and emerging technologies. That way, when a new crisis does develop, they know they will be ready to use it to increase their power and wealth over Western societies.

This immensely influential collection of organizations and their innumerable systems designed to take advantage of disasters is the foundation of the Propaganda Industrial Complex. It's not a conspiracy theory. It's a conspiracy fact. And if you know where to look, you'll soon discover just how important it has become in shaping our understanding of truth in the modern world.

The Climate-Change Case Study

Perhaps the best illustration of the Propaganda Industrial Complex at work is seen by looking at the issues of global warming and climate change. Elites have been shrieking about the alleged "climate crisis" for the past three decades. Two generations of Americans have been hearing about it for so long that it probably seems to them as though it's always been part of the American policy debate. Of course, those of us who are a little more experienced—yeah, let's go with *experienced*, because *old* just doesn't have the same ring to it—remember a time when no one had ever heard of global warming. In fact, maybe you remember when global *cooling* was the crisis of the day.

In 1970, for instance, the *Washington Post* published an article titled "Colder Winters Held Dawn of New Ice Age." In 1974, *Time* magazine published "Science: Another Ice Age?" In April 1975, *Newsweek* infamously published a dire article titled "The Cooling World," which described a catastrophic global cooling trend that could soon consume the planet. The next month, a headline in the *New York Times* read, "Scientists Ask Why World Climate Is Changing; Major Cooling May Be Ahead." Then, just four months later, the *Times* sounded its alarm bells even louder, declaring, "A Major Cooling Widely Considered to Be Inevitable."[60]

Of course, that "inevitable" cooling trend turned to warming by the late 1990s, and then evolved into the catch-all "climate change" shortly thereafter.

It would be crazy to say that elites caused global temperature to drop in the middle of the twentieth century or to rise in the decades that followed the cooling craze of the 1970s. Obviously, they didn't, just as American politicians didn't deliberately release COVID-19 into the world in the hopes of increasing their power. But what the Propaganda Industrial Complex did do was take advantage of climatic changes. So, as temperatures have fallen or risen over the past century, elites have capitalized on that opportunity, expanding their power and wealth in the name of "saving the planet."

This is why every time there's a major snowstorm, heat wave, hurricane, tsunami, drought, or pretty much any other significant weather event, journalists publish a slew of stories about how that disaster is somehow linked to human-caused climate change. This is all related to the first part of the Propaganda Industrial Complex's blueprint that I mentioned in the section by that title. Industrial Complex media need to convince people that climate change is a bigger problem than it actually is, so they beat people over the head with easily refuted arguments and utilize scare tactics.

News media outlets aren't the only ones pushing this agenda, of course. Hollywood regularly inserts climate change as elements into movies and television shows. Colleges teach courses on the "climate crisis" and train their students to become eco-warriors well prepared to save the planet from calamity. And K–12 schools regularly indoctrinate young children into believing the world is on the brink of entering a climate-related death spiral.

These intense campaigns have set the table for the second component of the Propaganda Industrial Complex—calls for a dramatic expansion of government action, spanning three decades.

In 1997, governments from around the world, including the United States, developed the Kyoto Protocol, which "operation-alizes the United Nations Framework Convention on Climate Change by committing industrialized countries and economies in transition to limit and reduce greenhouse gases (GHG) emissions in accordance with agreed individual targets."[61]

In February 2002, the George W. Bush administration "commit-ted the United States to a comprehensive strategy to reduce the greenhouse gas emission intensity of the American economy by 18 percent by 2012."[62]

In 2009, the first year of Barack Obama's presidency, the U.S. Environmental Protection Agency declared that greenhouse gas emissions are "pollution" that endangers the health and welfare of the American people. It also imposed regulations meant to coerce businesses and individuals to join in the transition away from tradi-tional energy sources.[63]

In 2015, the United Nations, with strong support from the Obama administration, developed the Paris Agreement, an inter-national treaty designed to promote an "economic and social transformation" meant to reduce climate change. Under the agree-ment, nations, including America, agreed to dramatically reduce their greenhouse gas emissions. According to the deal, "greenhouse gas emissions must peak before 2025 at the latest and decline 43% by 2030."[64] Also in 2015, the Obama administration announced its Clean Power Plan, along with a laundry list of other regulations and programs meant to push the United States into adopting a "clean energy" economy.[65]

In 2018, newly elected socialist congresswoman Alexandria Ocasio-Cortez released her plan for a Green New Deal, a climate proposal that would have completely overhauled the U.S. economy, just as the Paris Agreement demanded. Among other things, the Green New Deal would have required the United States to eliminate nearly all carbon-dioxide emissions over a ten-year period. It would have also created a government jobs guarantee, a universal health care program, and an expensive green housing plan. In total, the Green New Deal could have cost more than $90 trillion, according to estimates from the American Action Forum.[66]

From 2021 to 2024, the Biden administration passed the most radical set of climate policies in American history. Biden committed to slashing total GHG emissions by at least 50 percent by 2030, a goal that would single-handedly crush the U.S. economy if fully adopted.[67] Biden and congressional Democrats also passed the absurdly named Inflation Reduction Act, which did absolutely nothing to reduce inflation while creating nearly $400 billion in new green-energy programs.[68] Additionally, Biden issued countless energy-related regulations, including particularly egregious plans to reduce methane emissions and impose the sale and use of electric vehicles.[69]

As I noted earlier, though, the Propaganda Industrial Complex demands more than just government action. The third component, and arguably the most far-reaching, involves powerful public-private partnerships between government and big corporate and financial institutions.

When it comes to climate change, large private institutions have played a particularly active and important role. Corporations have injected into their own business plans numerous commitments to reduce the use of carbon-dioxide emissions, limit consumers' use of fossil fuels, and impose a wide variety of other environmental policies that are too extreme to make their way through the lawmaking process. Many of these policies were developed to create economy-wide changes, whether consumers want them or not.

For example, the largest banks in the United States have all agreed to phase out fossil fuels from their entire business models by at least 2050, including customer accounts and lending.[70] That means that in the near future, it will likely become increasingly difficult for businesses and individuals to operate and live as they do now. Soon, you may not even be able to purchase a gasoline-powered car, and not because it will be illegal, but rather because banks and insurance companies could make it impossible to do so.

Financial institutions are not the only ones who have joined in the government's crusade against affordable energy. The vast majority of large U.S. corporations have adopted environmental, social, and governance (ESG) standards, including limits on land use and carbon-dioxide emissions. Accounting firm KPMG reported that in 2022, "nearly all of the world's top 250 companies (G250) report on sustainability," using ESG social credit scores.[71]

As these policies show, some of the most far-reaching components of the Propaganda Industrial Complex that are alive and kicking today come from the private sector, not the government.

From the beginning of the climate-alarmism movement, there have been highly qualified critics of the assertion that climate change is a catastrophic problem, both from within and without the scientific community. The oft-repeated claim that 97 percent of scientists agree about the causes and consequences of climate change is, as two experts noted in the *Wall Street Journal*, nothing but a "myth" that has now been debunked numerous times and by multiple researchers.[72]

Dozens of highly successful, prominent scientists reject the assertion that humans have caused and continue to cause a climate change catastrophe. Some examples include the following:

+ David Legates, professor emeritus of climatology at the University of Delaware, visiting fellow at the Heritage Foundation's Center for Energy, Climate, and Environment, and director of research and education at the Cornwall Alliance for the Stewardship of Creation. Legates is also the former visiting research scientist at the National Climate Data Center[73]

+ Roy Spencer, PhD, the principal research scientist at the University of Alabama in Huntsville and former senior scientist in climate studies at NASA's Marshall Space Flight Center[74]
+ Willie Soon, a renowned physicist with the Center for Environmental Research and Earth Sciences who formerly worked at the Harvard-Smithsonian Center for Astrophysics and the Mount Wilson Observatory[75]
+ William Happer, PhD, cofounder and chair of the CO2 Coalition, the Cyrus Fogg Bracket Professor of Physics emeritus at Princeton University, and a former senior director at the White House National Security Council[76]
+ John Christy, PhD, distinguished professor of atmospheric science and director of the Earth System Science Center at the University of Alabama in Huntsville[77]

Of course, the Propaganda Industrial Complex doesn't tolerate opposing viewpoints. That's why its fourth component is to silence all dissenters, and boy, has the Complex embraced that strategy when it comes to climate change. Academic blacklists have been developed to keep skeptics of climate alarmism out of universities and away from research laboratories.[78] And most of the largest social media companies have pledged to ban or flag posts that question establishment talking points about climate change, although many left-wing activist groups and alarmist climate scientists say that even more censorship is needed.[79]

Lawsuits and other legal activities have been filed or threatened to create a chilling effect. In 2015, alarmist scientists and members of Congress even went so far as to call on the Justice Department to launch a RICO (Racketeer Influenced and Corrupt Organizations) criminal investigation of corporations and policy organizations that have produced research or other materials promoting climate change realism, alleging that these groups should be prosecuted as though they were organized criminal enterprises, such as the Mafia.[80]

The Propaganda Industrial Complex has used these same strategies on numerous other issues, too, from the coronavirus pandemic to Black Lives Matter. The details may change, but the overarching four-part strategy remains the same:

1. Anticipate the next big problem and then exaggerate or invent the idea that it has become a full-blown "crisis."
2. Develop massive government programs that will increase elites' control over society, all in the name of solving the alleged "crisis."
3. Establish a partnership between government agents and large private businesses and financial institutions to accomplish objectives that would be difficult or impossible for the government to achieve on its own.
4. Silence the opposition to the maximum extent possible.

Reality Dies in Darkness

These highly organized attempts to change the Western world have had a significant downstream effect: when it comes to a long list of important issues, millions of people have become completely detached from reality.

For example, despite the belief held by millions of Americans that climate change has become an existential threat to humanity and that our world is becoming increasingly uninhabitable, there is *no* scientific evidence that our changing climate has made life worse. In fact, most of the available data suggests people are much better off today than they were in previous decades.

Over the past fifty years, there has been no increase in the frequency or severity of hurricanes.[81] The number of intense tornadoes, defined as category F3 or higher, has declined "dramatically" since 1970.[82] The U.S. Heat Wave Index shows that over the past century of American history, the worst decade by far for heat waves was the 1930s, long before carbon-dioxide emissions were considered a problem.[83] Deaths related to extreme temperatures have also been declining in recent decades, and in the period from 2000 to 2019, there were roughly ten times more cold-related deaths recorded than heat-related deaths.[84]

There's also no evidence that crop or food production is in decline. In fact, data from the UN Food and Agriculture Organization shows global production in key crops sets new records almost every year.[85] And the situation in America is especially good. A review of government crop data conducted by the Heartland Institute in 2022 shows that "since 2015, almost every important U.S. crop has set a record for yield per acre, according to the U.S. Department of Agriculture (USDA). For example, USDA reports the three highest records for corn yields occurred in 2017, 2018, and 2019. Further, the five highest rice yields ever recorded occurred from 2015 through 2019, and the wheat yields recorded from 2011 to 2019 are among the top 10 highest wheat yields in U.S. history."[86]

The delusions about climate change developed by the Propaganda Industrial Complex and now held by many Americans today have extended to renewable energy sources, such as wind and solar. These are commonly referred to as "green energy" because the color green evokes the idea that they are good for the planet, but that's yet another myth perpetuated by the ruling class.

It's extremely difficult to recycle wind turbines and solar panels, which typically last only a few decades before needing to be replaced. CNBC reported in 2023, "Currently, about 90% of end-of-life or defective solar panels end up in landfills, largely because it costs far less to dump them than to recycle them." Some businesses are working to fix that problem, but it's unlikely it will ever be solved entirely.[87]

The situation with wind turbines is not any better. In fact, it could end up being much worse. Wind turbine blades are composed of extremely hard material, making them expensive and time-consuming to recycle. As a result, wind turbine "grave-yards" have been created by companies looking to profit from green-energy waste. In 2023, *Texas Monthly* magazine published a report featuring one such graveyard in the West Texas town of Sweetwater. Over the past decade, thousands of decommissioned wind turbine blades have piled up in Sweetwater, "eventually blanketing more than thirty acres, in stacks rising as high as basketball backboards."[88]

Wind and solar energy are also environmentally harmful because their facilities require huge amounts of rare earth minerals and much larger swaths of land to operate than traditional energy sources. One academic study that measured the environmental impact of the Green New Deal—which calls for America to transition to a nearly 100 percent renewable energy grid—found that replacing conventional energy sources such as natural gas, oil, and coal with solar energy would require at least 19 billion solar panels. Those solar panels would consume a land area roughly the size of the states of Vermont and New York combined.[89] Researchers at Harvard University found that if conventional energy were replaced by wind turbines, it would require consuming about one-third of the land in the continental United States.[90]

You don't have to take my word for it, though. Even some radical climate alarmists admit that green energy isn't good for the planet. In fact, director Jeff Gibbs, who coproduced left-wing propaganda films like *Fahrenheit 9/11* and *Bowling for Columbine*, released a stunning documentary in 2020 called *Planet of the Humans*, which is focused almost entirely on highlighting the catastrophic environmental impacts of wind, solar, and other forms of green energy.[91] Michael Moore—yes, *that* Michael Moore—served as the film's executive producer.[92] If Jeff Gibbs and Michael Moore, two of the biggest climate alarmists on planet Earth, are willing to admit that wind and solar are bad for the environment, you know it's got to be true.

Americans' detachment from reality goes far beyond environmental and climate issues. In the wake of the death of George Floyd, an African American man who died while being arrested by police in 2020, protests and riots, operating under the banner of Black Lives Matter, broke out across the United States. These demonstrations were spurred in large part by the widespread belief perpetrated by the Propaganda Industrial Complex that black Americans are regularly, unjustifiably killed by police.

A national survey conducted in 2021 by Rasmussen Reports and the Heartland Institute asked likely voters how many unarmed African Americans were shot and killed by police in 2020. The results are stunning. According to Heartland's analysis of the poll results, "81% of MSNBC viewers, 77% of CNN viewers, and more than 70% of ABC, CBS, and NBC viewers said they believe there are at least 50 fatal police shootings of unarmed African Americans every year."[93]

Further, Heartland noted, "about one-quarter of CNN viewers said at least 500, and 9% reported 1,000 or more. Similarly, 11% of ABC viewers said 1,000 or more, with 5% of the total reporting at least 5,000 fatal police shootings of unarmed African Americans every year."[94]

The real number for 2020, according to a comprehensive *Washington Post* database, is 18. And since 2020, the number has dropped. In 2021 and 2022, it was 11 and 13, respectively, and in 2023, the most recent year available, the number recorded was 16.[95]

The Rasmussen/Heartland survey also revealed other commonly held false beliefs, all of which can be traced back to the Propaganda Industrial Complex:

Viewers who identified CNN, MSNBC, ABC, CBS, or NBC as their "favorite" TV news outlet are significantly more likely to overestimate the number of homicides that occur each year in the United States involving rifles, including so-called "assault rifles."

For example, 46% of CNN viewers and 41% of NBC viewers overestimated the number of homicides involving rifles, compared to just 19% of those who say they don't watch network news.[96]

There's also strong evidence that suggests that the greater the crisis is perceived to be, the greater the departure from reality that's experienced by millions of Americans who are victimized by the Propaganda Industrial Complex's efforts.

There are seemingly endless examples from the COVID-19 pandemic that I could draw from, but perhaps the clearest is the effectiveness of mask mandates. For nearly three years, the mainstream press, government agencies, Hollywood stars, and countless corporations repeated the ridiculous claim that requiring people to wear flimsy masks would prevent the spread of the coronavirus, even though common sense and scientific data showed repeatedly that mask mandates were not working. However, excluding some rare exceptions, it wasn't until early 2023—three years after mask mandates went into effect—that establishment media organizations acknowledged this reality.

In February 2023, after publishing untold numbers of articles *supporting* mask mandates, *New York Times* writer Bret Stephens authored an article titled "The Mask Mandates Did Nothing. Will Any Lessons Be Learned?"[97] In it, Stephens wrote what millions of Americans already knew: the mask mandates were ineffective and pointless. According to Stephens:

The most rigorous and comprehensive analysis of scientific studies conducted on the efficacy of masks for reducing the spread of respiratory illnesses—including Covid-19—was published late last month. Its conclusions, said Tom Jefferson, the Oxford epidemiologist who is its lead author, were unambiguous.

"There is just no evidence that they"—masks—"make any difference," he told the journalist Maryanne Demasi. "Full stop."

But, wait, hold on. What about N-95 masks, as opposed to lower-quality surgical or cloth masks?

"Makes no difference—none of it," said Jefferson.

What about the studies that initially persuaded policymakers to impose mask mandates?

"They were convinced by nonrandomized studies, flawed observational studies."[98]

Here's a little tip for the *New York Times*: in the future, you don't need to wait for academics to conduct months- or years-long studies to know that a small mask barely clinging to one's face won't on its own do much to stop the spread of a highly contagious virus. This is especially true when hundreds of people are trapped in a small, confined airplane traveling 20,000 feet above sea level for hours-long flights, and when people are taking off their masks to eat and drink airline refreshments and regularly touching surfaces after putting their hands all over their faces and blowing their noses.

The reason it took so long for the *Times* and other big left-leaning media outlets to come to their senses isn't because the Propaganda Industrial Complex is full of stupid or mentally incompetent people—Joe Biden excluded, of course. It's because the coronavirus pandemic served a useful purpose for elites: the expansion of the size and influence of the ruling class. The truth is, they didn't want the pandemic to end. Endless pandemics are good for those looking for a justification to transform the world as we know it. Or, as then Prince Charles said in the early days of the pandemic, the coronavirus is a "golden opportunity to seize something good" and to "reset ourselves on a more sustainable path."[99]

This *golden opportunity* way of thinking is the common thread that binds together all the alleged crises that I have discussed in this chapter thus far, from climate change and police shootings to the coronavirus and assault rifles. When people are afraid, they become more willing to do the bidding of those in control of the most powerful institutions in the world. That's not to say the ruling class is totally selfish, though. I think many in government, Davos, corporate boardrooms, academia, and on Wall Street really do believe everyone would be better off if elites had more control. And if the elites get rich or better status in life in the process, what's the harm in that?

In the ruling class's attempt to better manage nearly every part of society, it has increasingly resorted to undermining fundamental truths. To them, the ends always justify the means. As a result, America and much of the Western world are falling apart. We are more divided and confused than ever, and emerging technologies, which we will discuss more in chapter 4, are going to make these problems much worse. I know that might be hard to imagine, but just wait. If you think misinformation from the mainstream media and other elite institutions is a problem now, just wait until they get their hands on artificial intelligence—or even worse, when AI gets its "hands" on *them*.

Always Prepared

As I noted previously, the Propaganda Industrial Complex's strategy often takes years to fully develop for any one particular "crisis," which means elites typically do a lot of preparation before attempting to enact these strategies on a wide scale. How can they achieve that impressive feat if they don't know what's going to occur in the future? The answer is, by being ready for almost anything.

At the start of this chapter, I described Event 201, a war game designed to help government and civic leaders prepare for a dangerous global pandemic. Event 201 occurred just months before COVID-19 became a household name, so it drew attention from citizens and some journalists concerned about the causes of the outbreak. But Event 201 is just one of many such events. The Propaganda Industrial Complex is nearly always toiling away to prepare for its next chance to use something occurring in the world to advance its progressive agenda, whether it be a severe weather event or a strange new virus. In many cases, the scenario elites prepare for never develops.

A good example occurred in 2005, when the Johns Hopkins Center for Health Security—the same people behind Event 201— hosted a similar war game called Atlantic Storm.[100] Atlantic Storm featured numerous leaders from government and the private sectors, including Madeline Albright, who had previously served as President Bill Clinton's secretary of state. Although, in Atlantic Storm, Albright managed to attain a small promotion for herself: she participated in the war game as "president of the United States."[101]

According to a description of Atlantic Storm published by the Center for Health Security:

> The exercise used a fictitious scenario designed to mimic a summit of transatlantic leaders forced to respond to a bioterrorist attack. These transatlantic leaders were played by current and former officials from each country or organization represented at the table. There was an audience of observers from governments on both sides of the Atlantic as well as from

the private sector, but the venue was designed to focus all attention on the summit principals and their discussions around the table.[102]

The Center for Health Security hosted a similar event in June 2001 called Dark Winter, a war game in which former senior government officials participated in "a fictional scenario depicting a covert smallpox attack on US citizens."[103]

Of course, neither the Atlantic Storm's mock bioterrorist attack nor Dark Winter's fictional smallpox assault ever occurred. But if they had, the leaders involved, as well as the countless others who learned from the war games and events like them, would have had a rough framework from which to build. That's the whole point of these efforts.

I could write an entire book that covers events like these and the strategies and recommendations that come from them. They and other, similarly creepy gatherings occur frequently, including in recent history.

Clade X, another Center for Health Security war game, occurred in 2018. Its purpose "was to illustrate high-level strategic decisions and policies that the United States and the world will need to pursue in order to prevent a pandemic or diminish its consequences should prevention fail."[104]

Similarly, at annual cybersecurity meetings called Cyber Polygon, leading technology companies, government officials, journalists, and corporations from around the world discuss potential threats related to cyberattacks and strategize about ways they can work hand in hand with government in the event of a future crisis. One of Cyber Polygon's biggest supporters over the past few years has been the World Economic Forum.[105]

Previous Cyber Polygon events have featured simulations of a future "cyber pandemic," where participants worked through a mock cyberattack that would cripple corporate supply chains and potentially wreak havoc on the global economy.[106] They have also included presentations that instructed participants about the dangers of "fake news," which Cyber Polygon organizers called "a new 'digital' pandemic."[107]

Pandemics, both the traditional biological kind as well as the cyber variety, are not the only things that have drawn the attention of elites in recent years. At the World Governments Summit, for example, leaders from the public and private sectors gather annually to discuss a wide range of topics and potential risks. In recent years, the event has been particularly focused on emerging technologies and how governments can use them to shape a new narrative for society.[108]

At the 2023 World Governments Summit, government officials and business leaders discussed topics such as "data-driven disruptions," "The Role of Digital Content and Postmodern Identity," how best to get financial institutions to pour mountains of cash into "climate finance," how governments can take advantage of artificial intelligence, and "A Blueprint for Governments: Designing Future Cities."[109]

However, if I had to pin down my all-time favorite World Governments Summit topic—a truly difficult task because I love them all so much—I would have to say the top spot goes to the 2022 panel discussion titled "Are We Ready for a New World Order?" In that illuminating discussion, hosted by Becky Anderson, an anchor with CNN, "thought leaders" discussed how emerging technologies, the COVID-19 pandemic, and geopolitical tensions have created the conditions to develop a completely new way of thinking about governments and international institutions.

One panelist, Dr. Anwar bin Mohammed Gargasha, a high-level official for the United Arab Emirates, explained that many societies are still foolishly clinging to a nineteenth-century "plane of thinking." That "plane of thinking" is one that embraces such outdated ideas as "nationalism" and "state sovereignty." Technological advancements, he reasoned, have changed things, and it is well past time for governments to rethink the international order as a result.[110]

I don't know about you, but boy, am I glad that someone finally said it. Who needs "America first" when you can have people like "his excellency" Dr. Anwar bin Mohammed Gargasha and the other World Governments Summit luminaries to lead our country instead? What could possibly go wrong with yet another reworking of the "world order"?

In November 2021, the World Economic Forum and the United Arab Emirates hosted an important "Great Narrative" event in Dubai. It focused on helping leaders "fashion longer-term perspectives and co-create a narrative that can help guide the creation of a more resilient, inclusive and sustainable vision for our collective future."[111]

The United Nations General Assembly meets every year, during which public- and private-sector officials craft international agreements, binding and nonbinding alike. The United Nations also hosts an annual Conference of the Parties, an international climate change event featuring the most powerful government officials in the world, as well as many business and finance leaders.[112]

I could go on forever discussing numerous other recent events that have brought together world leaders with the intention of redesigning the future. What we have discussed so far has merely scratched the surface. To say that elites meet regularly to figure out the best way to advance their agenda is an incredible understatement. Rarely does a month go by during which powerful private- and public-sector officials fail to host at least one planning session, war game, strategy meeting, or conference. While you live your day-to-day life, raising children and working hard to keep food on the table, the ruling class plots its next big transformation of Western societies.

The question is not whether this is happening, but rather, what do we do about it? How can we possibly stop a machine as big as the Propaganda Industrial Complex? I have a plan to do just that, which I will describe in the next chapter. It's going to require all of us who believe in individual rights to work together. Before I get into the details, though, I want to briefly shift to a slightly different topic.

Who's Afraid of Mice?

Have you ever seen a movie where a mouse breaks loose in a restaurant or at a party, and everyone goes absolutely nuts? I'm sure when you've watched these scenes you can relate, but it really doesn't make a whole lot of sense, does it? Why would a mouse cause people to screech in horror? This isn't *Jurassic Park*. We're not talking about a man-eating velociraptor or something. You might not want a mouse running around your house, eating your favorite brand of cereal, potentially spreading disease. I get it. But there's no need to panic.

It's not just a human problem, either. Elephants, one of the largest and most powerful animals on the planet, also freak out when a small mouse runs by their gigantic legs. Why? Believe it or not, academics have studied this issue. They found that it's not that elephants are afraid of mice per se, but rather that they get easily startled when something they can't control, predict, or understand surprises them.[113]

In my many years of experience of going toe-to-toe with massive institutions, spooky billionaires like George Soros, and powerful politicians in Washington, DC, I have found that the ruling class often acts the exact same way when it comes to people like you and me. They are terrified when someone calls attention to their schemes, even the "little guys" like us, who have nowhere near the same amount of wealth or influence that they do.

Of course, the main reason power-hungry elites are spooked by people like us isn't a result of being easily startled. It's because the importance of the numerous systems they've spent their entire lives profiting from, building, and being celebrated for is nothing but a giant illusion. The truth is, you don't need elites to micromanage your life, run the economy, or teach your children in institutions of higher learning. A lot of the readers of this book know that, but most of their neighbors do not. In America, elites' authority comes primarily from a misguided trust in their abilities and knowledge. When that trust erodes, so do their power and reputations. Eventually, the money dries up as well.

This is why the wealthiest, most influential people and institutions have been spending a lot of time in recent years talking to one another about ways for big corporations, banks, Wall Street firms, academics, and governments to improve trust and stifle speech by those who are believed to be responsible for damaging their reputations. Contrary to popular belief, big institutions are more like elephants than we think—easily scared of even the smallest creature that they can't control and don't understand.

I know it doesn't always feel like it, but powerful institutions and political and cultural leaders are more afraid of you than you think. And you have a lot more power than you realize. Thanks to the internet, we live in the golden age of information. Never before have people had so much access to data, good journalism, video content, and educational resources. Today, you can learn about almost anything, whenever you want, and then share what you find with friends, family members, or strangers, often for free. Every single day, millions of people are reached by folks just like you—yes, *you*—with information they might have never had the opportunity to see just a couple of decades ago. Social media has its flaws, a topic we're going to discuss a whole lot more in future chapters, but it's undoubtedly one of the most powerful tools ever developed for individuals, one that has given a voice to the previously voiceless.

We can leverage technology even more than we already have, and in so doing, call even greater attention to the schemes devised by the ruling class. If we can undermine the reputations of those irresponsible institutions that are actively working to steal away our freedoms, shining a bright spotlight on their corrupt systems and plans for the future, they will be forced to reverse course. At the very least, we will slow their progress.

In the next chapter, I will share the best methods for protecting yourself from misinformation, as well as my proposal for a new grassroots movement to uncover the schemes of the ruling class. It's not going to be an easy fight, but Americans have faced difficult periods in history before, and they have always risen to the occasion. We can and, indeed, *must* do it again. The free world is counting on us.

3

A POLITICALLY INCORRECT
GUIDE TO DISCOVERING AND
UNCOVERING THE TRUTH

HAVE BEEN BLESSED IN MORE WAYS THAN I CAN COUNT, BUT one of the truly greatest honors of my life is that I have had the opportunity to build a long-lasting relationship with my radio and television audiences. Every week, millions of people across the country and even around the world hear my radio program or watch my show on BlazeTV or through a social media platform. Many in my audience have been tuning in for years.

There are a lot of reasons why the audience continues to watch and listen, and I will gladly give much of the credit to my production and research teams, who go way above and beyond each week so that the audience has the most important and thoroughly researched information available. But I think one of the other pivotal reasons for the show's long-term success is that my team and I have dedicated more time than just about any other radio or television program in America to finding important stories that others aren't talking about. In many cases, these stories are narrowly focused on attempts by powerful groups, including governments, to take away your freedom or wealth.

My show was the first or one of the first to fully uncover the following issues and influences:

+ the Great Reset movement
+ the threat posed by environmental, social, and governance (ESG) metrics and other social credit scores
+ the truth behind the COVID-19 origin story
+ the radical socialist and progressive figures behind the rise of Barack Obama
+ the threat of a global jihad by radical Islamicists
+ the essential details about the Biden crime family
+ the dangers of Common Core
+ the various ways the Washington, DC, political class use their positions of power to become filthy rich
+ the destabilization of the financial system in the run-up to the 2008 crisis
+ the extent of the Obama-era Benghazi cover-up
+ the dangers of deepfakes
+ the methods elite institutions are using to embed emerging technologies with left-wing ideology and the reasoning behind them

How have we been able to see through the lies of so many elites and to consistently find groundbreaking stories before nearly every other radio and television program? There's a five-part process that has helped us discover the truth about the Propaganda Industrial Complex and its methods, as well as protect us from its lies. And I'm going to share it with you now, because, as I said in chapter 2, a couple of the best things that we can do to stop the Propaganda Industrial Complex and the destruction of truth in America are to learn the best practices for determining the truth and to understand the greatest strategies for pulling back the curtain on the ruling class and its plans for the future.

These difficult endeavors require a lot of time and manpower, and frankly, my team isn't big enough to do it on the scale that's needed to save this country. But together, we can see through elites' lies and uncover the stories and problems that others are missing.

The following is our five-part process for discovering and uncovering the truth, as well as a sixth section that provides suggested actions designed to help you share with others the information that you find by using this guide. In the chapters that follow the guide, we will outline some of the greatest dangers to truth and freedom, both today and in the future, with a special emphasis on emerging technologies that are today or will soon make it harder for people to separate fact from fiction. In each of these additional chapters, we will apply the lessons provided in the guide that follows so that you will be better prepared for the tremendous challenges ahead.

It is important that you learn the methods and information contained in this guide, not only to protect yourself from the Propaganda Industrial Complex but also because, soon, I'm going to launch one of the biggest grassroots journalism projects in American history, and as I said in chapter 2, I want you to be a part of it. So, if you can, grab a pen and paper—or, more realistically, open an app on your smartphone—and start taking some notes. We have a lot of work to do.

Part One: Guard Yourself against Lies

As I have illustrated throughout the past two chapters, the biggest institutions in North America and Europe have been colluding together for years to transform Western civilization. One of their most effective tactics has been to create new narratives about virtually every part of our lives, from economics to human biology. "Facts" have essentially become whatever ruling-class elites say they are. They can and often do change, typically to suit the purposes of those in power. As a result, individuals are constantly being barraged with false or misleading information, all of which is designed to advance the ruling class's agenda.

In my 2023 book *Dark Future: Uncovering the Great Reset's Terrifying Next Phase*, I explained how these efforts have recently expanded into the field of emerging technology.[114] Artificial intelligence, the Metaverse, augmented reality, virtual reality, and numerous other technologies are now being designed with progressive ideology embedded within them, making it even more difficult for people to know what is true. (By the way, if you haven't gotten a chance to read *Dark Future* yet, don't worry. We'll discuss emerging technologies again later in this book, in chapter 4.)

Unless Americans develop the skills necessary to know a lie when they see it, there will be no way for them to effectively resist the rising authoritarianism of elites. That's why my first section in this guide to help you fight back against the ruling class is to learn a good system for evaluating the trustworthiness of information. The following are several guidelines that should constantly be on your mind when you are confronted with news and information. My team and I have been using them, to varying degrees, for years.

Of course, none of what appears in this section should be taken as a rigid framework offering simple solutions to extremely complex problems. This section of our guide is not comparable to a slide ruler that you can whip out of your pocket to determine the validity of something you just saw on your favorite streaming service or cable news network with mathematical certainty. Learning how to decipher the truth is more like exercising muscles. Muscles require constant attentiveness and dedication to build and retain their strength. And if you stop exercising them, they degenerate. Take it from someone who has *a lot* of experience in this area. I haven't hit the gym since the Clinton administration, and now my body has basically transformed into a giant jelly-filled donut. I could go on, but I'm starting to get hungry, and I think you get the point. Don't let your mind become a jelly-filled donut. You need to work at this whole truth-finding business.

The following subsections include tests our team uses when determining the veracity of the information we find, whether it be from a source, a government or private-sector report, or a news outlet.

The Liar, Liar Test

Not everyone who's wrong is a liar—otherwise, we'd all be liars, because at one point or another, we're all wrong about something. I know I can come across as a smart guy—at least, sometimes—but just ask my wife about *that time Glenn was wrong* and she'll tell you, likely in agonizing detail, just how wrong I've been over the years. What she won't say, however, is that *Glenn is a liar*. Like you, I try my best to be honest, and to pursue the truth wherever it leads, even if it means ending up in some very uncomfortable places.

Unfortunately, I cannot say the same is true about a lot of people in the mainstream press, government, Wall Street firms, academia, and other institutions. The ruling class is overflowing with liars, and you need to figure out quickly who you can trust and who is unworthy of your time.

As a rule, when a large institution or powerful person lies to me, I forever hold that institution or person to a significantly higher standard than I do for others. I call it the Liar, Liar Test. And I don't only use it when consuming information from sources that usually disagree with me, either. It goes for people on both sides of the aisle, across the ideological spectrum. It's easy to ignore liars with whom you rarely agree. It is much harder to hold people on your own side to the same standard when they are caught bending the truth. But it is *vital* that you do so. Our overarching goal must always be to find the truth, not the thing that we would like to be true.

It may sound like a strange practice but consider keeping a list of prominent individuals and institutions, including government agencies, that have been caught red-handed lying to you, especially big lies. That way, in the future, if one of these same institutions or individuals tells you something important, you know to hold the source to a higher standard.

Take the UN World Health Organization (WHO), for example. In the 1990s and much of the pre-COVID-era 2000s, I had little reason to doubt information that came from the WHO. In my mind, the WHO was composed of a bunch of honest research scientists and doctors providing free vaccines to impoverished parts of Africa. They seemed harmless. In fact, if I were in those years to name the parts of the United Nations that I was most concerned with—and there were and still are plenty—the WHO would not have been one of them. But now we know the WHO not only belongs on that list, but it could very well be the most troubling of all the UN agencies.

In early 2020, when Americans first heard whispers of the COVID-19 virus, the United States relied on the WHO for important information, including how the virus spread and its likely origin. But to appease the Chinese government, the WHO lied to the American people and put the interests of foreign governments ahead of our own—over and over again.

In 2023, the U.S. House of Representative's Select Subcommittee on the Coronavirus Pandemic hosted a hearing that outlined many of the WHO's failures, including the misinformation it spread in the pandemic's earliest days. The committee's "key takeaways" included, "The World Health Organization caved to political pressure from the Chinese Communist Party and placed CCP interests ahead of global public health. It is now time to hold China accountable for its intentional coverup of COVID-19."[115]

During the hearing, the Select Subcommittee's chairman, congressman Brad Wenstrup, further noted:

> We saw the WHO deny that COVID-19 was spread via human-to-human transmission, based entirely on the word of the Chinese government. The WHO delayed naming COVID-19 a Public Health Emergency of International Concern, a World Health Organization procedure that, amongst other things, would have allowed for the procurement and distribution of scarce supplies, all because the Chinese Communist Party told them the spread was under control. The WHO delayed serious measures to counter the global spread of COVID-19, because the CCP was only worried about their own bottom line. When the WHO produced a report evaluating the possible origins of COVID-19, it became unquestionably evident that the entire report was nothing but more Chinese propaganda.[116]

The WHO lied to you—and, indeed, to the whole world. And it lied at a time when people were counting on the WHO more than ever. So now, responsible citizens cannot take the WHO at its word.

I wish this problem were limited to the WHO and United Nations, but it isn't. Countless other government agencies, international institutions, and influential organizations have proven themselves to be untrustworthy in recent years. As a result, whatever they say needs to be subjected to a higher level of scrutiny. How, exactly, can you do that?

The best way is to confirm information you receive from these sources by finding other sources that agree but also have a long track record of pursuing the truth. The best sources are the ones that have shown they are willing to publish information that conflicts with their own ideological or political views.

Now, I'm not suggesting that you forever ignore institutions and individuals who have been caught lying. There wouldn't be a government or other major institution on the planet you could trust if you were to consistently live by that rule. However, you should hold proven liars to a much higher standard. Don't just take them at their word, even when it comes to complicated scientific topics. If an institution or individual has blatantly lied once before, it could happen again.

The "What Is a Woman?" Test

Another good strategy for determining whether you can trust a particular person or institution is that if that person or organization is claiming to be an expert on any topic—it doesn't matter which one—find out what that person or organization's position is on an issue where there is no doubt what the correct answer is.

One of the questions I have been using most often in my professional life is the "What Is a Woman?" Test. If an alleged expert or organization is unwilling or incapable of clearly and accurately answering the question, "What is a woman?," then you know immediately that this source is completely unreliable. It doesn't matter how many degrees he or she might have or how many so-called experts work for the organization. If you can't definitively tell the difference between a man and a woman, you're not an expert in anything—other than delusion.

Of course, you don't need to limit yourself to "What is a woman?" Get creative. Perhaps you could have a "Should a Guy with a Penis Chestfeed Newborn Children?" Test. Or maybe an "Is Hamas an

Evil Organization?" Test. Reasonable people can disagree on a lot of things, but these no-brainer queries aren't among them.

If a person, organization, or news outlet is willing to look you in the eye and tell you with great confidence that something is true, even though common sense clearly indicates it isn't, then you must not trust that entity or individual. So, if anyone tells you "math is racist" or "biological men *should* compete in the UFC against women," you know that he or she is hopelessly guided by something other than truth, facts, and reason.

The Egg-Throwing Gorilla Test

Back in 2021, radio commentator and all-around brilliant guy Larry Elder was running for governor in California's recall election. Critics of his campaign engaged in the typical anti-Republican attacks. They labeled Elder a bigot, called him uncompassionate, and more. But the most ruthless attacks of all concerned Elder's alleged views on race. According to his critics, Elder is not only a racist; he's also a white supremacist.

For example, *Los Angeles Times* columnist Jean Guerrero lamented to CNN that Elder "has been able to reach the minority of voters in California who embrace his white supremacist worldview." Guerrero also warned that Elder "poses a very real threat to communities of color."[117] For those of you who don't know much about my friend Larry, he's a *black* man from inner-city Los Angeles.

Now, you might think that the *Los Angeles Times* would have received a wave of criticism from the left-wing, alleged anti-racists of California for making such an outlandish allegation against a successful, self-made black man. But the opposite occurred. Many of California's liberals ruthlessly attacked Elder, doubling down on the *LA Times'* insane arguments. In fact, at one campaign stop, a progressive activist even went so far as to sport a gorilla mask while hurling eggs at Elder.[118]

If you come across an individual or a news outlet that honestly believes that Larry Elder is the racist one in this altercation, not the bigots at the *LA Times* and the woman in the gorilla mask, throwing eggs at a black man, then that person or organization is a lost cause. They have been so irredeemably consumed by Clown World that you can't trust anything that they say.

The Beware of Bias Test

This test is an incredibly simple yet effective way of protecting yourself from lies. Generally speaking, people and institutions are more likely to mislead and lie when they believe that their dishonesty will benefit an ideological, political, or religious cause with which they are already aligned. Rarely will an institution or influential person deliberately lie about something if that lie is likely to hurt their cause.

We use this theory about human nature to help guide us when determining how much research we need to conduct about a particular news story or other information we find. If the source of the information—say, the *New York Times*—reports something that favors Republicans or conservative causes, there's an increased likelihood the *Times* is telling the truth. But if the *Times* publishes a story that perfectly fits its existing left-leaning narratives, then we hold that report to an even higher standard of review. The same would be true for almost any media outlet or information source, regardless of its ideological and political leanings.

This is why you will sometimes see the *New York Times* and CNN cited in the reference section of this book and other books I've written. It's not that I love reading the *Times* or watching CNN, but I have found that when I can use the Left's own reporting to prove my point, then people who normally don't believe the things I say find the arguments I make more compelling.

The Bloodthirsty Tyrant Test

Another useful guideline is the Bloodthirsty Tyrant Test. This should be common sense, but in today's Clown World, it isn't. If a tyrannical government, political leader, activist organization, academic institution, or some other person or group has regularly called for or approved of violent action against innocent civilians, you shouldn't trust information coming from that source without significant corroborating evidence. A warped sense of morality is a telltale sign that an institution or person is capable of spreading falsehoods. After all, if you're willing to support killing or inflicting pain on innocents, what's wrong with a little lying?

The Original Source Test

One of the hardest guidelines to follow is that you should never rush to a conclusion but always make the effort to go to the original source. I know that's difficult. I am as guilty as anyone of wanting to rush to share important news stories. But over the past few years, so much misinformation has spread like wildfire because people haven't been patient enough to wait for more information to emerge or taken the time needed to find original sources.

There are literally hundreds of examples of this phenomenon occurring, but one of the most egregious in recent memory comes from the recent war between Israel and Hamas, a terrorist organization that also operates the government of Gaza.

On October 17, 2023, dozens of major American and European news outlets—including the *New York Times*, CNN, and MSNBC—reported that the Israeli government had allegedly attacked a hospital in Gaza, killing roughly 500 people.[119] The explosion at the Ahli Arab Hospital in Gaza City occurred just ten days after Hamas launched a brutal, barbaric terrorist campaign against innocent Israeli citizens on October 7. During the October

7 attack, Hamas kidnapped and raped women, deliberately targeted innocent civilians, and murdered elderly adults and infant children. In total, about 1,200 Israelis were killed on October 7, making it the deadliest terrorist attack against Israelis since 1948, the country's modern founding date.[120]

In the immediate wake of the explosion at the Ahli Arab Hospital, most media outlets framed the deadly event as an overzealous assault by the Israeli government, one that could violate international human rights laws. Initially, and incredibly, their only source of information about the attack came from a spokesperson for Hamas's health ministry. The Israeli government denied that it was responsible for the explosion, instead claiming that it was the result of a failed rocket launch by a soldier for the Palestinian Islamic Jihad, a group allied with Hamas.[121]

On October 18, American officials announced that U.S. intelligence officers agreed with the Israeli government's assessment, but by that time, the damage had been done.[122] Millions of people around the world believed that Israel had unjustly killed 500 innocent people at a hospital in Gaza. Many others didn't know what to believe. Those aligned with Gaza continued to claim that Israel was responsible for the attack and that hundreds had been killed, including American congresswoman Rashida Tlaib, who refused to apologize for blaming Israel for the explosion, despite reports to the contrary from U.S. officials.[123]

In the wake of the hospital explosion and the media's reaction to the event, some traditional liberals and conservatives in the media heavily and justifiably criticized outlets like the *New York Times* for giving any credence at all to reports provided by spokespeople for terrorist organizations. If news organizations like the *Times* had their own Bloodthirsty Tyrant Test, they never would have made the mistake of issuing false reports about the explosion.

However, even most of the critics of the *Times* and other media didn't get the story quite right. It turns out that the misinformation surrounding the Ahli Arab Hospital explosion was even more significant than most people realized.

On October 28, David Zweig, a writer who has authored articles with left-leaning outlets such as *New York Magazine*, *Wired*, and the *Atlantic*, published a truly remarkable article about the coverage of the Ahli Arab Hospital explosion and its death toll.[124] In the article, Zweig recounts his astonishing attempt to find the original source for the claims that 500 people had died in the hospital explosion and that the Israeli government was responsible.

Zweig reported that despite numerous written requests and phone calls seeking to track down the original source of these assertions, "not one reporter" responded. "I began to wonder," he wrote, "was it possible none of these journalists had actually seen or heard the original statement? Maybe one outlet reported it, and then everyone copied them, so the journalists didn't know the original source."

Zweig goes on to say that shortly after having that revelation, he and Kelley Krohnert, an investigator, launched a "deep dive" online search to find a source, any source, for the widely repeated claims about the hospital attacks. What they found was incredible.

Zweig wrote, "Finally, we found what appeared to be the source. At 1:50pm ET on October 17, Al Jazeera's Arabic Twitter [now called X] account posted a video clip (presumably of an interview that aired on its TV network) of an interview with Ashraf Al-Qidra, the Ministry of Health spokesperson."

Zweig then had Google translate the post. According to Google's translation, the post read, "Ministry of Health spokesman in [Arabic script] to Al Jazeera: More than 500 victims in the bombing of Al-Ahly Baptist Hospital in downtown Gaza City."

Zweig then wrote, "This is the moment where your eyebrows should arch. Notice that the text refers to more than 500 *victims*. A victim can mean a death, but it, of course, can also mean someone injured in any capacity. Had the spokesperson not said that more than 500 were killed, but merely said more than 500 were victims?"

It was at that time that Zweig had two different Arabic translators listen to the interview posted by Al Jazeera's Arabic X account. They confirmed that the health ministry official never said 500 people *died*, but rather that 500 people were *victims*, suggesting the number counted injuries as well as deaths. If true, this would mean that nearly every major media outlet in the Western world had issued a wildly erroneous death count, not because a Hamas official provided the number, but because media had mistranslated reporting by Al Jazeera.

Zweig's investigation didn't end there, however. He later found that what happened was possibly "far worse" than media mistranslating Al Jazeera's Arabic X video. According to Zweig:

> A short while after seeing the Al Jazeera Arabic tweet I found a tweet [on X] from the Al Jazeera English account that had been posted 11 minutes before the Al Jazeera Arabic tweet.
>
> The Al Jazeera English [X] account wrote "At least 500 Palestinians killed in an Israeli air strike ... says health ministry." It linked to an Al Jazeera post that said, "The Gaza health ministry said at least 500 people died in the hospital blast." But, like all the other reports, there was no link to the original statement. (Note: one of the authors of this Al Jazeera post was among the reporters I had contacted.)
>
> It seems most likely that some of the American journalists had been tracking the Al Jazeera English [X] account—not the Arabic one I had seen and translated—and immediately copied

its erroneous reporting. And the rest of them began copying each other from there.

In other words, the claim that "500 people died" in a hospital attack in Gaza was due entirely to the media's sloppy reporting and a translation error by the person in charge of Al Jazeera's English-language social media accounts. Not one large news outlet bothered to verify that Al Jazeera's translation was correct, nor did they bother to credit Al Jazeera as the source of the claim, making it extremely difficult for others to check the truthfulness of their articles.

It is stories like these that prove why it's so important that you always do your own homework. Never take anyone's word for it, even someone you trust. If you make an effort to seek out original sources, or even just to avoid sharing information if you don't have the time to find an original source, it will go a long way toward limiting the spread of misinformation and lies.

The Crazy Uncle Test

Eggnog, Christmas carols, big Thanksgiving turkeys, parades, fire-works—Americans have *a lot* of holiday traditions. But of the many pastimes shared by Americans, being trapped in a completely absurd conversation with a Crazy Uncle is one of my favorites. The Crazy Uncle is usually a nice guy. Almost always attends family events. You can usually find him striking up conversations with many of the younger high school or college-age members of the family. They're still too young to know that it's best to avoid getting stuck in conversations with Crazy Uncle.

Unlike the Angry Uncle or Passive-Aggressive Aunt, the Crazy Uncle isn't typically loud or abrasive, but he always has something to say. Something you've never heard before. Something secret he learned from "the blogs" or, even better, online forums.

Crazy Uncles come in all shapes and sizes, and with a wide range of ideological views. But the one thing they all have in common is that they have something to share that you've literally never heard before. And no one else around you has either. Maybe it's a new study that reveals that your favorite holiday food is one of the world's worst carcinogens. Or maybe it's about a video showing Nancy Pelosi shifting momentarily into a lizard. Whatever the topic is, there's rarely, if ever, any evidence provided to support his claims. The Crazy Uncle doesn't need evidence, because he knows better. He has all the evidence in his mind. "Just trust me," he whispers. Of course, you don't trust him. He's your Crazy Uncle.

Although it's true that not every family has a less-than-reliable uncle, there's almost always someone who fills the role—an aunt, a nephew, or perhaps even a grandpa. The title Crazy Uncle isn't so much about how a person is related to others as it is how a family member behaves. Being a Crazy Uncle is a state of mind more than anything else.

If your Crazy Uncle called you up to tell you about an unbelievable breaking news story, one that he can offer absolutely no support or citations for, would you trust him? Probably not. Your Crazy Uncle isn't a reliable source. That doesn't mean he's always wrong, of course, only that he's wrong often enough that you can't take his word for it. Often, you don't even need to think about whether you should trust him or not. It's practically an instinct.

All Americans need to learn that they should treat the entire social media industry as though it were their Crazy Uncle. You should never accept anything you see on social media as fact until you've taken the time to verify the claim using outside, reliable sources. This doesn't mean you need to completely ignore social media or delete all your applications—although, after you read chapter 4, you may think differently. What it does mean, however, is that you *must* have a healthy dose of skepticism online, especially on social media platforms.

My team and I never assume something that we've found on social media is true, even audio and video. As you go further along in this book, you'll see why we feel so strongly about this, and I am willing to bet that by the time you finish, you will never look at the internet the same way again.

Going on the Offensive

If you follow the guidelines referenced in this section, you will effectively guard yourself against most forms of misinformation and disinformation. That's important, but we can't win the battle for the soul of America solely from a defensive posture. We need to go on the offensive and take the fight directly to the ruling class. We can do that by learning and uncovering their methods and plans for the future and then showing them to the world. So much of what elites do requires that most of the public never learns or fully understands what they are up to. And as we've seen in recent years in the fights over the Great Reset, pandemic lockdowns, and many other important topics, when the people fully learn what's going on, they often push back hard. Knowledge is truly powerful.

The next four parts of this guide, parts two through five, will provide you with the tools necessary to better understand and reveal the ways the ruling class are working to undermine your wealth and freedom. Then, part six will offer tips for sharing what you find with friends, family, coworkers, and the rest of America.

Part Two: Assume the Worst in the Ruling Class

On November 13, 1789, Benjamin Franklin wrote a letter to Jean-Baptiste Le Roy, a notable French physicist who had previously served as the director of the French Royal Academy of Sciences.

In the letter, Franklin noted that America's "new Constitution is now established," and that "everything seems to promise it will be durable." However, Franklin concluded, "in this world, nothing is certain except death and taxes."[125]

With all due respect to Dr. Franklin, I think he left one thing out of his oft-quoted list. If history has taught us anything, it's that nothing is certain except death, taxes, *and* that there will always be attempts by those in power to expand their wealth and control over society. It's a tale as old as time, and I doubt Franklin would disagree.

One of the greatest errors Americans have made over the past few decades, although the problem has become less common among conservatives in recent years, is that they often think that if their political party of choice were to have enough control, then all of life's problems would be solved. The truth is, if you're looking for salvation in politics—or anywhere other than a church, for that matter—you have gone to the wrong place. The only powerful people in politics whom I trust are those who never wanted to be powerful in the first place. Nearly everyone else will eventually prove themselves to be unworthy of the responsibilities they have been given, abusing their positions to attain greater standing, glory, or cash.

The first step to dismantling the ruling class and uncovering its plans to undermine individual freedom is to always assume that it's up to no good. At all times, there is more than one component of the ruling class seeking to limit your rights. If that sounds paranoid to you, then I'd recommend you pay more attention to what's occurring in the news.

The reason this is the first step in our process is because my research team and I have found repeatedly that if we look hard enough and long enough at any part of American society—whether it be banking, Wall Street, Main Street, Hollywood, academia, the intelligence community, policymaking, and so on—we will eventually find a scandal or a clear-cut, systematic, wide-scale attempt to undermine individuals and their freedoms. The most important stories in America right now are probably those that we do not yet know about. That might seem hard to believe at first, but give it time and you'll see. The more I have learned about those in power, the worse my opinion of them has become.

So, the first step to uncovering the ruling class's attempts at gaining more authority and wealth is to assume that the ruling class is attempting to gain more authority and wealth. But who, exactly, are the members of the elite, anyway? In previous eras, I think many people—conservatives most of all, perhaps—would have struggled with that question. But today, those of us who want to limit the power of government and have been paying attention to the world around us know that most of the institutions in the United States are working together to reduce your autonomy—from big news outlets to schools and brand-name corporations. There are very few safe havens remaining. Even many of America's churches have become political tools of the ruling class.

It's not hard, then, to find a group, government agency, or industry that's worthy of our attention. They all are. The scope of the problem has become *that* massive, which is precisely why now is the time for all of us to band together and fight back.

Part Three: Make a List; Check It Regularly

One of the most remarkable aspects of the Propaganda Industrial Complex is that much of what its members do to achieve its goals has been posted online. In the case of government agencies, this is usually because there's a legal requirement for transparency, but even private corporations and activist groups regularly make their most radical ideas available to the public. You just need to know where to look.

There are dozens of important websites, conferences, and insider publications that offer invaluable resources, but because they aren't popular news websites, most people ignore them. Start making a list of sources you find valuable, and then check those websites regularly. Place a special emphasis on websites that allow you to see original sources and are not curating news for you. In other words, try to avoid looking solely at news outlets when you're seeking to discover something entirely novel.

One of my team's informational gold mines in recent years has been the official website of the World Economic Forum (WEF), the organization that hosts an outrageously lavish event for elites in Davos, Switzerland, each year.[126] The WEF is also the group that launched the Great Reset movement in 2020.

There are thousands, perhaps tens of thousands, of posts on the WEF's website. You could read an article there almost every day and never see all the most important information the WEF makes available. The WEF is the meeting place for many of the most influential organizations, activists, and academics. Many people already know that, but what few realize is that the WEF allows many of those prominent figures to post their ideas on its official website.

The World Economic Forum has countless important initiatives that cover nearly every issue imaginable, from environmentalism to global tax structures. If you make a habit of reading the WEF's website once every few days, you'll have no trouble finding something worth talking about.

Another good source is events websites. Some of the best resources for uncovering elites' plans come from conference sites and announcements. The WEF's annual event in Davos includes hundreds of hours of speeches, panel discussions, and informational sessions each year. These videos are posted online and feature leaders from corporations, the banking and finance industries, government, academia, and more. My team has only managed to watch a fraction of the video content available from the 2024 Davos event, and that's just one year's worth of content.[127]

Davos isn't the only conference worth keeping an eye on. The WEF hosts numerous other high-profile gatherings. In 2024, for example, it hosted a Special Meeting on Global Collaboration, Growth, and Energy for Development in Saudi Arabia, an Industry Strategy Meeting in May in New York City, an Annual Meeting of the New Champions in June in China, and the Sustainable Development Impact Meetings in September in New York City.[128]

As I mentioned earlier in this chapter, another important annual event is the World Governments Summit, which takes place in Dubai. The 2024 meeting featured more than 23 ministerial meetings, more than 200 speakers, and 15 different forums. More than 120 government delegations and 85 international and regional organizations reportedly attended.[129] Like the WEF, the World Governments Summit has countless hours of video content to watch.

Here are some other organizations, events, and sources worth following:

- trade publications focused on "sustainability" or ESG (there are many of them out there)[130]
- websites that cover banking and financial regulations[131]
- the Johns Hopkins Center for Health Security[132]
- *Governing* magazine and *Heartland Daily News*, two publications that specialize in state policy issues[133] (few major print and digital publications pay close attention to state policy, but that's often the area where significant action, both good and bad, takes place)
- the *UN Chronicle*, the official news publication of the United Nations[134]

+ Principles for Responsible Investment, one of the leaders of the global ESG movement[135]
+ the "Insights" section of BlackRock's website[136]
+ the official press statement sections of the websites of the U.S. Department of State and the U.S. Mission to the United Nations[137]
+ the Atlantic Council's "Central Bank Digital Currency Tracker," which shows users the progress made by governments across the planet toward the creation of liberty- and privacy-killing digital currencies[138]

Part Four: Understand *Their* Terms

As you discover continuously more information, you're going to quickly find that many in the ruling class use terms that sound as though they refer to one thing but that carry a lot of hidden meaning as well. For example, when most people hear the word *sustainability*, they think of environmental stewardship and avoiding waste. But when elites and large institutions talk about "sustainability," they could be referring to a whole host of other ideas that have nothing to do with the environment.

For instance, the UN Sustainable Development Goals are the foundation of the majority of the United Nations' efforts. In many respects, they are the UN's guiding principles. They are also the framework for virtually all Western ESG and other social credit scoring systems, including those outside the United Nations. The UN Sustainable Development Goals go way beyond environmental concerns. They include 169 targets grouped into 17 issue areas, such as "No Poverty," "Zero Hunger," "Gender Equality," and "Reduced Inequalities."[139]

Those and many other parts of the Sustainable Development Goals are clearly not focused on environmentalism, although we usually think of sustainability as a concept limited to things like reducing consumption and making sure that people put their plastic forks in the right recycling container at their local restaurants. Why, then, did the United Nations choose to use the word "sustainable" for its broad goals about social and economic transformation? Well, because "sustainable" sounds good. It is no different from the decision by Alexandria Ocasio-Cortez to include the word "green" in the title of one of the most ambitious socialist proposals ever offered in the United States—the Green New Deal.

Another good example is elite institutions' use of the terms *diversity*, *equity*, and *inclusion* (DEI). No one wants to stand in the way of fairness and diversity, right? But that isn't what DEI means—at least, not typically. DEI has become shorthand for corporate and government policies such as racial and gender quotas in workplaces, as well as limits on freedom of expression, such as bans on so-called hate speech.

By unlocking the meaning of key words used by elites and their institutions, you will quickly find even the most innocuous-sounding programs or statements are filled with importance. Perhaps the best example from my own career is from the early days of my investigation of the Great Reset movement.

The Great Reset was a worldwide initiative launched by the World Economic Forum in the midst of the COVID-19 pandemic, in 2020.[140] It aimed to "push the reset button" on the global economy, social contracts, and virtually every part of life in the Western world.[141] At the time of the Great Reset's rollout, it seemed as though virtually every major politician and wealthy institution was behind the movement, and the rhetoric they used consistently at the time of the announcement was radical and pointed to a coming total transformation of the world.

Almost immediately, I knew the Great Reset was important, but much of the language used by its supporters was vague. At times, it seemed like a slogan, not an overarching plan. At other moments, though, in interviews and meetings, those involved in the Great Reset spoke about it in a way that suggested it did involve specific, sweeping reforms.

My big break in understanding the Great Reset came after reading a World Economic Forum article titled "Now Is the Time for a 'Great Reset,'" authored by WEF executive chairman Klaus Schwab. In the article, Schwab explained, "The Great Reset agenda would have three main components. The first would steer the market toward fairer outcomes. To this end, governments should improve coordination (for example, in tax, regulatory, and fiscal policy), upgrade trade arrangements, and create the conditions for a 'stakeholder economy.'"[142]

The term "stakeholder economy" grabbed my attention. It sounded odd, but it was clearly part of Schwab's vision to "steer the market toward fairer outcomes."

Later in the same article, Schwab wrote that rather than use coronavirus relief funds, both from the public and private sectors, "to fill cracks in the old system, we should use them to create a new one that is more resilient, equitable, and sustainable in the long run. This means, for example, building 'green' urban infrastructure and creating incentives for industries to improve their track record on environmental, social, and governance (ESG) metrics."[143]

Environmental, social, and governance metrics—there's another term I had never heard of before. What are these metrics, I wondered, and how could they be used to help elites "reset" the Western economy?

With these two terms in mind—"stakeholder economy" and "ESG"—I set out on a wild investigative journey that resulted in my 2022 book, *The Great Reset: Joe Biden and the Rise of Twenty-First-Century Fascism.* As I explained in detail in *The Great Reset,* ESG and stakeholder economics, also commonly referred to as *stakeholder capitalism*, refer to the use of social credit scores by Wall Street firms, governments, banks, and other wealthy institutions. Those social credit scores were and still are being used to "reset" and transform the societies of North America and Europe. ESG and stakeholder economics were the keys to understanding the Great Reset, and the only reason I was able to make the connection is because I took the time to fully grasp the meaning of the important terms Schwab used in his article.

Part Five: Follow the Breadcrumbs

Once you have amassed a good list of potential sources for important information, are checking those sources regularly, and have a good understanding of the terms being used, you will soon find yourself stumbling on articles, legislative proposals, and other information that raises red flags. Maybe you'll even come across something that appears to be a full-blown scandal. When this exciting moment comes, whatever you do, *do not stop digging.* I can't tell you how many times I've found a bigger problem, danger, or scandal by looking a little more closely at a surface-level issue. Do not stop searching until you've hit a dead end or think you have your arms wrapped all the way around a problem.

Follow whatever breadcrumbs you can find, especially financial incentives, and see where they lead. As I mentioned earlier, put a special emphasis on finding original sources. You'd be surprised how much important information you can discover online, sometimes proudly posted by influential organizations and governments.

For example, in February 2021, leaked documents revealed that Coca-Cola had been secretly instructing employees using radical, racist materials demonizing white people. The course, titled "Confronting Racism," included materials that made statements such as, "In the U.S. and other Western nations, white people are socialized to feel that they are inherently superior because they are white." Another part of the materials asked employees to "try to be less white" by following guidelines such as "be less oppressive" and "break with white solidarity."[144]

As you'd probably expect, conservative media went wild when the news broke, and rightfully so. But what so many of those covering the story missed was the reason behind the racist materials. What was the root cause of Coca-Cola teaching its employees to be "less white"? Was it really because the entire leadership team at Coca-Cola had drunk too much of the Ibram X. Kendi, 1619-project Kool-Aid? Or was something else going on?

At the time the racist Coca-Cola materials reached my desk, I was already far down the Davos-stakeholder-capitalism rabbit hole, so I was able to recognize the reason behind Coca-Cola's policy right away—ESG social credit scores. Our research team immediately investigated Coca-Cola's self-produced ESG report, something virtually all major companies publish annually, and pieced together the bigger picture at Coca-Cola. Most of the conservative media missed it because they weren't looking closely enough.

Part Six: Spread the Word

Okay, so you've found the next big bombshell story. Now you're probably thinking, *What am I supposed to do about it? I'm not a television or talk radio show host, politician, or the president of a major media outlet. How can I, of all people, make a difference?*

If I had to identify the single greatest threat to individual freedom today, it would be the hopelessness so many people feel when they start to learn about the problems facing the country. I know what that's like; believe me. There are many mornings that I wake up, read what's going on in the news, and think, *We've lost. We're never going to get America on the right track.*

Then, without fail, an inspirational person comes into my life, or those of us fighting for freedom experience an important victory, and I realize that I've had it wrong. Have we lost the country we once loved and cherished? Yes. We're all citizens of Clown World now, remember? But the spirit of America remains strong with tens of millions of people like you and me, in thousands of communities across the country. In fact, if you were to take out a map of the United States, hang it on the wall, and throw a dart at the map, chances are, if your experience is anything like mine, you're going to hit your executive producer with a tiny sharp object. But if you have more athletic ability than I do—and for your sake, I hope you do—then you will likely throw that dart and hit a spot where the American dream is still alive. In many small and medium-size communities across the country, there is still hope that our American way of life can be preserved.

I think it's also vital to remember that the United States has been through many dark times before, and in those moments, its people felt just as lost and hopeless. If you were an advocate of limited government living in America in December 1944, you would have just witnessed tens of millions of people dying in World War II, which had still not reached its conclusion. Franklin Delano Roosevelt, one of the most progressive, liberty-killing presidents in history, would have just been elected to his fourth consecutive term in office. (And you thought the Obama era was a long, painful period.) Additionally, voters would have just cast enough ballots to keep both the U.S. House and the Senate firmly in the hands of Democrats. Not since January 1933 had Republicans been in control of either the House or Senate, nearly twelve years earlier.[145]

Dozens of large government agencies and radical new laws had been created over the previous decade, many of which imposed vast new regulations on businesses and families or coerced hundreds of thousands or even millions of people into becoming dependent on government.

For example, the Agricultural Adjustment Administration and the Agricultural Adjustment Act gave the federal government greater control over America's farms. Writing for the Mises Institute, scholar Thomas DiLorenzo noted, "The Agricultural Adjustment Act sought to cartelize the agriculture industry by paying farmers huge sums for not growing crops and raising livestock. Farmers benefitted for a while from this program, but many poor sharecroppers became destitute because of it." [146]

The Securities Act of 1933 gave the federal government greater authority over the stock market and other securities trading. The National Recovery Administration imposed hundreds of far-reaching regulations on business activity. [147]

According to DiLorenzo:

> Over 700 NRA industrial codes were created and were rigorously enforced by thousands of government code enforcers who, according to Roosevelt biographer John T. Flynn, "could enter a man's factory, send him out, line up his employees, subject them to minute interrogation, take over his books on the instant." A hapless New Jersey tailor named Jacob Maged became nationally famous after he was arrested, convicted, and imprisoned by the code police for the "crime" of pressing a suit of clothes for 35 cents when the Tailors' Code fixed the price at 40 cents. [148]

Many of Roosevelt's New Deal–era programs were ruled unconstitutional by the Supreme Court throughout the 1930s, but by the start of his fourth term in office, the Supreme Court had been completely transformed by Roosevelt and was no longer defending the rights of individual people. The national government took advantage, often resorting to unquestionably tyrannical tactics.

For example, the Roosevelt administration's War Relocation Authority built government concentration camps of Japanese American citizens, which in December 1944 were still in operation. By the end of World War II, approximately 120,000 people had lived within their barbed-wire-fenced borders.[149]

Imagine how hopeless it would have seemed to freedom-loving Americans living in that horrific era. It took decades to reverse many of Roosevelt's policies, and it wasn't until the Ronald Reagan revolution of the 1980s and the Republicans' Contract with America in the 1990s that conservatism regained a significant foothold in the United States. But in the end, progress was made. In many respects, the United States in the 1980s and 1990s was freer than it had been in 1944. We can experience a similar revival again, but the only way that can happen is if everyday Americans decide to push back, every single day, in whatever ways they can.

I believe the most important thing we can do to reignite the flame of liberty today is to uncover the ruling-class forces undermining freedom. Unlike in 1944, it isn't obvious to most conservatives who the real threats are. Elites have managed to undermine truth in our modern world so effectively that most people have completely lost touch with reality, or they focus most of their time expressing outrage about the wrong issues. We must get people to pay attention to what really matters, and that starts by undermining the reputations of the institutions destroying our country. We can do that by comprehensively revealing their plans to amass more control and wealth.

The first five components of the guide outlined above explain the steps you can take to guard yourself against misinformation and uncover nefarious actors, but how do you reach people with the new information that you discover along the way? There are several strategies that you should consider. Some will be a better fit for you than others, but I guarantee that you'll be able to do at least one of the following:

First, tell at least one new person every month about some of the interesting things you've found. That person could be a friend, a coworker, a classmate, or a family member. Use original sources and keep it simple. If you're talking to people who don't share your political views, keep politicians out of it. Focus instead on elites in private-sector institutions or others who do not have an overtly political affiliation. Millions of people listen to my radio show each week. If just one million members of my audience were to agree to talk to one person every month for a year, they would reach 12 million people, far more than enough to change the outcome of elections and to create grassroots momentum for substantial policy changes.

Second, if you are a good writer, consider publishing some of what you find online. Publishing platforms such as Substack and Medium allow writers to share their ideas with the world. It's also never been easier or more affordable to start your own website with a platform such as WordPress. Publishing your findings and then sharing them can be a great way to get others, including people in your personal life, to learn information that they otherwise would never see. In all your writing, remember to show original sources.

Third, consider sharing some of your findings using long-form posts or short videos on social media sites that support free speech, such as Elon Musk's X platform.

Fourth, following the release of this book, Blaze Media is going to launch a new program for subscribers that will allow them to submit important stories that they find, along with links to sources. Those stories will be shared with my research team, the news writers and editors at Blaze Media, and the production teams for all the television and podcast shows at BlazeTV. If you've done your homework and found something important, it could end up being shared with millions of people across the country through Blaze Media.

Once the program is fully up and running, it will be one of the greatest amplifiers of grassroots journalism in the United States. Davos and its friends in government, banking, academia, media, Wall Street firms, and left-wing activist groups are in for a rude awakening.

The Battles Ahead

Now that we have established a good framework for uncovering and discovering truth, I am going to spend the remaining chapters of this book discussing some of the most important topics and problems Americans are likely to face over the next few years and longer. In each of those areas, I will provide you with the critical information you need to protect yourself from falsehoods and to prepare you and your family to more closely investigate what Davos, governments, Big Tech companies, foreign nations, and other powerful interests are doing to erode your rights.

Our first challenge will be to tackle emerging technologies, the topic of chapter 4. If you thought the misinformation and disinformation problems are bad now, just wait until we reach the height of the coming Fourth Industrial Revolution. Things are about to get crazier and creepier than you ever imagined possible.

4

YOU CAN'T BELIEVE YOUR EYES: HOW EMERGING TECHNOLOGIES ARE MANIPULATING YOU AND YOUR CHILDREN

HAVE BEEN A PART OF THE MEDIA INDUSTRY FOR A LONG TIME. In the early 1980s, I took my first job in the industry at age eighteen at a radio station in Provo, Utah. That means—doing some back-of-the-envelope math—I've been working in media for somewhere north of . . . let's go with twenty years. Although, now that I think about it, maybe it has been more. Math has never been my strongest suit.

My career in media has taken me from working in local radio stations to national radio to cable television to creating my own media network, TheBlaze. I have literally witnessed firsthand the evolution of the news industry, which began to change rapidly in the 1990s. It was at this time that the static nature of print media and network television gave way to opinion talk radio and cable news. Then the development of the internet and affordable home computers made internet-based publications more influential in the early 2000s. Cable news became a juggernaut during this period, but then slowly bled customers during Barack Obama's presidency.

Today, the future of traditional cable news outlets looks bleak. Internet-based streaming services and independent shows hosted by larger online platforms are beginning to dominate much of the space. Soon, they will completely overwhelm cable news networks, whose audience is getting increasingly older in age.

Each improvement in technology experienced over the past four decades has brought with it new advantages, efficiencies, and challenges. But the problems we face today and those that will soon come our way are much more difficult to manage than anything we've ever witnessed before.

Social media platforms have become one of the primary battlegrounds for information dissemination, further blurring the lines between news and entertainment and giving people a warped sense of reality.

Now, more than ever, what we see on television and the internet is not only changing *what* people think but also *how* people think. It's shaping their personalities and manipulating their feelings, all of which is then impacting the rest of our society, often for the worse.

It's becoming harder than ever to know what's real and what isn't, and the establishment news media isn't making it any easier. As I showed in chapters 1 and 2, as part of the Propaganda Industrial Complex, the media regularly promote misinformation to achieve ideological and political goals.

I wish I could say this is the worst of our problems, but it's far from it. As I'll show in this chapter, advancements in media algorithms, the development of advanced artificial intelligence (AI), and improvements in deepfake technology are forcing all of us to venture into uncharted territory.

Of course, these technological marvels are not all bad. They present exciting positive opportunities for the future too. But only if people are prepared. And right now, most Americans are anything but ready for the future that's hurtling toward them.

During the next few years, AI will continue to reshape how information is generated and disseminated. The convergence of social media, artificial intelligence, and generative technologies will usher us into an era where the very fabric of reality and truth will be at stake.

This chapter will provide you with the information needed to navigate those difficult times, but before we can discuss the future, we first need to better understand our world today.

Echo Chambers

Let me ask you an easy question: Does it seem as though people are angrier than ever? Like they are increasingly on edge, ready to launch into a tirade about anything and everything? At social gatherings, do you find yourself biting your tongue instead of chiming in on a conversation about social issues because you're afraid a loved one might get triggered over a political, religious, or social viewpoint? Does it feel as if everyone has an aggressive opinion on every issue—even the type of car you choose to drive or the food you eat? This phenomenon goes way beyond political matters. Today, it feels as though if you admit that you enjoy a particular movie or musical artist, you're also simultaneously making some sort of social or political statement, one that's often subject to vehement criticism.

America is more polarized than ever. The widening gap between political ideologies has seeped into nearly every aspect of public discourse, from social issues to pop culture. Some political commentators have described the perceived societal rifts in the United States as a kind of "cold civil war"—and lately, it seems as though that *cold war won't stay chilly for long*.[150]

Some will smirk at these observations, writing them off as nothing new. I get it. I've lived through other periods where America also seemed very polarized, to say the least. But when I talk about the growing rift in our society and discourse, I'm not falling into the trap of engaging in recency bias. Data supports the claim that America appears to be on the verge of ripping itself apart.

For example, the American National Election Studies (ANES) has been surveying the public on these matters for more than seventy years.[151] One of its assessments, referred to as the "feeling thermometer," asks people how they feel about their own political party as well as rival parties. In 1978, the average person's feelings rating toward his or her own party was 71.1 out of 100 possible points. When asked about the respondent's feeling toward his or her rival party, the number dropped to 48, a 23-point gap between the two perceptions. Since 1978, the gap has grown substantially.[152]

From 1978 to 2020, ANES's feeling thermometer for "own-party feeling" has remained relatively consistent around the low-70s score. The "rival-party feeling," on the other hand, has steadily declined. In 2020, it was 19.3, and the gap between the positions soared to 52.2 percentage points, the largest it has ever been since the ANES started measuring this metric in the late 1970s.[153]

In addition to the feeling thermometer, ANES also has been tracking the "strength of partisanship" since 1952. In the ANES partisanship survey questions, respondents are asked to label themselves with one of the following identifications, regardless of their political position: independent, leaning independent, weak partisan, or strong partisan. In 2020, the percentage of respondents who self-identified as "strong partisan" reached 44.2 percent, the highest number ever recorded and nearly double the rate recorded in 1978.[154]

The ANES findings clearly indicate the American public is becoming increasingly stratified in terms of political allegiance, and ANES is not the only group observing this trend. Organizations such as Rice University, Stanford University, and Pew Research Center have also identified an increase in polarization in the United States.

For instance, a study conducted in 2024 by researchers at Rice University and Stanford University show that "people are more polarized than ever."[155] Similarly, the Pew Research Center published a widely referenced feature article in 2017 that showed the growing division between Democrat and Republican voters since the mid-1990s. According to Pew, America's right-leaning voters are becoming more conservative and Democrats are becoming significantly more progressive or socialistic.[156]

All of this begs the question, What is driving these shifts? Some will argue increased polarization is a result of Donald Trump's venture into politics, or perhaps the Left's over-the-top response to Trump. This is a fine enough theory, but it does not correlate with the observations of the organizations mentioned earlier. The studies I referenced previously also clearly show an increase in polarization before Trump announced his first run for president.[157]

Others might point to "fake news" and an increase in partisan propaganda to explain the growing rift. This is a better theory, but it still can't explain everything we're experiencing. Fake news and propaganda are not new concepts, by any stretch of the imagination.

Jacob Soll, a professor of history at the University of Southern California, wrote a feature for *Politico Magazine* in 2016 outlining an abridged history of fake news. According to Soll, fake news predates objective journalism. He points to examples dating back hundreds of years. In the era of modern daily newspapers, which began in the United States in the nineteenth century, criticisms of "yellow journalism," "sensationalism," and "gate keeping" have been leveled for more than a century. For example, it was common for New York newspapers in the early 1900s to run an issue featuring a baseless but captivating story on the front page, as well as for publishers to align closely with politicians or political parties.[158]

So, if bias and a willingness to publish fake news aren't the causes driving the increased polarization in the United States today, what is? There are many contributing factors, including several related to the way America's news and information are being disseminated.

For most of human history, the distribution of news and information was very slow. Even in the modern era of print newspapers, information needed to be collected by a journalist, formed into an article, proofed by an editor, laid out in a newspaper, printed, and then delivered to the reader. Want an update to the news story you read today? You'll have to wait for tomorrow's paper.

Broadcast news, which began in the early twentieth century with the advent of commercial radio technology, sped up news dissemination. Short news bulletins would air between programs as early as the 1920s. During the 1930s, the radio was a popular medium to relay information about World War II, including advertisements for war efforts and propaganda.[159] The Golden Age of American radio began in the 1940s, when radio stations started to produce more sophisticated news shows, featuring interviews, analysis, and investigative reporting.[160]

In the 1950s and '60s, people increasingly turned to their televisions for news. As televisions proliferated in American homes, news anchors like CBS's Walter Cronkite, "the most trusted man in America," became the primary avenue by which people received their news and information.[161]

The speed of news once again increased with the creation of CNN by Ted Turner in 1980. CNN was the first network to broadcast nothing but news twenty-four hours a day, seven days a week.[162] Turner's gamble turned out to be a success. Viewership grew, and CNN added opinion programming, like *Crossfire* and *Larry King Live*. CNN revolutionized the industry. Journalists now had the ability to inform people about what was going on in real time. The speed of news dissemination greatly increased. CNN's model contributed to the globalization of news, making information more immediate and accessible to audiences everywhere. People regularly tuned in to CNN to see live coverage of breaking stories. For example, CNN was the only national station covering the *Challenger* space shuttle disaster in 1986 as it occurred.[163]

With the demand for all-day programming firmly established, corporations soon rushed to fulfill it. In the mid-1990s, MSNBC and Fox News were launched.[164] In the following years, dozens of the most recognizable news shows originated on one of these all-news-all-day channels.

There's no denying that a 24/7 news cycle can foster an environment that prioritizes sensationalism, haste, and selectivity over accuracy, depth, and comprehensive reporting. This undeniably contributed to the polarization of viewpoints in America, as individuals became exposed primarily to content that reinforced their existing beliefs, leading to "echo chambers" and a lack of constructive dialogue. Furthermore, the constant bombardment of information has overwhelmed individuals, leading to information fatigue and a decreased ability to critically analyze news and information, forcing viewers to adopt "sound-bite" takes on complex issues.

The rise of 24/7 news cycles also exacerbates societal tensions and perpetuates misinformation, as news outlets compete for audience attention and ratings rather than focusing on objective reporting and journalistic integrity.

A lot has changed since the creation of CNN and Fox News. Currently, the media landscape is cluttered with numerous news channels, streaming services, podcasts, YouTube shows, live streams, and social media influencers. There is so much content being produced that you couldn't possibly hear everything everyone has to say, even if you literally spent every minute of your life watching and listening to as much content as you can find. This magnification of the 24/7 news cycle has created a lot more space for diverse viewpoints, and it's easier than ever to find news stories and insights that the mainstream press in the past would never have shared with the American people. However, some parts of the population are now more ill-informed than ever.

In the contemporary media landscape, the prevalence of sound-bite journalism has become increasingly pronounced, incentivizing content creators to focus on developing shallow, sensationalist coverage. This shift has led to a prioritization of capturing audience attention over delivering substantive content, resulting in the degradation of nuanced reporting on complex issues. As news organizations compete for clicks and views in a fiercely competitive environment, the emphasis on generating clickable headlines and shareable sound bites has contributed to the erosion of journalistic standards at large institutions as well.

Social media platforms like X (formerly Twitter), Instagram, Facebook, and TikTok have only made the problem of sound-bite media worse, as these platforms largely focus on and promote short-form content. All too frequently, users of these platforms will boil down a topic by so much to fit it into 140 characters or a one-minute video that it has lost all of its important context. Consumers of this material only receive a tiny sliver of information on some of the most important issues going on in the world.

Further, at the height of the cable-news era, political strategists would often talk about the news cycle in terms of twenty-four hours. A politician could win or lose the news cycle for the day with just one story. Today, the news cycle is hour-to-hour. I cannot tell you how many times I have lined up all the stories that I thought would be important for the day before a broadcast, only to be completely blindsided by a developing story just minutes before showtime.

News is moving at such a high speed that it almost *requires* the use of sound-bite takes on important issues. If you take the time to develop a well-informed, researched, and nuanced take on a story, by the time you are ready to voice your opinion, the news cycle will have moved on to another story, two or three times over. Additionally, in many cases, while you are taking the time needed to establish your stance on an important news story, it's common for everyone on at least one side of the debate to label you an enemy or an extremist for not immediately coming to their side.

The presence of a multitude of content providers who produce content regularly has also resulted in people choosing to silo along highly specific ideological lines. Instead of being challenged by viewpoints that run counter to their established ideology, people now have a seemingly unlimited number of choices in media, including some that conform perfectly to their ideological positions. This should be cause for great concern, because the primary reason for news media is to supply information, not to affirm your current belief structure.

While listening to a bunch of people who agree with you might feel nice, it is this sort of mindset that causes echo chambers to develop and then thrive. The term *echo chamber*, as it is popularly used in modern times, refers to an environment in which a person primarily receives news, information, or opinions that only serve to reinforce that person's already-established worldview.[165] A media landscape composed of echo chambers can exacerbate political polarization. If only one side of a debate is presented during a discussion, listeners will lack an understanding of the other side's perspective. This can lead to a lack of empathy and erode potential for a constructive dialogue between sides.

While the issue of echo chambers has been a problem for generations, it's getting much worse in our modern era of niche-audience podcasts and YouTube channels. It's getting to a point now where even the biggest cable news networks don't seem to operate in the same universe anymore.

Back in the 1990s and the early 2000s, you could switch between the major news stations and see how each side was talking about a news story or event that was taking place. You could turn on MSNBC in 1998 and listen to the anchors discussing the impending impeachment of Bill Clinton. Then you could switch over to Fox News and hear their anchors talking about the Clinton impeachment, but with perhaps a more right-leaning perspective.

Today, major news stations often don't talk about the same stories at all. If you turn on Fox News today, you might see extensive coverage of the border crisis and broken policies that allow for millions of illegal aliens to stream into America, but if you turn on CNN for that network's perspective on the matter, you will likely see something else entirely, such as yet another report on the supposed Trump-led insurrection on January 6, 2021. How are loyal viewers of each of these stations even supposed to have a conversation in real life when they are increasingly not even being exposed to the same news stories?

Before I go any further, let me address something I've been thinking about a lot while writing this chapter: *Am I guilty of contributing to this sense of increased polarization in America?* I have been in media for most of my life, and I did establish TheBlaze, one of the largest conservative media platforms in the world. I am sure many could and will level charges against me for fomenting echo chambers or contributing to sensationalism. I am cognizant of this and have been working for years to focus on the truth, not promoting one side over the other.

For example, my radio show is a long-formed medium for news and information for millions of Americans, the opposite of the sound-bite media industry that's developed over the past decade. Instead of three-minute television segments that you regularly see on cable news, my team and I spend massive amounts of time and money to produce in-depth coverage of complex issues others aren't discussing, both on radio and television. We also produce hour-long weekly specials that dig deep into important, timely stories, and we produce a weekly podcast, *The Glenn Beck Podcast*, where I host long-form conversations with a single guest that covers a wide range of topics. I don't claim to be perfect, but I am always striving to do better.

Social Media, Big Tech, and Weapons of Mass Deception

If the introduction of cable news was an evolution in the way we consume media, then the dawn of social media is a full-blown revolution. It fundamentally altered how information is disseminated, consumed, and interacted with on a global scale.

When social media platforms first emerged, they were often lauded as groundbreaking tools for connecting people and facilitating communication on a scale never seen before. Platforms like MySpace and Facebook promised to transform the way individuals interacted, offering new avenues for sharing personal updates, photos, and thoughts with loved ones, friends, and other acquaintances. For the first time ever, you could share a picture from a party or your views on the latest blockbuster movie with all your contacts, and you could do it simultaneously and instantaneously.

It feels as if Facebook has been around forever, but it's not very old at all. If Facebook were a human—and thank God it isn't, because can you imagine how screwed up that guy would be?—it still would not be able to legally drink alcohol in America. Launched in 2004, Facebook was designed as a networking site for college students. By the end of 2004, it had accrued more than 1 million active users. In the following couple of years, creator Mark Zuckerberg opened the platform to the public and Facebook grew like wildfire. Within three years of opening its digital doors to the public, Facebook amassed 350 million users. By 2012, active users for the platform eclipsed 1 billion.[166] Today, active users exceed 3 billion, including 250 million in the United States alone.[167]

Just a few years after Facebook launched, Twitter once again changed the media landscape. Twitter, with its strict character limit for posts and early adoption by many influential people, shifted social media away from a relatively narrow network of friends and family to a much broader audience. Twitter allowed users to communicate with anyone, not just friends, including many famous and influential people.

Social media became a democratizing force in America, empowering ordinary individuals to have a voice and participate in public discourse. Almost overnight, platforms like Twitter, YouTube, and Instagram became wildly popular and then vehicles for the promotion of social and political change. YouTube now has roughly 2.5 billion users.[168] Instagram has 2 billion users.[169] X, formerly Twitter, has a user count of 600 million.[170]

The ability for users to post content in real time on social media allows for the rapid dissemination of news. Stories often break on social media long before traditional media outlets can publish a report. Citizen journalists now take to social media, uploading stories, pictures, or videos within seconds of an event taking place, giving their firsthand account. The first coverage of a train derailment won't be from CBS News anymore. Instead, it often comes from an X account named something like @TurdFergeson69.

According to research by the Pew Research Center, a staggering number of people regularly get their news from social media sites. In 2023, 50 percent of U.S. adults said they get their news from social media "often" or "sometimes." Thirty percent of adults in the United States said they regularly get their news from Facebook, and 26 percent said YouTube. Fourteen percent said they get news from TikTok, and 12 percent said they get news from X.[171] (Author's note: I'm not sure who you lunatics are that get your news from dancing tweens on TikTok, but if one of you happens to read this book, please consider getting help. You don't have to live like this anymore.)

In the 2010s and 2020s, social media amplified the problems Americans first experienced from 24/7 cable news outlets. One of the first things many people do today when they wake up in the morning is grab their phone and immediately check their news feeds on social media. Many people don't even make it out of bed before getting their strong daily dose of social media insanity. People also take their phones with them everywhere they go and regularly check them for news and information, making people more exposed to the news than ever before.

Media has become so ubiquitous in the modern age that there is virtually no way to increase the level of consumption for the population. We're maxing out. Scholars have been warning about this for decades. Back in the 1960s, Nobel Laureate Herbert A. Simon coined the term "attention economy" when describing the impending "bottleneck of human thought" that would soon limit people's ability to effectively understand their environment. In 1997, theoretical physicist Micheal Goldhaber similarly warned this same limitation would shift our economy from a material-based economy to an "attention-based economy," where markets compete for consumers' attention, not the money in their wallets.[172]

In an "attention economy," a consumer's time is considered a scarce resource. As with any scarce resource, the price correlates positively with the demand for that resource. In this context, the demand for attention is high, fueled by the proliferation of digital platforms and content competing for users' limited time and focus. As a result, businesses and content creators vie for consumers' attention through various strategies, such as targeted advertising, engaging content, and personalized recommendations.[173]

The commoditization of attention has profound implications for society, influencing everything from media consumption habits and consumer behavior to the dynamics of public discourse and political engagement.

Due to this major shift in media consumption, established news sources have also adopted social media as a way of promoting their content. Practically every media company in existence has created profiles on social media platforms to share their content in the hope of expanding readership and redirecting users to their sites. As these platforms have become more cluttered with companies competing for users' attention, social media companies realized they could boost revenues by charging advertisers progressively more for advertisements.

In the United States alone, billions of dollars are spent every year advertising on social media. In 2022, an estimated $66 billion was spent advertising on platforms like Facebook, YouTube, and Twitter. This number is only expected to grow in the coming years. Studies show 90 percent of companies in the United States use social media to advertise their products.[174] Facebook and other social media sites have essentially become the largest media companies in the world, and they've managed to do it in record time. Establishment media has been losing ground in the attention economy to these platforms for years, all while pouring ad dollars into their coffers.

Perhaps most important, these developments have had a massive impact on nearly every part of life, not just the way people consume the news.

The Addicting and Mentally Impairing Power of Social Media

When you are out in public, are you noticing more and more people hunched over, arms folded up, heads lowered, and eyes glued to their phone screens? You see them walking down the street, seated at a restaurant, even behind a steering wheel—but always with their phones in their faces. Heck, you don't have to go in public to see them. I'm willing to bet you have at least one obsessive screen-scroller in your house.

The proliferation of social media is a testament to the quality of product offered to consumers. These platforms feature intuitive interfaces, incorporate various customizable elements, and provide services that fulfill the needs and desires of its users. These features have contributed to the exponential growth of social media, leading to these platforms becoming an integral part of daily life for billions of people worldwide.

There is another important factor that has contributed to the growth of social media, though: it's highly addictive. Americans have been told repeatedly that social media platforms were merely designed to enhance communication, facilitate social networking, and increase users' ability to easily interact with friends and family. But the features that make social media platforms so appealing are also designed to facilitate addictive behaviors, resulting in numerous negative psychological outcomes.

This is no longer a theory built on wild speculation. Social media addiction has become so well recognized by scholars that it has justified its own section on Addiction Center, an online guide for addiction, owned by Recovery Worldwide.[175] On the Addiction

Center's website, social media addiction is described as "a behavioral addiction that is characterized as being overly concerned about social media, driven by an uncontrollable urge to log on to or use social media, and devoting so much time and effort to social media that it impairs other important life areas." This dependence, according to the Addiction Center, has many of the same qualities as other substance-use disorders. Those suffering from an addiction to social media may experience mood modification, increased tolerance, withdrawal symptoms, conflicts in their personal lives, and relapse after attempts at quitting.[176]

The idea of an addiction to social media may sound strange to some, but the psychology behind it is similar to that of gambling or recreational drug use. Studies show that the notifications, follows, comments, and other interactions on these platforms trigger the brain's reward centers, releasing dopamine in a manner similar to when a person consumes certain drugs. This effect from social media use can result in both physical and psychological addiction. When a user sees a notification related to an interaction, the brain produces dopamine, causing that user to feel pleasure.[177]

The allure of these artificial dopamine boosts is particularly strong for young people, says psychologist and founder of the Center for Internet and Technology Addiction, David Greenfield. Speaking of the internet, Greenfield says research widely shows that many young people "can't put it down. They're all about impulse and not a lot about the control of that impulse."[178]

According to Greenfield, one of the tactics used by social media companies is "intermittent reinforcement," giving users a feeling they may get a reward at any time. "But when the reward comes is unpredictable. 'Just like a slot machine.'"[179] This sporadic reward schedule can lead to compulsive and addictive behaviors, as users become increasingly engaged in seeking out the next potential reward. This process rewires the brain, making the user crave his or her next interaction fix.[180]

According to recent polling conducted by the Pew Research Center, 95 percent of teens in the United States now use a smartphone, and the number jumps up to 98 percent if you only include those between the ages of fifteen and seventeen. Even more troubling, 35 percent of teens reported using social media "almost constantly," and one-third of teen respondents acknowledged their time spent on social media is likely "too much." Most teens also admitted it would be somewhat or very difficult to give up social media.[181]

In October 2023, forty-one states and the District of Columbia filed a lawsuit against Meta, the parent company of Facebook, alleging their products were knowingly addictive to children. "Meta has harnessed powerful and unprecedented technologies to entice, engage and ultimately ensnare youth and teens," said the plaintiffs in the case.[182] As of the writing of this book, the case is pending in federal court.[183]

Not only has social media been shown to be addictive; many studies now exist that suggest social media use is correlated with an increase in mental health problems, especially among younger people. One important academic study published in *JAMA Psychiatry* in 2019 investigated how mental health problems relate to time spent on social media platforms. The study, titled "Associations Between Time Spent Using Social Media and Internalizing and Externalizing Problems Among US Youth," tracked the social media use of nearly 6,600 adolescents in the United States. The study found a direct correlation between social media usage and reported anxiety, depression, and other serious mental health problems.[184]

The association between mental health and social media use is particularly troubling considering that we're seeing mental health rapidly decline among Americans in Generation Z, which uses social media at a disproportionately high rate. (Generation Z includes those born between 1997 and 2012.) Recent studies conducted by the Walton Family Foundation, John Della Volpe, and Social Sphere reveal staggering statistics about the mental health condition of younger generations. They found that 42 percent of Gen Z "is about twice as likely as Americans over 25 ... to battle depression and feelings of hopelessness." Eighteen percent of Gen Z is so distraught they believe they would be better off dead.[185]

Scholars have also found an increase in several strange behaviors that have been linked to excessive social media use. For example, during the COVID-19 lockdowns, there was an increased number of cases involving teens who had developed tics like those associated with Tourette's syndrome. At first, many of these cases were written off as isolated incidents, but then scholars realized this was happening all over the world. Doctors and psychologists began reporting sudden-onset tics—the shouting out of random words, phrases, and swear words; seemingly inadvertent hand and arm movements; and hitting of oneself or other people and objects.[186]

After further study, researchers determined that the sudden explosion of these tics was not linked to Tourette's. Pediatric neurologists have instead claimed that teens developed these strange behaviors after watching social media influencers on apps like TikTok.[187]

This development of odd mental health conditions is not limited to tics. Other recently published literature discusses a "sick-role subculture" revolving around TikTok and other social media platforms, where adolescents adopt characteristics of rare psychiatric conditions. Some of these characteristics are related to eating disorders, autism, and dissociative identity disorder.[188]

The detrimental effects of social media have become so pronounced and impossible to ignore that the U.S. government has also investigated the association in recent years. In 2023, U.S. surgeon general Vivek Murthy issued a mental health warning about our nation's teenagers and their social media use.[189] In the surgeon general's advisory, Murthy said, "At a moment when we are experiencing a national youth mental health crisis, now is the time to act swiftly and decisively to protect children and adolescents from risk of harm."[190]

Since Murthy's warning, other government actions have been taken as well. In January 2024, the CEOs of Meta, X, TikTok, and other social media companies were called before Congress to address concerns over the platforms' effects on young users.[191] Legislators have also proposed bills to protect children from the potential maleffects of social media use.[192] A notable example of such legislation was signed into law in March 2024 by Governor Ron DeSantis in Florida. The law bans children under the age of fourteen from using social media. It also requires parental consent for fourteen- and fifteen-year-olds.[193]

Many of the issues relating to the mental harms of social media discussed in the previous section can be seen as unintentional. Social media is a relatively new concept in the grand scheme of things, and industry advocates will likely argue internal actions could and should be taken to offer better protection to its users, especially younger people. However, many actions taken by social media companies are 100 percent designed to be manipulative and may be even more detrimental to our society than the previously discussed mental health crisis.

Big Tech Censorship and Government Collusion

Anyone paying even a little bit of attention to the news over the past several years knows about alleged Big Tech censorship on social media. What started as mere accusations and anecdotal evidence of stifling conservative content has since become established fact. We now know beyond a shadow of a doubt that there has been collusion between social media companies and government to control speech on many of the internet's most powerful social media platforms. The reason for this is obvious: government knows how much influence social media has in the world today, so if it can tip the ideological scales of these platforms even a little, it could have massive impacts on society and even election outcomes.

Initially, concerns about Big Tech censorship centered around claims of biased moderation and suppression of conservative voices on platforms like Facebook, X (before Elon Musk took over), and YouTube.[194] These platforms, which are dominated by liberal Silicon Valley elitists, unfairly targeted conservatives and others critical of the government, thereby undermining free speech and manipulating the public discourse.

As time progressed, the trend became more pronounced. High-profile incidents of content suppression stacked up. In 2017, popular conservative media group PragerU sued YouTube for restricting some of PragerU's video content.[195] In 2018, Facebook, YouTube, and Apple removed Alex Jones and his media company from their platforms for allegedly spreading misinformation.[196]

Even after these cases, the debate continued as to whether these platforms should be allowed to remove content they don't like from their sites. But during the COVID-19 pandemic, the story of Big Tech censorship took on entirely new dimensions. Under the banner of fighting misinformation and disinformation, platforms ramped up their efforts to throttle conservative speech, suppress legitimate debate and opinion about important public policy decisions, and promote politically driven narratives that benefited Democrats.

However, during the pandemic, the full story behind Big Tech companies' decisions to stifle free speech did not come to light. Since the pandemic has ended, however, much more information has been unearthed, revealing a widespread, systematic manipulation of communication and news dissemination by companies such as Facebook, Twitter (now X), and Google.

During the pandemic, these platforms claimed their decisions to censor were made simply to enforce reasonable terms of service on their platforms. It appeared something more was going on, but the companies were not interested in pulling back the curtain.[197] Then something incredible happened. Billionaire Elon Musk bought Twitter.

After years of criticizing social media companies for their indifference to the principles of free speech, Musk took control of Twitter, a publicly traded company, in October 2022.[198] Then Musk opened the doors to select investigative journalists to identify potential systematic suppression of conservative content. "The public deserves to know what really happened," stated Musk after announcing he was going to make the relevant information public. Later, on Twitter, he added, "This is a battle for the future of civilization. If free speech is lost even in America, tyranny is all that lies ahead."[199]

Musk allowed journalists Matt Taibbi, Bari Weiss, and Lee Fang, along with authors Michael Shellenberger, David Zweig, and Alex Berenson, to sift through mountains of files, emails, and internal communications from Twitter relating to the handling of content on the platform. In December 2022, the team started releasing their findings, which were dubbed the "Twitter Files."

"The 'Twitter Files' tell an incredible story from inside one of the world's largest and most influential social media platforms. It is a Frankenstein tale of a human-built mechanism grown out [of] the control of its designer," wrote journalist Matt Taibbi in the first batch of findings.[200] Over the following months, different members of the team released additional batches of the "Twitter Files."

Each batch confirmed essentially every accusation conservatives had been making for years about Big Tech censorship. Before Musk's takeover, content had, indeed, been secretly shadow banned, prominent conservative figures had been blacklisted, and politically disfavored messaging had been throttled.

One Twitter engineer was quoted as saying, "We control visibility quite a bit. And we control the amplification of your content quite a bit. And normal people do not know how much we do."[201]

Some of the files showed that Twitter's terms of service had also been weaponized against popular conservative accounts.[202] For example, internal communications at Twitter showed employees stretched the "hateful conduct" rules to suspend popular personalities and profiles. This was even the case when it came to banning President Donald Trump.[203]

Even more shocking than the internal bias of this social media giant was their willingness to work with political officials, FBI, and other government agencies to censor content. It appeared to be routine when Twitter folks would receive lists of troublesome Tweets flagged by the Biden presidential campaign. "More to review from the Biden team," reads one email with a list of links. "Handled" reads the reply.[204] The FBI and the Department of Homeland Security also developed a habit of requesting content or profiles be moderated.[205]

To make matters even worse, the Twitter Files uncovered evidence that executives at Twitter held regular meetings with the FBI. Over time, the FBI became intertwined with high-ranking employees at Twitter. Documents further revealed there had been direct lines of communication established between U.S. intelligence and the platform's moderation activities. The investigation uncovered more than 150 emails between the FBI and Yoel Roth, Twitter's trust and safety chief at the time. Twitter Files journalist Matt Taibbi even went so far as to say that Twitter was operating as an FBI "subsidiary."[206]

A particularly meaty example of Twitter's flagrant disregard for free speech principles revolved around the infamous Hunter Biden laptop story. As the 2020 election drew closer, the FBI repeatedly warned Twitter's Roth of a potential "hack and leak" operation from

Russia to influence the vote.[207] Not coincidentally, Meta CEO Mark Zuckerberg later told a similar story about the FBI.[208] Because of these warnings, the platforms were primed to censor a potentially explosive story that was expected to come out in the weeks leading up to the election.

So, in October, when the New York Post ran a story describing bombshell revelations about then presidential candidate Joe Biden, his corrupt son Hunter Biden, and their alleged influence peddling and overseas business dealings, social media platforms immediately decided to censor the content, in line with the FBI's warnings.[209] The leaked information about Biden's potential corruption and crooked business dealings could have cost him the election, if it weren't for the swift and dramatic actions taken by social media platforms.

Within hours, Twitter and Facebook censored the story on their platforms.[210] Twitter and Facebook blocked its users from sharing the Post's article, claiming the content was "potentially harmful" and "unsafe," a designation usually reserved for extreme cases, like child pornography.[211] Twitter even went as far as to lock the New York Post's entire account. Users couldn't even direct message the link to other users.[212]

At the time, Trump White House spokeswoman Kaleigh Mc-Enany was locked out of her account for simply tweeting about the story.[213] Once the dust settled, internal communications showed Twitter employees had expressed confusion over the censoring of the story, as it did not explicitly violate the community standards. For example, the former vice president of global communications at Twitter asked, "Can we truthfully claim that this is part of the policy?"[214]

The censorship of the news kept potentially millions of people from learning about the report, just days before the election. Polling conducted after the election was over found that a substantial percentage of Biden voters would have changed their vote if they had known about the snuffed-out story revolving around Hunter Biden's laptop.[215] Considering the margin of victory for Biden in certain key swing states was razor-thin, it is conceivable that the suppression of this story by social media giants Facebook and Twitter could have swung the election.

The publication of the Twitter Files gave the American public unprecedented insight into the inner workings of a massively influential social media company. However, it is important to note that the revealed censorship and government collusion demonstrated was not exclusive to Twitter.

In July 2023, a U.S. district judge ruled Biden administration officials could no longer contact social media companies regarding the "removal, deletion, suppression, or reduction of content containing protected free speech posted on social media platforms." In light of this court decision, the State Department canceled its monthly meeting with Facebook.[216]

In November 2023, the Committee on the Judiciary and the Select Subcommittee on the Weaponization of the Federal Government, led by Republican Rep. Jim Jordan, produced a report outlining how the Department of Homeland Security, the Cybersecurity and Infrastructure Security Agency, and the State Department colluded with American universities to fight "misinformation" on social media platforms. According to the report, these groups worked together with industry experts through the Election Integrity Partnership. Additionally, the report also outlined how the partnership worked to "censor Americans before the 2020 election, including true information, jokes, and opinions."[217]

In February 2024, documents called the "Amazon Files" revealed that the Biden White House "pressured" Amazon in early 2021 to censor books seen as critical of COVID-19 vaccines. These documents described how Andrew Slavitt, a former White House senior advisor, reached out to Amazon in the hopes that they would take action against the offending books. One Amazon official referenced "feeling pressure from the White House Taskforce" to do something about the book listings. Amazon eventually did take action, attaching a "do not promote" label on some of the "anti-vax" books.[218]

After the release of the files, Rep. Jim Jordan (R-OH) said, "Amazon caved to the pressure from the Biden White House to censor speech."[219]

Social media platforms are supposed to be a reflection of reality, open platforms where all voices share equal standing. But when these institutions squash speech, they manipulate this reflection of reality. It's not just that dissenting opinions are derided and criticized; it's that these perspectives are removed from the equation entirely, creating a massive echo chamber on vital topics. How can anyone who gets their news from social media make informed opinions about important matters if they are not exposed to important stories that conflict with the views of Silicon Valley elites? They can't.

Big Tech giants like Facebook, Google, X, TikTok, and just a few others wield massive power. Billions of people flock to these platforms every day, where they receive information about their world. These companies can censor, curate, and shape this information at will. These actions can enhance or reduce the influence of people, ideas, or political movements. They can alter public health choices and destroy debates about important public policy decisions. They can weave narratives that direct the actions of entire populations. This perversion of the world's most popular information networks is manipulating society.

As bad as social media has become, though, Americans now face even graver threats to the truth, threats that have the potential to create significantly more polarization.

Algorithms, Data Collection, and Artificial Intelligence

"I want you to imagine walking into a room, a control room with a bunch of people, a hundred people, hunched over a desk with little dials, and that that control room will shape the thoughts and feelings of a billion people. This might sound like science fiction, but this actually exists right now, today. I know because I used to be in one of those control rooms. . . . What we don't talk about is how the handful of people working at a handful of technology companies through their choices will steer what a billion people are thinking today."[220]

This depiction of the type of control wielded by social media and other big tech companies may sound overstated. Surely this is just an exaggeration, right? I promise you, it is not. This quotation is from Tristan Harris, president and cofounder of the Center for Humane Technology. Before his current role, Harris served as a design ethicist at Google, where he studied how "you ethically steer people's thoughts."[221]

Harris had a bit of a falling-out with Google after he came to the realization that many of Google's products, including Gmail, were deliberately designed to be addictive to users. Harris soon realized the worst qualities of the tech products and platforms we have all been using were not bugs. They were intentional features created by greedy Big Tech giants.

In 2020, Harris testified at a hearing before the House Subcommittee on Consumer Protection and Commerce titled "Americans at Risk: Manipulation and Deception in the Digital Age." There, in response to a question about some of the problems associated with social media companies, Harris said, "The platforms are not doing enough and it's because their entire business model is misaligned with solving the problem."[222]

Harris further explained how engineers at these companies study what gets users' attention and how to hold it. "Outrage works really well at getting attention," Harris said. "If Facebook had a choice between showing you the outrage feed and a calm news-feed, they would want to show you the outrage feed, not because someone consciously chose that, but because that worked better at getting your attention."[223]

Harris's claims are supported by a wealth of evidence. For example, in 2021, an internal document revealed how Facebook's content algorithm prioritized comments and posts that received "angry" reactions from users. On Facebook, you can "react" to a comment or post using a number of emoji faces, including laughing, crying, angry, and so on. Documents described how the "angry" reactions were ranked five times more valuable than a standard "like" when determining which content Facebook would show to more people.[224]

Let's stop right here for a moment. It's possible this one example alone accounts for a measurable degree of the extreme polarization we are experiencing today. Hundreds of millions of Americans are using Facebook. A large percentage of those users get their news on the platform. And now we know that Facebook has in the past prioritized controversial posts and comments to drive engagement. This must have had at least some impact on society. Yet, this is just one example and probably not even the most important one.

As technology continues to develop, we are going to see an exacerbation of all the problems we've discussed in this chapter so far. Advanced algorithms, data collection, and artificial intelligence are going to make media and the news industry even more susceptible to manipulation, misinformation, and polarization. These technologies have the potential to amplify echo chambers, tailor content to individual biases, and further blur the line between truth and lies.

Advanced Algorithms

Most of the time when conservatives criticize Big Tech companies like Facebook and Google, they focus on the perceived political bias of employees. For instance, they will often trot out polls showing that overwhelmingly, the engineers at these Big Tech firms donated to Democrats in past election cycles.[225] But the problem goes far beyond having too many left-leaning employees. In many cases, the most damaging aspects of these platforms are programmed directly into their algorithms.

A social media company like Facebook employs a vast number of algorithms across its platform. An algorithm is simply a step-by-step set of instructions or rules a computer follows to solve a problem or perform a task.[226] Some are simple computational procedures while others are unimaginably complex. Relatively simple algorithms sort news feed posts chronologically, while highly sophisticated machine learning algorithms are used for image recognition or personalized content recommendation.[227]

The content recommendation engine is a particularly interesting algorithm that has strengthened considerably since the early days of social media. This is an algorithm that tries to understand what you like. The better this recommendation engine is, the more likely the platform will retain your attention and keep you on the platform for long periods. Not every video and post is shown to every person. Videos are selected for you, based on your tastes, interests, and viewing patterns. This is on full display when you turn on streaming services like Netflix and see a "recommended for you" tab. If you typically watch action movies, Netflix will recommend other action movies you might like to keep you engaged with its product.

Every social media company uses a recommendation engine. Facebook uses it to suggest "friends you may know," to populate your newsfeed, and to curate ads you might be interested in. YouTube uses it when recommending channels you might like or the next video you should watch. These recommendations are based on the data you generate when interacting with the site. If you "like" a post, that will refine the algorithm applied to your account. If you quickly scroll past a news story with barely a glance, that action will refine your algorithm. If you watch the entirety of a video, that will refine your algorithm too.

This technology is not necessarily a bad thing. If I am not interested in a specific topic—say, video games or the best way to style your dog—then I am happy to avoid all the videos about those topics. But when algorithms become so powerful that they can manipulate people, often bringing out the worst qualities of the individual, they can have a far-reaching negative effect on society. This is exactly the sort of thing that is occurring with the billion-plus people using TikTok, an application that has taken recommendation algorithms to a whole new level of scary.[228]

TikTok is a social media platform that allows users to create, share, and discover short-form videos, typically ranging from fifteen to sixty seconds in length. Launched in 2016 by the Chinese company ByteDance, TikTok quickly gained popularity worldwide, particularly among younger demographics.[229] Along with its focus on short-form video, TikTok became extremely popular largely due to a powerful recommendation engine used to produce a never-ending stream of content for users to watch. As before, these recommendation algorithms were constructed based on a user's interactions on the application. Quickly swiping to a new video, lingering on a video, or watching it entirely all create data that is used to paint a picture of the user and the content he or she is more likely to consume.

After just a short period of using TikTok, animal lovers will see more animal videos. Car guys will see more car videos. Those interested in politics will get more political content. As the algorithm gets to know you more intimately, the application will feed you increasingly niche content that is tailored to your very specific interests. Perhaps the animal lover is really into hedgehogs, or the car guy is particularly fond of 1980s muscle cars. The recommendation engine will quickly figure out each person's unique eccentricities. The political junkies will receive videos reflecting their precise flavor of social or political ideology, perhaps even pushing that worldview further toward the fringe. And if you give the algorithm enough time, it will often eventually expose vulnerable people to troubling content.

In 2021, the *Wall Street Journal* conducted an investigation into the power and influence of the TikTok algorithm. Investigators created one hundred fake TikTok accounts that were programmed to watch videos based on a set of basic personality traits. For example, one of these bot accounts was programmed to have an inclination for depressing content. Another bot was programmed to look for sexual content. Yet another bot looked for political content. The bots were instructed to interact with the app, allowing the algorithm to develop detailed profiles for the fake accounts. It wasn't long before the content became extreme.

Before long, the app began to show the sexual-content-orientated bot videos showcasing bondage and other more extreme sexual kinks and proclivities. The political bot started to see videos associated with the political fringe, including conspiracy theories. The most alarming finding in the investigation involved the depression bot. This bot was eventually exposed to videos promoting suicide.

Guillaume Chaslot, founder of Algotransparency, is concerned about the power and influence of TikTok over its users. "The algorithm on TikTok can get much more powerful and it can be able to learn your vulnerabilities much faster," said Chaslot. "We are training them, and they're training us."[230]

Algorithms like those used by TikTok don't only target and manipulate vulnerable individuals. They also can have society-wide impacts.[231] In November 2023, a troubling trend in videos started on TikTok. The videos revolved around young people's immediate reactions after having read Osama bin Laden's "Letter to America," originally published in 2002. (And in case you were wondering, yes, *that* Osama bin Laden.)

The videos showed people exclaiming how Osama bin Laden's letter opened their eyes to bin Laden's unique perspective. They shared how the letter showed them how everything they learned about September 11, 2001, and terrorism were lies, and that America is a "plague on the entire world." In a matter of days, dozens of these videos racked up millions of views. The trend eventually stirred enough of a controversy that TikTok removed some of the content from the platform.[232]

It is impossible to quantify the damage that has been done to our youth by these social media platforms. What percentage of our youngest generations has been exposed to this sort of extreme content? What will the future of the world look like when younger generations who have been groomed to be sympathetic to murderous terrorists or to embrace mental illness grow up and become the leaders of our country?

Data Collection and the Chinese Communist Party

Over the past few years, it has been increasingly acknowledged that data is becoming the most valuable resource on the planet, if it isn't already.[233] In the landscape of the modern economy, data stands as the cornerstone of innovation, efficiency, and progress. Its significance transcends industries. It shapes the way businesses operate, governments govern, and individuals interact with the world around them. These uses of data have improved innumerable products and services for people across the planet, increasing economic efficiency and people's quality of life. But there is also a dark side to data collection. It is regularly being exploited by authoritarian governments and other bad actors who use data to limit human rights or to take advantage of people.

As we discussed in the previous section, social media platforms and other online services have been designed to collect huge amounts of user data. Much of this data is used to customize users' experiences, making social media and other products more alluring for consumers. But this data has many other uses as well. One such use has been for years at the center of an ongoing high-profile debate in the United States about banning TikTok.[234]

As I noted previously, TikTok has had a detrimental effect on many of its users and society as a whole. But another fear driving the recent TikTok debates was that the popular video-sharing app had essentially been operating as spyware for the Chinese Communist Party (CCP).[235]

Along with all the other data collected on users, mentioned earlier in this chapter, TikTok also captures important personal information, including users' IP address, unique device identifiers, browsing and search history, screen resolution and operating system data, app and file names and types, keystroke patterns, and in some cases, even precise GPS information.[236] Instead of having pages of text in the "privacy policy" section of TikTok's website, it could probably have saved time by simply writing, "You have none."

The accusation that the CCP is using data farmed from TikTok has been around since the Chinese-owned app was launched in 2016, but the company has consistently denied the claim.[237] In 2023, however, a former executive for ByteDance, the parent company of TikTok, came forward with information about how the Chinese government has accessed user data for political purposes.[238]

In a June 2023 court filing, Yintao Yu outlined how the CCP used "backdoor" access to TikTok for the purpose of spying on pro-democracy protestors in Hong Kong during their 2018 demonstrations against the Chinese government. The CCP used this data to determine protesters' identities, locations, and some of their communications.[239]

In the wake of these and other revelations, governments around the world have begun to take steps to combat the potential privacy intrusions by the CCP through TikTok. In 2023, the U.S. government mandated all federal employees remove TikTok from their government-issued smartphones. Similar actions have been taken or discussed in other jurisdictions in the United States, the European Union, and Canada.[240] Further, as of April 2024, lawmakers in the United States are considering legislation that would completely ban the app nationwide.[241]

Issues related to data collection go way beyond the internet and social media. I dedicated a lot of time in my previous book, *Dark Future*, to discussing the magnitude and dangers associated with data collection.[242] As I noted in that book, surveillance systems, satellites, financial transactions, smart devices, smart watches and other wearables, interactions with businesses, GPS, biometric devices, and government records all generate information about you that can be used to create a highly detailed picture of who you are. The more information that is obtained, the more accurate the picture.

Yuval Harari is a historian, best-selling author, and frequent speaker at World Economic Forum events such as Davos. Harari speaks and writes often about the power of emerging technologies, data collection, and advanced algorithms.[243] On many issues, Yuval and I don't exactly see eye to eye. In fact, usually, his ideology scares the heck out of me. But on this issue, I agree with Harari. Here's what he has to say about data collection: "If you have enough data, and enough computer power, then you can create an algorithm that understands humans better than they understand themselves. This has been kind of the holy grail of governments and armies and corporations for thousands of years: to understand humans better than they understand themselves, to be able to predict them, to be able to manipulate them."[244]

For businesses, knowing the customer is key. This has been the case forever, but with new technology and business models built around the internet and social media, it has never been more important. Social media companies offer businesses the opportunity to micro-target their audience to a degree that has never been seen before. Businesses can target ads for their products and services to specific demographics, including age, gender, location, occupation, education level, and even the interests and behaviors of its users.[245] This allows them to spend their marketing dollars reaching only those people who are most likely to be interested. This arrangement incentivises social media companies to forever fine-tune their algorithms by collecting more data, giving more value to the hundreds of billions of dollars in advertisements they sell to businesses around the world each year.[246]

For governments, knowing their citizens means being able to better control them. If you have ever had the pleasure of dealing with the IRS, you know all too well just how much its agents want to get to know you. Government data collection and surveillance are also instrumental for law enforcement agencies, ensuring compliance with regulations, and detecting and preventing criminal activities such as tax evasion, fraud, and terrorism. By gathering comprehensive information about citizens' financial, social, and behavioral patterns, governments can identify potential risks to public safety and economic stability.

Of course, government surveillance and data collection raise serious concerns about privacy rights, civil liberties, and the potential for abuse of power. In extreme cases, authoritarian governments like China can use collected data from a massive surveillance state to power social credit score systems that punish citizens for virtually any act that runs counter to the will of the ruling Communist Party.[247]

For really bad actors, knowing a person inside and out could lead to scary levels of manipulation. The World Economic Forum's "2019

Global Risk Report" includes a section outlining how data collection and advanced algorithms could be abused to "identify emotionally receptive individuals and the specific triggers that might push them toward violence." Hypothetically, advanced systems could target a particularly susceptible person and radicalize him or her using multimedia and news stories. The report further adds, "Oppressive governments could deploy affective computing to exert control or whip up angry divisions."[248]

We live in a moment in history in which the systems that disseminate news and information are so powerful that they shape not only what we know but also how we perceive reality itself. This is not just a problem. It's a crisis. But if you thought that was bad, just wait until you read the next section, which covers advanced technology that's so powerful it's now making it virtually impossible to know what's real.

Generative AI and Deepfakes

In an era dominated by digital communication and online information, the adage *Don't believe everything you see or read online* has become a mantra for navigating the vast landscape of the internet. With the proliferation of social media platforms and user-generated content, the lines between fact and fiction have been badly blurred, making it increasingly challenging to discern truth from falsehoods. Misinformation, propaganda, and manipulated media spread far and wide, and at an alarming speed. This has caused many to approach online content with a healthy dose of skepticism. However, even an extreme sense of skepticism may not be enough in our emerging era, one that's likely to be heavily affected by generative AI and deepfake technologies.

In late 2022, progress in the field of artificial intelligence took a massive leap forward with OpenAI's release of ChatGPT. ChatGPT is an artificial intelligence program trained on an absurd amount of data.[249] It has been designed to provide important information to users and generate natural-sounding conversations. Its architecture enables ChatGPT to understand context, grasp nuances, and produce humanlike responses across a wide range of topics. Leveraging deep-learning techniques and a massive neural network, ChatGPT is capable of simulating engaging and coherent dialogue, making it a versatile tool for various applications, from customer service chatbots to language assistance and creative writing aids.[250] This form of content creation is known as *generative AI*.

After the release of ChatGPT, Americans witnessed a deluge of progressively more advanced generative AI products. These innovations span numerous domains, including image generation, music composition, and even code development. From generating lifelike images to composing original pieces of classical music, these generative AI tools have pushed the boundaries of automation far beyond what most experts believed could be done just a few years in the past. These tools are allowing for the rapid creation of some truly wonderful things. But they are also serving to completely erase the lines between fact and fiction and real people and automated bots.

You might think that you'd be able to escape generative AI by simply staying away from programs like ChatGPT. But it's becoming increasingly more difficult to avoid the effects of generative AI. For example, most people think that the internet and social media platforms are primarily composed of people interacting and communicating with one another from all over the world. But this is no longer the case. Online "bots," a term that means "fake users," are now everywhere, and they are increasingly being operated using AI.

Early iterations of these bots primarily served functional purposes, such as web crawlers used by search engines to index web pages or automated programs that performed repetitive tasks like sending automated emails or managing online forums. Over time, people began using these bot programs for other purposes too, including nefarious ones. Bots could be used to spread spam or artificially increase web traffic. Others figured out ways to use bots to initiate scams, steal data, or spread malware.[251] As technology advanced, these online bots became more sophisticated and are now used to achieve a growing list of goals, including influencing online discourse about important issues and current events.

Back when Elon Musk was negotiating the purchase of Twitter, one of the sticking points revolved around the supposed number of spam bots and fake accounts on the platform.[252] Musk alleged that 20–33 percent of Twitter's users were bot accounts.[253] While that number might seem high, it is supported by additional research and data from other social media platforms. For instance, in 2017, Facebook claimed its advertisements could reach upwards of 41 million Americans between the ages of eighteen and twenty-four.[254] However, U.S. Census Bureau data shows there were only 31 million people in America who fell into that age range.[255]

Numerous cybersecurity firms have conducted research on the extent of internet bots, and their conclusions are alarming. Imperva, a U.S.-based cybersecurity company, releases its "Bad Bot Report" annually. In its 2023 report, it found that nearly half of all internet traffic came from bots.[256] "Year-over-year, the proportion of bot traffic is growing and the disruptions caused by malicious automation results in tangible business risks," said Karl Triebes, a senior vice president at Imperva.[257]

Barracuda, another firm that specializes in cybersecurity, also released a study in 2023 showing a similar finding. According to Barracuda's research, bots make up roughly 48 percent of web traffic, and 30 of those percentage points are specifically related to "bad bots."[258]

These realizations are leading many people to seriously reconsider the "dead internet theory," which suggests the internet is now mostly composed of inauthentic posts, comments, and interactions generated by bots.[259] The theory has existed for many years now, but the recent flourishing of artificial intelligence, generative AI, and large language models like ChatGPT has dumped gasoline on the speculation fire.

Yoshija Walter, a researcher with the Institute for Management and Digitization, published a report in February 2024 titled "Artificial Influencers and the Dead Internet Theory." In it, Walter discusses how the AI revolution is adding yet another wrinkle to the constantly shifting digital media space. According to Walter, social media is transforming "from a space for genuine human interaction to a sophisticated domain dominated by consumption-driven algorithms."[260]

"Ten years ago," Walter writes, "the theory used to be rather speculative, but with the wake of generative AI, it can now be observed first-hand, and it highlights a disturbing trend: the blurring lines between human and AI-driven interactions. As AI proliferates in generating content, it increasingly shapes user perceptions and behaviors, directing the digital narrative toward its algorithmically determined objectives, often at variance with the inherently unpredictable nature of human discourse."[261]

Not only can generative AI tools be used to mimic human interactions online; they can also be used to generate content. This content includes, but is not limited to, entire articles, images, and even websites. A recent example of this surfaced in late 2023 when *Sports Illustrated* was caught using AI tools to generate stories, complete with AI-generated authors.[262]

While publications like *Sports Illustrated* might use generative AI technology to increase their efficiency and output, experts are becoming increasingly and rightfully more concerned about the use of generative AI by bad actors. There is already substantial evidence showing that generative AI is being used by foreign governments to promote political agendas through the use of fake news stories and misinformation.

In March 2024, a sensational headline was widely shared on social media, titled "Israeli Prime Minister's Psychiatrist Commits Suicide." Considering the ongoing conflict in Israel, the headline grabbed a lot of attention. That would have been fine, except that the story was fake. It had been generated by AI and posted to a bunch of propaganda-spewing websites. The fake articles even linked to other fake sites hosting an obituary for the nonexistent psychiatrist, to make the story seem even more authentic.[263]

Newsguard is a company that, among other things, tracks fake websites and AI-generated misinformation. As of April 2024, Newsguard has "identified 777 AI-generated news and information sites operating with little to no human oversight, and is tracking false narratives produced by artificial intelligence tools."[264]

Of course, this sort of fake news is possible without AI, but the generative AI tools that are now affordable and readily available to the public have significantly reduced the costs and barrier to entry of developing these kinds of complicated misinformation campaigns and websites. A small group of bad actors leveraging generative AI technology can create entire fake online ecosystems, with overlapping references and citations to give the illusion of authenticity.

I know it might be hard to believe, but the problem is even worse than what I've described so far.

As I mentioned earlier, generative AI technology is not limited to producing text, articles, and websites. Text-to-image generative AI technology has recently become available to the public, and it boasts incredibly impressive features capable of fooling most casual users. OpenAI's DALL-E, Google's ImageFX, DreamStudio's Stability AI, and other generative AI programs by Getty Images and Midjourney allow you to simply type in a brief text prompt and generate extremely high-quality images of basically anything you can imagine.[265] Sometimes, the images produced by these programs are indistinguishable from reality. For creative purposes, these tools can be incredible. Instead of spending hours using programs like Photoshop, graphic designers and artists can use generative AI to do much of the initial heavy lifting. However, these tools can also be used to push misinformation that looks and/or sounds real.

Journalists and historians know the power images harness. A powerful image taken during a global conflict can relay more information and emotion to an audience than any news article. Well, what if you didn't have to wait for a real powerful image and instead you could completely fabricate photographs to further your political agenda? This sort of thing is already happening, thanks to generative AI.

Since the Israeli operations in Gaza after the October 7, 2023, attacks by Hamas, websites and social media platforms have seen an explosion in AI-generated images crafted to illicit sympathy for civilians in Gaza or even Hamas terrorists.[266] One particularly striking image showed an abandoned Palestinian infant standing among the rubble of a bombed building in Gaza. The infant's hands and face were caked with blood. Although many of those who saw the horrifying image didn't know it, the picture was entirely AI-generated.[267] It was designed specifically to be as emotionally evocative as possible.

Oh, and it gets so much worse.

Fake AI-generated websites filled with fake AI-generated articles featuring fake AI-generated images are just the beginning. Text-to-video generative AI and deepfake technology are soon going to force you to second-guess everything you ever see online or television. You know the quote *Believe nothing you hear, and only one half that you see*? Soon, we are going to have to downgrade that to *Believe nothing you hear and only one-tenth of what you see*.

Much like the description of text-to-image generative AI, text-to-video leverages deep-learning techniques to understand and then translate text prompts into video content. In 2023, this technology was very limited, only producing dreamlike abstractions, but this all changed in February 2024 with the launch of OpenAI's Sora.[268] The videos produced by OpenAI's Sora program are nearly indistinguishable from real life. With just a simple, two-sentence prompt, a user can produce scenes that look plucked right out of a movie, featuring generated, hyperrealistic people, backgrounds, and movements.

This technology is already so good that you will likely see it used in television commercials and possible movies before this book reaches your hands. Studios will be able to save massive amounts of cash on filming, special effects, and other production costs because of programs such as Sora. And just as with other forms of generative AI, this advancement makes these achievements possible to a wide range of people that would normally never have the means or resources to create high-quality generative videos like these. Some people will be able to create wonderful art, videos, or films without the need for cameras or animation tools. But there will also be tremendous risks and potential for abuse.

At the time of publication of this book, Sora is not available to the public, but it's not hard to imagine how AI-generated videos will soon be used to spread misinformation and propaganda at a scale that once seemed possible only in science fiction movies.

Perhaps the greatest threat posed by this new technology is that it allows for the creation of deepfakes—lifelike images, audio, and video that closely match the appearance and/or voices of real people. Deepfake technology powered by machine learning has the ability to manipulate real-life video and audio content with unprecedented realism. By analyzing extensive datasets of facial expressions and speech patterns, deepfake algorithms can seamlessly superimpose one person's likeness onto another's or even copy their voice with astonishing accuracy.

In early 2024, an incredibly convincing video of Jennifer Aniston was shared online, appearing to show the actress sitting on a chair, saying, "If you're watching this video, you're one of the 10,000 lucky people that will get a Macbook pro for just $10." The video also seemed to show Aniston saying, "Jennifer Aniston here, and I'm doing the world's biggest Macbook giveaway. Just go to my site below and claim yours now."[269]

If you're one of the many people who clicked on that link and are still waiting for your Macbook, I have some bad news for you. Despite the video looking and sounding exactly like Jennifer Aniston, it was nothing but an AI-generated fabrication.

There are countless scams just like that one happening every day across the country and throughout the world. In some cases, scammers are calling victims using the voice of one of their loved ones.[270] In these cases, people think they are helping a friend or family member who's asking for money or needs help, when in reality, they are handing their hard-earned money and/or personal data over to a complete stranger.

Although the technologies I have discussed in this chapter are undeniably spectacular and will create incredible opportunities, they are also eroding the foundations of reality, and they are doing it at a remarkable pace. America is heading for a future where people are constantly being influenced and manipulated by AI-generated news, websites, images, and videos. There is even a start-up in Los Angeles planning to roll out a news station equipped with AI-generated anchors.[271]

As these advancements continue to make it more difficult for people to know what's real and what isn't, it will become crucial for every one of us to develop discerning critical thinking skills, hone our media literacy, and exercise skepticism when encountering information online. Furthermore, learning and following the first step of the guide outlined in chapter 3, titled "Guard Yourself

Against Lies," will be important for you to protect yourself and your family from the threats posed by emerging technologies.

More specifically, be sure to utilize my Crazy Uncle Test and the Original Source Test. Both of these strategies will keep you from falling into misinformation and disinformation traps.

In an era where AI-generated content can easily sway opinions and shape narratives, it's essential that individuals learn how to question the authenticity of sources, verify information, and remain vigilant against manipulation. By actively engaging with content responsibly and seeking out diverse perspectives, we can empower ourselves and our loved ones to navigate the digital landscape of the present and future with clarity, resilience, and integrity.

As I mentioned earlier in this chapter, information and propaganda wars have been raging for the whole of human history. Propaganda isn't new. What has changed, however, are the modern weapons being waged in propaganda wars. They have the power to reshape the fabric of entire nations and bend the arc of history toward those who wield them. Because of emerging technologies, we are now entering the nuclear-bomb age of the propaganda wars, where the dissemination of misleading or manipulated content will have profound and far-reaching consequences, challenging the very foundations of democracy and societal cohesion.

Our elections are especially vulnerable to these threats. Because of advancements in deepfake technologies and Americans' lack of understanding of them, the United States is poised for a deepfake election catastrophe that could tear our country apart, if we don't learn how best to handle this growing danger. It is a problem that's so important that I have devoted the entire next chapter of this book to addressing it.

5

THE ~~WILL~~ CONTROL OF THE PEOPLE: ELECTIONS IN THE ERA OF MISINFORMATION

ON JANUARY 11, 2017, LESS THAN TWO WEEKS BEFORE DONALD Trump was sworn in as president, *Politico* published a headline-worthy, damning article about the 2016 election. It had it all: a massive scandal, coordination between a presidential candidate and a foreign government, and fear of retribution. It sounded like something that might make its way into a Tom Clancy novel. And unlike other investigations that had been launched by establishment media outlets in the immediate aftermath of Trump's election victory, the January 2017 *Politico* article claimed to have strong evidence that the 2016 presidential race had truly been impacted by foreign operatives.[272] It wasn't just a theory anymore. *Politico* had the proof, and now the American people would have it too.

When the writers for the January *Politico* article, Kenneth Vogel and David Stern, published their bombshell piece, I am sure they believed it would steal headlines nationwide. But, curiously, it didn't.

Many Americans have never even heard of it. Why? Because Vogel and Stern's investigation did *not* find a coordinated effort between the Trump campaign and the Russian government. Instead, it found *Ukrainian* operatives had been working with the *Hillary Clinton* campaign as part of a secret effort to stop Trump from becoming president.[273] How should we characterize this incredible story of intrigue? I don't know about you, but one important word keeps coming to mind: *collusion.*

"Donald Trump wasn't the only presidential candidate whose campaign was boosted by officials of a former Soviet bloc country," Vogel and Stern wrote.[274]

"Ukrainian government officials tried to help Hillary Clinton and undermine Trump by publicly questioning his fitness for office," Vogel and Stern also reported. "They also disseminated documents implicating a top Trump aide in corruption and suggested they were investigating the matter, only to back away after the election. And they helped Clinton's allies research damaging information on Trump and his advisers, a *Politico* investigation found."[275]

Vogel and Stern said there is "little evidence" of a "top-down effort by Ukraine" to alter the outcome of the 2016 election. Ukrainian officials might have been acting without a directive from the nation's president or legislature, they said. However, Vogel and Stern couldn't have been clearer when they declared, "The Ukrainian efforts had an impact in the race."[276]

What, exactly, was the "impact" of the Ukrainian interference? According to Vogel and Stern, "A Ukrainian-American operative who was consulting for the Democratic National Committee met with top officials in the Ukrainian Embassy in Washington in an effort to expose ties between Trump, top campaign aide Paul Manafort and Russia, according to people with direct knowledge of the situation." Those efforts helped "to force Manafort's resignation" and further advanced "the narrative that Trump's campaign was deeply connected to Ukraine's foe to the east, Russia."[277]

If true, this story is tremendously important. Russia and Ukraine played central roles in two different impeachment campaigns led by the Democrats against Trump. One envisioned Trump as a Russian asset who had been compromised by Vladimir Putin's regime, perhaps in return for Russia's help in the 2016 election. The other asserted that Trump illegally used his position as president to attempt to get the government of Ukraine to start an investigation into Joe Biden and his family's scandalous business dealings in the country.[278] Both accusations caused significant damage to Trump during and after his time in office. But what about Hillary Clinton's alleged collusion with Ukrainian officials?

Clinton's involvement with Ukraine was a hot topic among Republican members of Congress during Democrats' 2019 Ukraine-focused impeachment investigation of Trump. Some Republicans said that it was reasonable for Trump to be concerned about Ukraine in light of the various reports that had emerged about the Biden family's business dealings in the country, as well as Clinton's ties to Ukraine during the 2016 election.[279]

You might think that this would have made the reporters over at *Politico* happy. Their fine journalism was finally getting the attention it deserved, and that's a good thing, right? Not according to *Politico*. At the height of the Trump-Ukraine impeachment fervor, in 2019, *Politico* published a story that largely dismissed the conclusions contained in its prior report.[280] The outlet did not, however, renounce any of the specific evidence that it had previously presented as proof of coordination between Democrats and Ukraine, nor did it retract its 2017 article. As far as I can tell, *Politico*'s official position on the Clintin-Ukraine connection is *both* that everything it had previously reported is true *and* that there's nothing to see here.

We shouldn't be too hard on *Politico*, though. At least it reported its findings at some point in the past. Most media outlets have completely ignored the Clinton-Ukraine relationship, as well as ignored or downplayed the alleged corruption involving the Biden family and Ukrainian businesses and government officials.[281] The media was all too eager to report every whisper and scant piece of evidence suggesting a Trump-Russia relationship, but when it came to Hillary Clinton, there was virtually silence. No calls for wide-scale investigations. No demands for special prosecutors. No army of journalists beating down witnesses' doors. Other than *Politico*, it seems few, if any, outlets bothered to talk about it, and even *Politico* undermined its own reporting in a feeble attempt to get Trump.

Election Propaganda

Undermining or upholding the validity of elections, depending on the circumstances, is one of the many misinformation tactics used by the Propaganda Industrial Complex to consolidate its power. When it can't convince people to vote for the *right candidate*, the Complex insists that its opponent is a monster, a cheater, or part of an election conspiracy.

The propaganda surrounding elections has reached a fever pitch over the past two and a half decades. In 2000, when Republican George W. Bush won a tightly contested race in Florida, the Propaganda Industrial Complex declared that Florida governor Jeb Bush, George's brother, "disenfranchised" thousands of "eligible voters," a move that allegedly cost Democrat Al Gore the election.[282] Democrats repeatedly claimed that Gore, not George Bush, had won the state, and the presidential election as a result. They sued in court. They challenged the certification of Florida's Electoral College votes.[283] One writer for the popular left-wing publication *The Nation* said the election had been "stolen" and that the Supreme Court's decision to end Gore's legal challenges was "treasonous, though . . . not technically." [284]

As I noted previously, following Hillary Clinton's loss to Donald Trump in 2016, Democrats spent years investigating a fictitious Russian collusion conspiracy theory. Clinton herself referred to Trump as an "illegitimate president" and insisted that "he knows" the election had been stolen. [285]

Trump "knows he's an illegitimate president," Clinton said. "I believe he understands that the many varying tactics they used, from voter suppression and voter purging to hacking to the false stories—he knows that—there were just a bunch of different reasons why the election turned out like it did." [286]

Clinton's claims are particularly blood-boiling considering that the genesis of so many of the Russian-collusion conspiracy theories that bubbled up in 2016–18 were directly related to a report paid for by the Clinton campaign. Christopher Steele, the author of the so-called Steele dossier, used "false secondhand accounts designed to tie Trump to the Kremlin that were subsequently fed to corporate media reporters and government officials." [287] That dossier was then used by the FBI and others to launch additional investigations into the Trump campaign.

To make matters worse, the court responsible for issuing FISA surveillance warrants used to spy on the Trump campaign based its decision in large part on the Steele dossier, primarily because the court was not informed about the dossier's ties to Clinton. [288] The Clinton campaign also failed to properly disclose to the Federal Election Commission (FEC) the payments it made to fund the dossier. In 2022, the FEC fined the Clinton campaign and Democratic National Committee a combined total of $113,000 for violating election law. [289]

So, to say Clinton's crybaby claims about the legitimacy of the Trump presidency is infuriating is to wildly understate how I feel about the situation. The imagery of blood shooting out of my eyes is probably more accurate.

Speaking of head-exploding levels of frustration, have I mentioned the 2020 election?

In 2020, Democrats used fears over the COVID-19 pandemic to justify some of the most substantial changes to U.S. election integrity laws ever made. Unsecure, widespread mail-in balloting became the norm in states across the country.[290] Many states and allowed people to drop off their votes at unsecured ballot boxes for the first time.[291] Signature verification requirements were relaxed.[292]

As a result of these changes, voter turnout surged well beyond anyone's expectations. According to the Pew Research Center, "About two-thirds (66%) of the voting-eligible population turned out for the 2020 presidential election—the highest rate for any national election since 1900."[293] Joe Biden, an elderly man who hid in his basement during much of the 2020 campaign season, received more votes than any presidential candidate in history, including Barack Obama.[294]

It was also one of the closest elections in history. Three swing states were decided by fewer than 21,000 votes each—Arizona, Georgia, and Wisconsin.[295] All three were won by Biden. Had Trump won those three states, he likely would have been president.[296] Out of 155 million votes cast in 2020, the election ultimately came down to fewer than 50,000 votes.[297]

With all of these important considerations in mind, you might think election officials, government agencies, journalists, academics, and other prominent figures and organizations would be cautious about declaring Biden the unquestionable winner of the race in the days immediately following Election Day. But elites had their victory, and they weren't going to do anything to risk another four years of Trump as president. So, as soon as it possibly could, the Propaganda Industrial Complex declared Biden the indisputable winner and then demanded that all Americans accept him as the president-elect. Anyone who dared to speak about election fraud was silenced.

The "Most Secure Election" Myth

The Propaganda Industrial Complex justified its decision to silence claims about voter fraud without providing any meaningful evidence, and without a single serious investigation. In fact, just ten days after the election, the Propaganda Industrial Complex declared the 2020 contest "the most secure in American history."[298]

CBS News reported, "2020 Election 'Most Secure in History,' Security Officials Say."[299]

Vox reported, "Trump's Own Officials Say 2020 Was America's Most Secure Election in History."[300]

Fortune declared, "The 2020 Election Was the 'Most Secure in American History.'"[301]

CNN reported, "Election Officials, Including Federal Government, Contradict Trump's Voter-Fraud Conspiracy Theories."[302]

What many of the articles and reports published by the Propaganda Industrial Complex didn't tell the American people, however, is that the statement by government officials most often used to justify their "most secure election" mythology was not about all forms of voter fraud. In fact, it didn't have anything to do with *most* kinds of fraud, which is why it was produced so soon after the election ended.

On November 12, 2020, just one day before countless media reports were published upholding the safety and reliability of the 2020 results, officials at the Election Infrastructure Sector Coordinating Council (EISCC) and the Election Infrastructure Government Coordinating Council (EIGCC) issued a press statement that read, in part, "The November 3rd election was the most secure in American history. Right now, across the country, election officials are reviewing and double checking the entire election process prior to finalizing the result."[303] Both the EISCC and EIGCC are part of the U.S. Department of Homeland Security.

That statement sounds like an open-and-shut case, doesn't it? Two election-focused government agencies declared the race the "most secure in American history," just as the media reported. But what most media outlets did not report is what kind of "security" those agencies were referring to.

The EISCC and EIGCC generally do not investigate things like stolen ballots, ballot box security, forged signatures on ballots, voting multiple times, or many other common kinds of fraud. Their only concern is cybersecurity and other electronic voting systems. That's why a little further down in the same press release that inspired the Propaganda Industrial Complex's media blitz about 2020 being the "most secure election," the EISCC and EIGCC clarified their remarks with the statement, "There is no evidence that any voting system deleted or lost votes, changed votes, or was in any way compromised." They also wrote, "Other security measures like pre-election testing, state certification of voting equipment, and the U.S. Election Assistance Commission's (EAC) certification of voting equipment help to build additional confidence in the voting systems used in 2020."[304]

None of these issues have anything to do with most kinds of voter fraud, but the Propaganda Industrial Complex didn't care. It ran with the "most secure election" slogan and still hasn't looked back.

We now know that it is likely election fraud was widespread during the 2020 race, and that it probably had a significant impact on the outcome of key swing states.[305] There's no way to know the precise extent to which fraud happened, of course, but that's because fraud was so easy to commit that it would be difficult to accurately measure.

It also doesn't help that there have been no serious government-led investigations into many common kinds of voter fraud, such as mail-in ballot fraud involving members of the same family. In many states, election officials don't have the tools or protocols in place to know whether one person filled out his or her spouse's ballot, or whether an adult child voted on behalf of his or her elderly parent. That seems like an important thing to worry about in an election in which tens of millions of additional people were able to vote by mail. There are, however, very good reasons to think a ton of illegal voting occurred.

In December 2023, the Heartland Institute published the results of a survey it conducted with Rasmussen Reports about the 2020 election. The survey, which consisted almost entirely of likely 2024 voters who also cast ballots in 2020, found a stunning percentage of voters admitted to casting votes illegally. According to Heartland,

> Seventeen percent of mail-in voters admitted that in 2020 they voted in a state where they are "no longer a permanent resident."
>
> Twenty-one percent of mail-in voters admitted that they filled out a ballot for a friend or family member.
>
> Seventeen percent of mail-in voters said they signed a ballot for a friend or family member "with or without his or her permission."
>
> Nineteen percent of mail-in voters said that a friend or family member filled out their ballet, in part or in full, on their behalf.[306]

All told, the Heartland Institute/Rasmussen poll found at least one in five mail-in voters acknowledged that they had engaged in voting activity that was likely illegal.[307] A subsequent report published by Heartland determined the total percentage of mail-in voters who had committed at least one kind of illegal voting could have been as high as 28 percent.[308]

Perhaps even more shocking was that Heartland analysts determined that even if a high percentage of the illegal voting found by their poll with Rasmussen Reports could be explained by some respondents misunderstanding questions, it is still likely that mail-in fraud impacted the outcome of the 2020 election. According to Heartland researchers, if just 6 percent of mail-in ballots were cast illegally, then Donald Trump, not Joe Biden, would have captured enough Electoral College votes to win the presidential election in 2020, assuming those illegal votes had been prevented or caught before being counted.[309]

At the 4 percent and 5 percent mail-in fraud levels, there would have been a tie in the Electoral College, which means state delegations in the U.S. House of Representatives would have decided the outcome of the race. Because Republicans controlled a majority of state delegations, it's likely that Trump, a Republican, would have been named president under this scenario.[310] (It's also likely crazy left-wing activists would have burned the country down to the ground in a fit of rage.)

Just as a reminder, the Heartland survey found that at least 20 percent of mail-in voters admitted to engaging in at least one illegal voting activity, far more than the 4–6 percent thresholds referenced previously.[311]

The Next Crisis

There's so much more I could discuss about misinformation in American elections. In chapter 4, I explained the importance of election-related social media censorship and the Hunter Biden "laptop from hell" scandal.[312] And I could go on for days talking about the details of the Russian-collusion catastrophe; Special

Counsel Robert Mueller and his bogus investigation of Trump; the horrifying level of corruption at the FBI, especially as it pertains to its treatment of Trump; and the media's endless stream of lies about the Trump administration's policies.

But let's be honest. You didn't buy this book so you could read about the depressing election news of the past. You bought this book so you could read about the depressing election news of the *future*. And I'm sure you're not interested because you enjoy being miserable. (Although, I bet it is the case for some sick, twisted freaks.) You're interested in what's coming our way because you want America to give up its Clown World ways and return to the values that made this place the greatest country on earth. That's what I want too. I truly believe we can get there, but it's going to be a difficult road.

The election challenges ahead are daunting. We've already entered the era of election fraud. Out of the past six presidential elections, three have resulted in roughly half the country believing its candidate of choice was screwed, to the benefit of the other half of America. If that trend continues, the United States won't survive long. There are good reasons to worry, too. Many news outlets only provide viewers, listeners, and readers with what they want to hear, not well-established facts. Some government agencies, law enforcement, and courts have been weaponized to serve political purposes.

Technological changes are occurring that will undoubtedly alter the way people think about elections. As I explained in chapter 4, algorithms and artificial intelligence are dramatically transforming the way we experience and think about the news. They are shaping our thoughts and feelings, often in unhealthy ways that further detach people from reality.

But when it comes to our elections, the most dangerous threat of all is that we are losing our ability to trust what we see and hear. As

I noted in the previous chapter, deepfake images, audio, and video are reaching a level of sophistication that far surpasses anything we've seen before. Now when you see your favorite or most hated politician say or do something, you cannot be sure it really is him or her. The uncertainty will grow in the coming years. At some point, there will likely be a deepfake crisis. It could spark severe economic and/or political instability. It is avoidable, but only if people soon understand the threats we face before it's too late. Americans also must be better prepared to know how to tell the difference between truth and lies, and to recognize the threats posed by large institutions and powerful politicians who often benefit from crises, just as I outlined in chapter 3.

The remainder of this chapter will show you how serious a problem election deepfakes have already become, as well as warn you about the potential problems coming our way. I will also discuss how some of the lessons we learned in chapter 3 apply to the dangers posed by deepfakes, so you will know how to help your friends, family members, and coworkers manage the pitfalls of a potentially calamitous future election crisis.

Americans are becoming increasingly more divided over the integrity of elections. In February 2024, a Rasmussen national survey found "52% of Likely U.S. Voters say cheating is likely to affect the outcome of the next presidential election, including 27% who think it's Very Likely." The same survey found 54 percent of likely voters believe government officials have not "done enough to prevent cheating in elections."[313]

A free society cannot survive if half its voters believe elections are rigged or so full of cheating that no one can trust the outcome is legitimate. That's the unfortunate situation we've found ourselves in, and as I'm about to show you, things could get a lot worse soon.

A Most Dangerous Game

The phone rings. It's an unknown number. *Probably just another salesperson or politician looking for a vote*, you think. You know you shouldn't pick up, but the phone number's area code is local to you.

What if it's about my kid? you wonder. *What if it's an important call about that costly medical bill I just paid?*

You can't help yourself; you accept the call, hold it quickly up to your ear. Now you're curious. You *need* to know who is on the other line.

"Hello?" you say. Then a voice you recognize eagerly responds.

"What a bunch of malarkey," the voice mumbles.

Who could this possibly be? you wonder. *It sounds like—no, it couldn't be him. But it does sound like him.*

Confusion suddenly sets in. The voice calling out to you on the phone—from a local number, no less—is unmistakably the voice of Joe Biden. You would recognize his muttering, bizarre cadence anywhere.

"It's important that you save your vote for the November election," Biden's voice says.

What is he talking about? you think to yourself. *Is he talking about the upcoming Democratic primaries?*

It's a cold, snowy, bright January day in New Hampshire. You know the Democrats' 2024 presidential primaries are coming up soon, and getting recorded calls from candidates has become a daily occurrence for you and your family. On more than one occasion, you've wanted to throw your phone out of a moving car just to put a stop to the flood of stupid phone calls, but you have that whole I-need-a-phone-to-have-a-job-to-put-food-on-the-table problem, so you always stop yourself at the last moment.

There's something different about this call, though. It sounds as though Biden's recorded voice just asked you to "save your vote for the November election." *Why would the Biden campaign want voters to stay home?* you think. *Maybe I misheard him.*

Then the voice calls out again.

"Voting this Tuesday only enables the Republicans in their quest to elect Donald Trump again. Your vote makes a difference in November, not this Tuesday."

Now there's no doubt in your mind. The Biden campaign is telling voters *not* to vote in the state's presidential primaries—or is he?

In January 2024, New Hampshire voters found themselves in the exact situation described above. And in case you're wondering, yes, the quotes used in my short narrative are from the real calls, including his opening "What a bunch of malarkey" line.[314]

The New Hampshire attorney general's office issued an urgent warning to voters just days before the election about calls featuring an artificially generated version of Joe Biden's voice. The calls were not produced by the Biden campaign, but rather by opponents of the president. "These messages appear to be an unlawful attempt to disrupt the New Hampshire Presidential Primary Election and to suppress New Hampshire voters," the state's attorney general said in a statement. "New Hampshire voters should disregard the content of this message entirely."[315]

NBC News reported, "The investigation comes after a prominent New Hampshire Democrat, whose personal cellphone number showed up on the caller ID screens of those receiving the call, filed a complaint."[316]

My research team and I weren't able to track down the number of voters who received the call. It's possible election officials still aren't sure. And it's even less clear what the true purpose of the scheme was. Biden, of course, was in no danger of losing the primary in New Hampshire. And even if he had been, Democrats had removed all of New Hampshire's primary delegates as a punishment for refusing to move its primary later in the year. In 2023, at Biden's request the Democratic National Committee rearranged the party's primary schedule, moving New Hampshire out of its spot as the first-in-the-nation primary, disrupting a tradition that goes back a century.[317] It appears that the calls, which were in clear violation of election law, were motivated solely by a desire to embarrass Biden.

Now, imagine for a moment what would happen in a similar situation in the future, except that the calls were being made days before the general election, and in a state where the outcome could play a significant role in deciding who the next president of the United States will be. What would happen if a sizable number of voters were tricked into staying home for an election, or told to cast their mail-in ballots in the wrong manner, or directed not to sign a mail-in ballot envelope? How many fooled voters would it take to create a full-blown election catastrophe? Remember, out of 155 million votes cast, the 2020 election ultimately came down to fewer than 50,000 votes in three states—Arizona, Georgia, and Wisconsin.[318]

Additionally, if a deepfake scenario like the one that occurred in New Hampshire in early 2024 were to occur again in an important future general election, it would give plenty of ammunition to the election loser to claim that a deepfake changed the outcome of the race, *whether it did or not.* One of the most painful lessons learned over the past two and a half decades of U.S. elections is that perception is often more important than reality.

If this sounds too hypothetical to warrant significant attention, you should know that a deepfake may have already had a significant effect on at least one prominent U.S. election.

In early 2023, Chicago was in the midst of a hotly contested mayoral race between Paul Vallas, Democrats' establishment candidate, and Democrats' socialist-leaning candidate, Brandon Johnson. In February, just before the election commenced, a video circulated on social media that appeared to show Vallas making controversial comments about police shootings.

According to CBS News in Chicago, the video "shows a photo of Vallas with a voice underneath that very much resembles his voice—saying that back in his day, cops would kill 17 or 18 people and 'nobody would bat an eye.'"[319]

The video further says that Chicago should start "refunding the police."[320]

The deepfake—which featured a fake news agency, Chicago Lakefront News—was clearly meant to severely damage Vallas, especially among African American voters. Johnson, an African American with strong ties to the city's black community, needed significant support from African Americans to win the race.

The video was viewed thousands of times on X alone before being flagged as misinformation and taken down.[321]

"You can cause great harm getting something like this wrong, because it'll take so long to get it back," said Al Tompkins, a senior faculty member at the Poynter Institute, according to a report by CBS News in Chicago. "You can't stuff the genie back in the bottle once the damage is done, particularly in a political campaign where these things get circulated not just in media, but in social channels and conversations."[322]

There's no way to know how many Chicago voters saw the video or heard from a friend or family member about its contents. There's also no way to know how many people believed the deepfake was real. What we do know, however, is that Vallas ultimately lost the mayoral race. Johnson won by fewer than 27,000 votes in a runoff election, despite having been widely considered the election's underdog.[323]

As bad as the problem is becoming in America, it's already been far worse in other parts of the world. *Wired* reported in October 2023:

Just two days before Slovakia's elections, an audio recording was posted to Facebook. On it were two voices: allegedly, Michal Šimečka, who leads the liberal Progressive Slovakia party, and Monika Tódová from the daily newspaper *Denník N*. They appeared to be discussing how to rig the election, partly by buying votes from the country's marginalized Roma minority.

Šimečka and *Denník N* immediately denounced the audio as fake. The fact-checking department of news agency AFP said the audio showed signs of being manipulated using AI. But the recording was posted during a 48-hour moratorium ahead of the polls opening, during which media outlets and politicians are supposed to stay silent. That meant, under Slovakia's election rules, the post was difficult to widely debunk. ...

The election was a tight race between two frontrunners with opposing visions for Slovakia. On Sunday it was announced that the pro-NATO party, Progressive Slovakia, had lost to SMER, which campaigned to withdraw military support for its neighbor, Ukraine.[324]

Similarly, in March 2024, the Associated Press (AP) reported:

In Moldova, an Eastern European country bordering Ukraine, pro-Western President Maia Sandu has been a frequent target. One AI deepfake that circulated shortly before local elections depicted her endorsing a Russian-friendly party and announcing plans to resign.

Officials in Moldova believe the Russian government is behind the activity. With presidential elections this year, the deepfakes aim "to erode trust in our electoral process, candidates and institutions—but also to erode trust between people," said Olga Rosca, an adviser to Sandu. The Russian government declined to comment for this story.[325]

AI deepfakes have also been used recently in Taiwan to fool citizens into believing the United States plans to interfere in the country's elections. The AP reported in March 2024:

> In Taiwan, a self-ruled island that China claims as its own, an AI deepfake gained attention earlier this year by stirring concerns about U.S. interference in local politics.
>
> The fake clip circulating on TikTok showed U.S. Rep. Rob Wittman, vice chairman of the U.S. House Armed Services Committee, promising stronger U.S. military support for Taiwan if the incumbent party's candidates were elected in January.
>
> Wittman blamed the Chinese Communist Party for trying to meddle in Taiwanese politics, saying it uses TikTok—a Chinese-owned company—to spread "propaganda."[326]

In light of these stories, and considering that about "70 countries estimated to cover nearly half the world's population—roughly four billion people—are set to hold national elections" in 2024,[327] it's hard to imagine that there won't be at least one deepfake election catastrophe before the year is over. We've already seen deepfakes in the United States that are sophisticated enough that had they been posted a day or two before an election, they would have likely affected some voters' views.

For example, in February 2023, conservative "Jack Posobiec tweeted a video seeming to show President Biden announcing a military draft to answer Russia's offensive in Ukraine, he described it as a 'sneak preview of things to come,'" according to a report by the *Washington Post*.

Posobiec was asked about the tactic at the Conservative Political Action Conference in March 2023. He acknowledged that he had received a lot of criticism for the video, but rather than apologize,

Posobiec defended his decision to post the video. "Screw them all," he said.[328]

Friendly Deepfake Deceptions

It is tempting to think of deepfakes as primarily a problem for campaigns, but some candidates overseas have realized that deepfakes have tremendous potential to help present political figures in more positive ways too.

In 2022, the campaign of Yoon Suk-yeol, a presidential candidate in South Korea, produced deepfake versions of Yoon to improve public opinion, especially among younger voters.[329] According to a report by the *Wall Street Journal*:

> The so-called AI Yoon—as in Artificial Intelligence Yoon—sounds, looks and gestures much like the real-life, conservative politician who is in a close race for South Korea's presidential election on Wednesday—although with much more mischievous humor.
>
> A sharp-tongued former prosecutor, the 61-year-old Mr. Yoon is new to politics and wanted an efficient way to reach out to the electorate. He needed to pursue young voters and sought a softer public image, and had just roughly three weeks to officially campaign by law.
>
> "We want voters to see the human side of Yoon—not the stern image he projects on television," said Baik Kyeong-hoon, head of the campaign's AI Yoon team.

Yoon's campaign produced more than eighty different deepfake video clips of the candidate. The videos were typically short, about thirty seconds or less.

The *Wall Street Journal* noted that AI Yoon discusses a wide range of topics too, "including North Korean missile launches and fake news. The character also delves into the K-pop girl group Blackpink (one of their songs is AI Yoon's 'karaoke go-to') and his grocery shopping list that day (eggs, green onions, anchovies and beans)."

The Yoon campaign has also learned that the deepfakes can be used to improve his real-life human interactions as well.

The *Wall Street Journal* reported that "Mr. Yoon has adapted what he brings up on the campaign trail, and how he says it, based on the popularity of the online videos," according to Lee Jun-seok, the man who first developed the plan to launch AI Yoon, and the head of Yoon's People Power Party.

It's true that deepfakes can be a campaign manager's worst nightmare, but as AI Yoon shows, they can also be a miracle for campaigns forced to promote less-than-ideal candidates or stuck with difficult circumstances. Now, thanks to the power of AI, when a campaign finds itself trapped with an unlikable candidate, or a painfully old candidate, or a gaffe-machine who likes to tell stories about children playing with his leg hair, or, in the case of Joe Biden, all three, the campaign can just use AI to make the candidate *appear* more likable.[330]

In more ways than one, Biden really is a prime candidate for utilizing deepfakes to a candidate's advantage. Imagine campaign ads where Biden is speaking eloquently—no stammering, mumbling, or stuttering. He sounds sharper and moves with ease, casually strolling from one end of a room to the other. Perhaps he even looks a little younger too. All of these things are possible with deepfake technology. Sure, campaigns can carefully edit their shots, use makeup and lighting to make their candidate look good, and film multiple takes to achieve the best possible version of their guy. But deepfake technology can propel that strategy to an entirely new level of deception.

However, improving one's public persona is just scratching the surface of the potential political benefits of using deepfake AI technology. Deepfakes have become so advanced that they are now helping candidates campaign in ways that were previously impossible.

Take former Pakistani prime minister Imran Khan, for example.[331] His party "has used an artificial intelligence voice clone of him to campaign from prison." In December 2023, the BBC reported:

> Mr Khan had his three-year sentence for corruption suspended in August, but remains in jail.
>
> His Pakistan Tehreek-e Insaf (PTI) party used AI to make an audio clip to address an internet "virtual rally."
>
> Mr Khan's speech was generated from text he had written from prison and had approved by his lawyers, PTI said.
>
> The four-minute audio message, marred by internet disruptions, was played over an AI-generated image which appeared to be speaking.

Khan used the power of AI to tell voters that he is a political prisoner and that his party is being unjustly silenced by Pakistani officials. The BBC further reported:

> "Our party is not allowed to hold public rallies," Mr Khan said, as he urged supporters to turn out in large numbers at the country's general elections set for 8 February.
>
> "Our people are being kidnapped and their families are being harassed."

Khan's political party, PTI, claims that its online rally featuring deepfake Khan was viewed by 6 million people across several major social media platforms.

The Associated Press reported in March 2024, "In Indonesia, the team that ran the presidential campaign of Prabowo Subianto deployed a simple mobile app to build a deeper connection with supporters across the vast island nation. The app enabled voters to upload photos and make AI-generated images of themselves with Subianto."[332]

Although campaigns using deepfakes to improve the image and circumstances of their candidates isn't as dangerous as more nefarious deepfake strategies, it's still an incredibly deceptive tactic. Voters choose leaders for all kinds of reasons, including candidates' temperament, values, and communication abilities. It's bad enough that politicians regularly lie and misrepresent themselves to get elected, but AI deepfake technology is taking things to a whole new level. And we're still in the earliest stages of the AI revolution. Just wait until deepfakes become completely indistinguishable from real-life video and audio. People will have absolutely no idea who they are electing.

Imagine the Possibilities

The use of artificial intelligence and deepfakes in elections isn't limited to fooling people into believing misleading audio and video. AI-generated and user-altered images have also been utilized to cause confusion or as part of clever campaign tactics.

In January 2024, actor/political commentator Mark Ruffalo shared on Elon Musk's X social media platform, formerly called Twitter, "AI-generated fakes of former President Trump supposedly surrounded by young girls on late-pedophile Jeffrey Epstein's plane."[333]

In addition to sharing the fake photos, Ruffalo wrote, "Gross. #MAGA wants to paint everyone on those flights as pedophiles except the one guy who smiles in a group of young girls all headed to

Epstein's 'Fantasy Island' with him. My bet is there are some decent republicans left in America that may think this is going too far."[334]

Ruffalo later apologized for spreading fake news, but, of course, didn't take responsibility for his rush to share the images. Instead, he blamed Musk.[335]

"Be careful. Elon's X and his allowing so much disinformation here is driving the value of his app down by 55%," Ruffalo wrote.[336]

In June 2023, CNN reported, "The presidential campaign for Florida Gov. Ron DeSantis released a video on social media that appears to use images generated by artificial intelligence to depict former President Donald Trump hugging Dr. Anthony Fauci."[337]

"The images were included in a video posted Monday that first shows Trump as host of the reality TV show 'The Apprentice' firing people and then pivots to sound bites of Trump praising Fauci and explaining why he could not fire the former head of the National Institute of Allergy and Infectious Diseases," CNN also reported. "At one point, the audio is laid over pictures of Trump and Fauci, including several of the two men appearing to embrace. The words 'Real Life Trump' are transposed over the images."[338]

Trump was targeted again in March 2023. According to the *Washington Post*:

> Eliot Higgins, the founder of the open-source investigative outlet Bellingcat, was reading this week about the expected indictment of Donald Trump when he decided he wanted to visualize it.
>
> He turned to an AI art generator, giving the technology simple prompts, such as, "Donald Trump falling down while being arrested." He shared the results ...
>
> Two days later, his posts depicting an event that never happened have been viewed nearly 5 million times, creating a case study in the increasing sophistication of AI-generated

images, the ease with which they can be deployed and their potential to create confusion in volatile news environments.[339]

At the time of writing this chapter, Higgins' X post had been viewed 6.8 million times.[340]

War Games

In chapter 2, I showed you how one of the most important strategies used by the Propaganda Industrial Complex is to develop detailed strategies for a range of potential crises, so that when a problem develops in the future, elites are ready to take advantage.

The threats posed by deepfakes are real. This technology has the potential to completely undermine Americans' confidence in an important election, to sow chaos and confusion, or to fool people into voting for the wrong candidate. It could spark violence, endless conspiracy theories, or something much worse. Something needs to be done, and we'll get to that later in this chapter, but that something isn't giving the Propaganda Industrial Complex more power over our lives. We need to have a plan of action for when the next election misinformation disaster occurs, because elites are now in the process of developing a plan of their own.

In March 2024, NBC News reported that former government officials, journalists, and activists gathered together for an event titled "The Deepfake Dilemma."[341] According to NBC News, "the exercise illustrated how AI-enabled tools threaten to turbocharge the spread of false information in an already polarized society and could sow chaos in the 2024 election."

"Rather than examining a singular attack by a group or hostile regime, the exercise explored a scenario with an array of both domestic and foreign actors launching disinformation, exploiting rumors and seizing on political divisions," NBC News reported.

NBC News walked readers through some of the scenarios experienced by participants in the "Deepfake Dilemma" war game:

It's Election Day in Arizona and elderly voters in Maricopa County are told by phone that local polling places are closed due to threats from militia groups.

Meanwhile, in Miami, a flurry of photos and videos on social media show poll workers dumping ballots.

The phone calls in Arizona and the videos in Florida turn out to be "deepfakes" created with artificial intelligence tools. But by the time local and federal authorities figure out what they are dealing with, the false information has gone viral across the country.

Event participants gathered around a mock White House situation room, where each played a unique role, including the head of law enforcement and intelligence agencies. Players "sifted through the alarming reports from Arizona and Florida and numerous other unconfirmed threats, including a break-in at a postal processing center for mail-in ballots."

NBC News reported:

Conferring with the tech companies, players who were "government officials" struggled to determine the facts, who was spreading "deepfakes" and how government agencies should respond. (MSNBC anchor Alex Witt also took part in the exercise, playing the role of president of the National Association of Broadcasters.)

In the exercise, it was unclear initially that photos and video of poll workers tossing out ballots in Miami were fake. The images had gone viral, partly because of a bot-texting campaign by Russia.

Eventually, officials were able to establish that the whole episode was staged and then enhanced by artificial intelligence to make it look more convincing.

Participants then developed a series of strategies for dealing with the crisis. In some cases, they couldn't agree on the best way to handle it.

"It was jarring for folks in the room to see how quickly just a handful of these types of threats could spiral out of control and really dominate the election cycle," said Miles Taylor, according to NBC News.

"One of the big debates in the room was whose job is it to say if something's real or fake," Taylor told NBC News. "Is it the state-level election officials who say we've determined that there's a fake? Is it private companies? Is it the White House?"

"That's something that we think we're also going to see in this election cycle," Taylor said.

Taylor is a former senior official from the U.S. Department of Homeland Security (DHS). He helped organize the event on behalf of a group called The Future US. Taylor is well known among powerful left-wing media figures for secretly subverting the Trump administration while he was working for the DHS.

In 2018, while serving as the chief of staff at DHS, Taylor anonymously authored an op-ed for the *New York Times*, titled, "I Am Part of the Resistance Inside the Trump Administration." In it, Taylor wrote, "Although he was elected as a Republican, the president shows little affinity for ideals long espoused by conservatives: free minds, free markets and free people."[342]

Taylor also hurled numerous insults at Trump, including that "Trump's impulses are generally anti-trade and anti-democratic," and that the former president's leadership style is "impetuous, adversarial, petty and ineffective."[343]

Nick Penniman, CEO of Issue One, was another of the event's participants.[344] Issue One is an organization that "helped lead the congressional push to establish a 9/11-style commission to investigate the January 6th attack on the U.S. Capitol."[345]

"Now, in the last few years, we in America are having to defend assaults on our elections from both domestic and foreign forces," Penniman said, according to NBC News report. "We just don't have the infrastructure or the history to do it at scale because we've never had to face threats this severe in the past."

"We know a hurricane is eventually going to hit our elections," Penniman also said, according to the NBC News.[346]

What did the war game participants recommend that the country do to avoid a future election deepfake crisis? Greater public-private partnerships between tech companies and governments, of course.

"The once close cooperation among federal officials, tech companies and researchers that developed after the 2016 election has unraveled due to sustained Republican attacks in Congress and court rulings discouraging federal agencies from consulting with companies about moderating online content," NBC News claimed.[347]

"Concerned about understaffed and inexperienced state election agencies, a coalition of nonprofits and good-government groups are planning to organize a bipartisan, countrywide network of former officials, technology specialists and others to help local authorities detect deepfakes in real time and respond with accurate information," NBC News also reported, citing promises from some of the participants of the war game.[348]

Do the participants of the March 2024 war game sound like the kind of impartial, nonpartisan people we need working on important election-integrity issues? Or do they sound like anti-Trump hacks looking for ways to take advantage of a future deepfake crisis? (I'll give you a hint: it isn't the first option.)

It's Time to Prepare

If you're not terrified by all of this, then you haven't been paying attention. America is on the verge of a catastrophic election-related misinformation event. A deepfake or series of deepfakes could be the trigger. Elite institutions, journalists, Davos-affiliated groups, big corporations, and technology companies are all preparing for the fallout, and if the past has told us anything, their plans will almost certainly result in people having fewer freedoms, not more.

How can the American people avoid this disturbing vision of the future? The first thing we all must do is learn the strategies for understanding the truth that I outlined in chapter 3. It is vital that you do not rush to judgment when new information emerges, especially in the period immediately before an election. Everyone loves a good "October surprise" that benefits your favorite candidate weeks or days before votes are cast, but we all need to learn to resist the urge to trade reliability for political gain. The truth must be paramount at all times.

We're entering an era where you can't believe your eyes or ears because of artificial intelligence and other emerging technologies. And that problem is going to get worse. Time and caution are going to be required on everyone's part. The truth will win out, if given the opportunity to do so.

As I mentioned in chapter 3, also remember that you should apply the Beware of Bias Test when learning about breaking news and important information. The American people must collectively demand more evidence and apply a higher burden of proof on institutions that make important truth claims that reinforce their ideology or help them achieve stated goals.

We must also resist the urge to depend on government agencies, technology experts, mainstream media outlets, and other large institutions, especially those with a history of being dishonest. On issue after issue, many of them have proven that they are not reliable sources of information, especially when it comes to topics that affect elections. That doesn't mean you shouldn't hear what they have to say, but it is absolutely essential that Americans require big institutions making truth claims to show all their evidence, and for those on the opposite side of the debate to have time to evaluate it. We shouldn't just "trust the experts." It didn't work for those who blindly followed government and its allies in media and Big Tech companies during the coronavirus pandemic, and it certainly won't work in a future election-related deepfake crisis.

Of course, we can only control ourselves, and although we can work to inform the people around us of the dangers of deepfakes and other AI-generated content, especially near the time of elections, we cannot stop tens of millions of other Americans from falling into the trap. There are some in media with big audiences who will do their best, but there's no guarantee that will work either. That means you need to be prepared for a potential election disaster and its fallout.

Here are some of the things I plan on doing, now and in future elections:

- At the time of an election, plan to be in a location where you would feel comfortable for several days or even weeks. Don't plan any travel during an election or immediately afterward.
- Be prepared with plenty of food and water, in case a really dramatic election crisis causes other problems, like riots.
- Have cash on hand. Consider investing in some silver and gold. Gold is the ultimate hedge against insanity.
- If you have multiple residences, stay outside of major cities. If you don't have a residence outside of a city, consider staying with family in a more rural part of the country.

These simple actions may seem like overkill, but the danger of a serious election-related catastrophic event has never been higher, and the tensions surrounding such a situation would be incredibly high. When the stakes are elevated, it's better to be too cautious than to find yourself in the wrong place in the middle of a chaotic and potentially violent period.

The Risks Are Real

Technology is transforming virtually every part of our lives, but its impact on elections has been especially important in recent campaigns. That challenge is not going to go away. In fact, it's going to get worse soon. Not in ten years. Not in five years. Over the next twenty-four to thirty-six *months*. I hope a deepfake disaster never strikes. I believe it's possible for enough Americans to become informed on these important issues that a full-blown catastrophe never develops. But time is running out. And make no mistake about it: if a crisis hits, progressives in powerful institutions will be ready to seize the opportunity.

If you want to know what the most influential organizations, businesses, and governments are thinking, one of the best sources is the World Economic Forum (WEF), the people responsible for hosting a lavish conference of global elites in Davos, Switzerland, each year, as well being the mastermind behind the Great Reset movement.

Each year, the World Economic Forum publishes a "Global Risks Report."[349] It's based on two large surveys of leaders that the WEF conducts annually. In the WEF's "Global Risks Report 2024" edition, the WEF spoke to "1,490 experts across academia, business, government, the international community and civil society." It also collected survey data about expected risks over the next two years from more than "11,000 business leaders in 113 economies."

According to the WEF, out of dozens of potential risks, the leaders they spoke with identified "AI-generated misinformation and disinformation" as a significant current risk more often than nearly any other risk. The only risk deemed more important than AI-generated misinformation was "extreme weather."

Experts were also asked to identify risks over the next two years and ten years. In the two-year period, respondents said "misinformation and disinformation" was the number one risk. Over the next ten years, "misinformation and disinformation" was fifth overall. All four of the risks ranked above "misinformation and disinformation" were related to environmental issues, such as "critical change to Earth systems."

The WEF further explained in its report:

> Emerging as the most severe global risk anticipated over the next two years, foreign and domestic actors alike will leverage Misinformation and disinformation to further widen societal and political divides (Chapter 1.3: False information). As close to three billion people are expected to head to the electoral polls across several economies—including Bangladesh, India, Indonesia, Mexico, Pakistan, the United Kingdom and the United States—over the next two years, the widespread use of misinformation and disinformation, and tools to disseminate it, may undermine the legitimacy of newly elected governments. Resulting unrest could range from violent protests and hate crimes to civil confrontation and terrorism.

The WEF also noted that the leaders surveyed believe "as truth is undermined, the risk of domestic propaganda and censorship will also rise in turn. In response to mis- and disinformation, governments could be increasingly empowered to control information based on what they determine to be 'true.'"

There isn't a single part of those statements with which I disagree, although I have a completely different understanding of what is meant by "misinformation" and "disinformation." When the WEF uses those words, it simply means *anything that doesn't align with the views held by global elites.*

The most powerful figures and institutions in the world know we're headed for tough times. They are preparing for it, as they so often do. In the same way that elites were ready to take advantage of gigantic global pandemic in 2020, they are readying themselves now for an election crisis. Meanwhile, our neighbors, friends, and many of our family members are not preparing, or even thinking about these issues. Many have never heard the word "deepfake," and if they have, they probably think it poses few, if any, risks to election integrity. And even many of the people who are worried about deepfakes and other AI-generated content impacting elections have only heard about those concerns through mainstream media outlets, which, of course, are not going to promote individual liberty if a disaster does hit in the coming years.

We have an important chance to avert a future election-related crisis, or at least to be better prepared for its effects. But if we don't do the hard work today, I fear that our country will soon be in great peril.

6

PROPAGANDA WARS: PROTECTING AMERICA FROM FOREIGN MANIPULATION

THE TWENTIETH CENTURY WAS A PERIOD OF UNPRECEDENTED innovation and progress. New and improved technologies made life substantially easier than it had ever been before in human history.

It was in this era that manufacturers began to mass-produce the gasoline-powered motor vehicle, making it available to millions across the United States.

Household electricity went from being a luxury offered only to the wealthy to a universal utility that all Americans have access to.

Commercial airfare developed rapidly, making it easier than ever to travel the vast lands of the United States, and even around the world.

Man went from riding horseback to traveling to the moon, all in less than a century's time.

Nuclear technology transformed energy development and geopolitics forever.

The creation of the modern home computer and the birth of the Internet Age brought information to the masses in ways that few had previously thought possible.

However, despite these and many other remarkable achievements, the twentieth century was also a time of great horror, bloodshed, and warfare. About 16 million people lost their lives in World War I. The 1918 global influenza epidemic killed roughly 50 million.[350] Worldwide casualties due to World War II topped 85 million, and that's probably a conservative estimate. Some sources estimate that the number of civilians who died in China alone could have been greater than 50 million.[351]

New and emerging technologies provided individuals, private companies, and governments with greater opportunities to transform the world, and the wealthy and powerful took advantage—in some cases, for the better. In others, for the worse.

The use and influence of propaganda also underwent a radical change in the twentieth century. It's true that propaganda has existed since the dawn of human civilization, but as with warfare, travel, medicine, and other areas of life, technological changes have made propaganda increasingly more sophisticated and effective in recent decades.

During World War II, both Allied and Axis militaries heavily utilized paper propaganda leaflets. Allied government leaflet agencies produced an estimated 6 billion paper messages over the course of the war in Europe, and both sides developed a variety of innovative ways to distribute them. The British Online Archives notes:

> The 1940s brought new technological developments which aimed to increase the amount of leaflets that could be safely dropped by pilots. One of these innovations was suggested by

British Air Officers; a proposal to construct a special bomb to disperse leaflets over enemy territory. The most successful of these bombs was the "Monroe bomb," invented in 1943 by United States Army Air Forces Captain James Monroe. The Monroe bomb is said to have dropped over 500 million leaflets in Europe during the Second World War.[352]

These propaganda leaflets were used for many purposes, including psychological warfare. Their aim, depending on the audience, was to demoralize enemy troops and civilians, to spread misinformation, to encourage defection, and to boost morale among friendly forces. The leaflets were carefully crafted to appeal to the emotions and beliefs of the target audience, often featuring persuasive language, images, and promises of better conditions or surrender terms if the enemy were to comply.[353]

The effectiveness of these methods remains largely unknown, although many military historians agree that leaflet propaganda was most effective when enemy soldiers were already highly demoralized.

In March 1945, the Supreme Headquarters Allied Expeditionary Force's Psychological Warfare Division, which operated under the control of future president Dwight Eisenhower, airdropped some 80 million propaganda leaflets behind German lines. Shortly thereafter, 350,000 German soldiers surrendered. According to the Psychological Warfare Division, 90 percent of those prisoners of war had reported seeing a propaganda leaflet before giving up the fight.[354]

In the decades that followed World War II, propaganda radically spread across the world. More and more people purchased television sets, so governments took advantage by instituting sweeping TV propaganda campaigns. Across the planet, governments ramped up misinformation and infiltration efforts. In many countries, college campuses became breeding grounds for foreign intelligence propaganda operations.

In the 1990s, the internet became widely available to the public, especially in wealthier regions of the world. This created new opportunities for nations to engage in propaganda wars. False or misleading information seeded by adversarial intelligence and terrorist organizations was posted in online forums and on blogs and news websites. As internet technology improved, giving rise to the development of video and social media platforms, propaganda further evolved, becoming increasingly more persuasive in the early 2000s.

In all these periods, propaganda from foreign influences had a profound impact on social, cultural, and economic issues. But the present era presents much greater challenges. Technological innovations like those outlined in chapter 4—notably, artificial intelligence, data collection, deepfakes, advanced algorithms, and complex social media systems—have made it easier than ever for foreign powers to manipulate how people think and feel.

As I will show throughout the rest of this chapter, the propaganda threat for Americans has become especially troubling over the past decade and a half. Smartphone technology and the proliferation of the internet has allowed foreign actors to influence Americans in ways that were the stuff of science fiction just a decade or two ago. The United States has never experienced a propaganda assault like the one it's facing today, and if we don't learn how to recognize and avoid those attacks soon, we will inevitably fall victim to them. In many ways, we already have.

The following sections of this chapter will provide some important illustrations of foreign propaganda efforts. They feature propaganda operations in the United States and those occurring outside of its borders but that have had a prominent impact on Americans, directly or indirectly. By highlighting these operations, I am in no way suggesting that these are the only propaganda efforts going on today. This chapter only lightly scratches the surface of this gigantic problem. But by the time you finish this chapter, you will have the understanding needed to ensure that you and your loved ones are protected from other, similar forms of propaganda.

Russia and the Internet Research Agency

Beginning as late as 2013, an organization called the Internet Research Agency (IRA) became one of the Russian government's most important tools for spreading misinformation and sowing discord in foreign nations, including the United States. At its height, the St. Petersburg-based group employed four hundred staff, many of whom worked twelve-hour shifts. This included eighty dedicated "trolls," whose job was focused on sowing "discord in the U.S. political system," although U.S. intelligence claims that the IRA conducted operations in Russia and dozens of other nations as well, not just America.[355]

In June 2015, before wildly outlandish claims about Donald Trump "colluding" with Vladimir Putin became a regular talking point on left-wing cable news networks, the *New York Times* published an in-depth investigative story about the IRA. The article featured a trove of information provided by Ludmila Savchuk, a former Internet Research Agency employee.

According to the *Times*, based on Savchuk's leaked information:

The first thing employees [of the Internet Research Agency] did upon arriving at their desks was to switch on an Internet proxy service, which hid their I.P. addresses from the places they posted; those digital addresses can sometimes be used to reveal the real identity of the poster. Savchuk would be given a list of the opinions she was responsible for promulgating that day.

Workers received a constant stream of "technical tasks"—point-by-point exegeses of the themes they were to address, all pegged to the latest news.

Savchuk and her co-workers would post comments that disparaged the Ukrainian president, Petro Poroshenko, and highlighted Ukrainian Army atrocities. Russian domestic affairs were also a major topic. Last year, after a financial crisis hit Russia and the ruble collapsed, the professional trolls left optimistic posts about the pace of recovery. Savchuk also says that in March, after the opposition leader Boris Nemtsov was murdered, she and her entire team were moved to the department that left comments on the websites of Russian news outlets and ordered to suggest that the opposition itself had set up the murder.[356]

In 2014, Russian hackers leaked emails to the press that revealed additional details about the responsibilities demanded of IRA workers. In an article about the leaked emails, *BuzzFeed News* reported:

> The documents show instructions provided to the commenters that detail the workload expected of them. On an average working day, the Russians are to post on news articles 50 times. Each blogger is to maintain six Facebook accounts publishing at least three posts a day and discussing the news in groups at least twice a day. By the end of the first month, they are expected to have won 500 subscribers and get at least five posts on each item a day. On Twitter, the bloggers are expected to manage 10 accounts with up to 2,000 followers and tweet 50 times a day.
>
> They are to post messages along themes called "American Dream" and "I Love Russia."[357]

However, by 2016, the IRA's trolls, at the behest of the Kremlin, had turned most of their attention to the United States and its highly contentious presidential election.

According to a 2019 government report by the U.S. Senate Select Committee on Intelligence, in 2016 the IRA "used social media to conduct an information warfare campaign designed to spread disinformation and societal division in the United States."[358]

The Senate Select Committee further reported:

> Masquerading as Americans, these operatives used targeted advertisements, intentionally falsified news articles, self-generated content, and social media platform tools to interact with and attempt to deceive tens of millions of social media users in the United States.
>
> This campaign sought to polarize Americans on the basis of societal, ideological, and racial differences, provoked real world events, and was part of a foreign government's covert support of Russia's favored candidate in the U.S. presidential election.[359]

The IRA's operational focus "was on socially divisive issues—such as race, immigration, and Second Amendment rights—in an attempt to pit Americans against one another and against their government," the Select Committee wrote in its report.[360]

The IRA operatives attempted to accomplish this goal by using "hot-button, societal divisions in the United States as fodder for the content they published through social media in order to stoke anger, provoke outrage and protest, push Americans further away from one another, and foment distrust in government institutions."[361]

According to *BuzzFeed News*'s report on the leaked IRA emails, to trick social media users, trolls adopted one of numerous archetypes for each of their fake social media accounts, including "Handkerchief,

Gay Turtle, The Ghost of Marius the Giraffe, Left Breast, Black
Breast, and Ass, for reasons that are not immediately clear."[362]

The Senate Select Committee's 2019 investigation found that
the IRA's mission in America wasn't only to impact the 2016 election, but rather to accomplish a wide range of goals beneficial
to the Russian government. It also determined that one reason
for the IRA's success is that its trolls not only created fake social
media users; it also developed fake followers of those social media
accounts, to make them appear more realistic and to help amplify
propaganda campaigns.[363]

The *New York Times* included a good illustration of these tactics
in its 2015 report about the IRA's trolls and its propaganda projects.
According to the *Times*:

> One document outlined a project called "World Translation";
> the problem, it explained, was that the foreign Internet was
> biased four to one against Russia, and the project aimed to
> change the ratio.
>
> One account was called "I Am Ass." Ass had a Twitter
> account, an Instagram account, multiple Facebook accounts
> and his own website. In his avatars, Ass was depicted as a pair
> of cartoon buttocks with an ugly, smirking face. He filled his
> social-media presences with links to news articles, along with
> his own commentary. Ass had a puerile sense of humor and
> only a rudimentary grasp of the English language. He also really
> hated Barack Obama. Ass denounced Obama in posts strewn
> with all-caps rants and scatological puns. ...
>
> Despite his unpleasant disposition, Ass had a half-dozen or
> so fans who regularly liked and commented on his posts. These
> fans shared some unusual characteristics. Their Facebook
> accounts had all been created in the summer of 2014. They all
> appeared to be well-dressed young men and women who lived

in large American cities, yet they seemed to have no real-life friends. Instead, they spent their free time leaving anti-Obama comments on the Facebook posts of American media outlets like CNN, Politico and Fox News. Their main Facebook interactions, especially those of the women, appeared to be with strangers who commented on their physical appearance. The women were all very attractive—so attractive, indeed, that a search revealed that some of their profile photos had been stolen from models and actors. It became clear that the vast majority of Ass's fans were not real people. They were also trolls.[364]

Because IRA operations were designed to divide Americans, they also had a tendency to target some demographics far more than others. The Senate Select Committee concluded in its report "that no single group of Americans was targeted by IRA information operatives more than African-Americans. By far, race and related issues were the preferred target of the information warfare campaign designed to divide the country in 2016."[365]

According to the Select Committee:

Evidence of the IRA's overwhelming operational emphasis on race is evident in the IRA's Facebook advertisement content (over 66 percent contained a term related to race) and targeting (locational targeting was principally aimed at African Americans in key metropolitan areas with), its Facebook pages (one of the IRA's top performing pages, "Blacktivist," generated 11.2 million engagements with Facebook users), its Instagram content (five of the top 10 Instagram accounts were focused on African-American issues and audiences), its Twitter content (heavily focused on hot-button issues with racial undertones, such as the NFL kneeling protests), and its YouTube activity (96 percent of the IRA's YouTube content was targeted at racial issues and police brutality).[366]

Unfortunately for the Russians, all good things eventually come to an end, including the IRA. After surviving numerous attacks by Western intelligence operations, the Kremlin disbanded the IRA in 2023.[367] The move came after the IRA's founder, Yevgeny Prighozin, briefly launched a boldly stupid rebellion against the leadership of the Russian Defense Ministry in June 2023, a move widely interpreted as a strong criticism of Vladimir Putin's handling of the war in Ukraine.[368]

In addition to being the proud owner of one of the world's biggest troll farms, Prighozin had been hand-picked by Putin to run a band of Russian mercenaries called the Wagner Group. The Wagner Group has played an important part in the Russia-Ukraine war. Like many in Russia, Prighozin wasn't happy with the Russian military's mostly poor performance in Ukraine, so he decided to send a clear message to Putin: either change the strategy and leadership of the war, or you're going to have a domestic crisis on your hands.

Unsurprisingly, Putin was more than just a little displeased with Prighozin's threats. Putin had plucked Prighozin from obscurity and made him one of the most powerful people in Russia. In 1981, Prighozin was convicted of assault and robbery. He was sentenced to twelve years in prison. When he was released, Prighozin did what most hardened criminals do: he got into the restaurant game. Prighozin opened a restaurant in the 1990s in St. Petersburg, where Putin was at the time serving as deputy mayor.

Through his restaurant, Prighozin developed a close relationship with Putin, which he then used to launch a catering business. In the following years, as Putin rose up the ranks of Russia's government, Prighozin became progressively more powerful and well-known among Russia's elite, and not just for his tasty Blini pancakes and Pelmeni dumplings. Prighozin became an influential figure in media and Russian internet troll farms too. Eventually, Putin decided this felon-turned-chef was the right man to run the murderous mercenary Wagner Group. (And you thought corruption and nepotism were serious problems in America. As bad as things are here, America still has nothing on the Russians.)

Most reporting about Prighozin's leadership of the Wagner Group suggests he was successful, at least as far as brutal, human rights-violating private military chiefs go. All that ended, though, when Prighozin pulled his little stunt in 2023. Prighozin's rebellion lasted just two days, ending abruptly while Prighozin and his mercenaries appeared to be on their way to seize Moscow. Putin, who initially called Prighozin a traitor, agreed to give his former favorite chef and the rest of the Wagner Group immunity in exchange for ending the conflict. Prighozin and other Wagner leaders reportedly met with Putin, agreed to the deal, and then took refuge in nearby Belarus. However, two months later, Prigozhin was flying in a small plane north of Moscow when it suddenly and mysteriously crashed, killing everyone onboard and surprising absolutely no one.

Just before Prighozin's untimely death, the IRA had been taken over by Putin, who then shut it down.[369] If Prighozin hadn't rebelled against Putin, the IRA would almost certainly still be in operation today.

It would be foolish to think that the death of Prigozhin and his troll farm means that Russia's internet misinformation and disinformation campaigns are coming to an end. The Internet Research Agency wasn't the only such group, and it won't be the last. In fact, evidence suggests that Putin has already resurrected the IRA, or perhaps launched a new, similar organization.

In March 2024, the *New York Times* reported

A handful of websites have appeared in recent weeks with names suggesting a focus on news close to home: D.C. Weekly, the New York News Daily, the Chicago Chronicle and a newer sister publication, the Miami Chronicle. In fact, they are not local news organizations at all. They are Russian creations, researchers and government officials say, meant to mimic actual news organizations to push Kremlin propaganda by interspersing it among an at-times odd mix of stories about crime, politics and culture.[370]

The *Times* further reported, "The sites, the researchers and officials said, could well be the foundations of an online network primed to surface disinformation ahead of the American presidential election in November."[371]

Patrick Warren, the co-director of Clemson University's Media Forensics Hub, told the *Times* that emerging technologies such as artificial intelligence have "made this even easier to do and to make the content that they do even more targeted."[372]

One specific example of false news pushed by the Russians through their disinformation sites is an article that featured a fake "leaked audio recording" of a Biden administration official "discussing a shift in American support for Russia's beleaguered opposition after the death of the Russian dissident Aleksei A. Navalny."[373]

It appears that Russia's online misinformation campaigns are still thriving.

Democrats have capitalized on these campaigns in the past. When Democrats' Russian-collusion conspiracy theories reached their height, it was common for reporters at the *New York Times*, the *Washington Post*, CNN, NBC, and many other outlets to claim that the only reason Donald Trump won the 2016 election is because of Russian misinformation efforts. That was a ridiculous theory then and it's even more ridiculous now that we know exactly what sorts of things the Russians were promoting online.

Remember that one X social media user cooked up by the Russians was called "I Am Ass." According to a report by the *Times*, "One characteristic post [by I Am Ass] linked to a news article about an ISIS massacre in Iraq, which Ass shared on Facebook with the comment: 'I'm scared and farting! ISIS is a monster awakened by Obama when he unleashed this disastrous Iraq war!'"[374]

Anyone who changes his or her vote for president because someone on that person's favorite social media site named "I Am Ass" told them to do so is an idiot who doesn't deserve to vote. In fact, I think that should be America's next constitutional amendment. This country can't agree on much, but I'm willing to bet I could get enough support for quick passage of the "I Am Ass" Amendment, because almost no voter is that stupid.

The Russians know this, of course. They aren't running misinformation campaigns to try to get you to vote for Trump, or Kamala Harris, or anyone else. Their sole mission is to deepen the ideological and social divisions that already exist in America. Some moron on social media named "I Am Ass" will never get you to change your vote, but he sure as heck can make you angry. He can make you feel like your country is lost and that the *other side* is too radical to be taken seriously. That's the real reason for Russia's propaganda war against the United States. Russia knows it cannot beat us one-on-one. It learned that painful lesson the hard way decades ago. So, Putin is working to destroy us from within.

The Russian-collusion investigations led by the Democrats played right into Putin's hands, and I think the Democratic politicians and mainstream media outlets knew it at the time they started peddling their own form of propaganda. They didn't care, though, because Democrats believed it would help them stop Trump, or at least wound him enough to slow his policy agenda. I think they succeeded, at least to some extent.

The question we all face now is, Will America let the Russians succeed again? I pray not, because I'm not sure the United States can survive another successful, vast Russian misinformation campaign. And perhaps more important, Russia isn't the only one playing this game. Another, even more powerful nation is working to undermine America too.

China's Propaganda War

In 2017, Neville Roy Singham and Jodie Evans hosted a beautiful "One Love Union"–themed wedding in Jamaica.[375] Singham and Evans's ceremony was, by all accounts, a lovely affair that featured esteemed guests from forty-five countries.[376] It was, in the words of the *New York Times*, "a 'Who's Who' of progressivism," one that included "Amy Goodman, host of 'Democracy Now!'; Ben Cohen, co-founder of Ben & Jerry's ice cream; and V, the playwright formerly known as Eve Ensler, who wrote 'The Vagina Monologues.'"[377]

I must admit, I am a little jealous. When Tania and I had our own One Love Union, I, too, wanted the skinnier guy from Ben and Jerry's and the lady from *The Vagina Monologues* to attend, but they never showed up. Their invitations must have gotten lost in the mail.

At first glance, Singham and Evans might have seemed like an odd match. Evans is a self-described socialist whose rise to leftist stardom came after she cofounded Code Pink, an anti-war activist group that played a prominent role in the Left's resistance to the War in Iraq.[378] Singham is a former wealthy tech guru who made a mountain of money from creating and then selling a software consulting firm called Thoughtworks. In August 2017, he sold Thoughtworks to a group called Apax Partners for a whopping $785 million.[379] Since Evans is a socialist, you would think marrying an absurdly rich guy who made a literal fortune from capitalism might be just a little bit problematic. But then again, being ideologically consistent isn't exactly socialists' strong suit.

If you look a little deeper beneath the surface, the relationship starts to make a lot more sense. You see, Singham isn't just a wealthy businessman. He's also a communist who has established deep ties with the ruthless tyrants running China, a connection that Singham and Evans have used to funnel untold mountains of money into various left-wing causes in the United States.

In August 2023, the *New York Times*, which is hardly a right-wing rag, published a detailed investigative report about Singham, Evans, and their connection to the Chinese Communist Party. According to the *Times* investigation, Singham is "at the center" of a "lavishly funded influence campaign that defends China and pushes its propaganda." Singham doesn't merely take money from Chinese-funded enterprises, either; he "works closely with the Chinese government media machine and is financing its propaganda worldwide."[380]

"From a think tank in Massachusetts to an event space in Manhattan, from a political party in South Africa to news organizations in India and Brazil, *The Times* tracked hundreds of millions of dollars to groups linked to Mr. Singham that mix progressive advocacy with Chinese government talking points," the report claimed.

Singham and Evans said that they are not working at the behest of the Chinese government, but the *Times* found that "the line between him and the propaganda apparatus is so blurry that he shares office space—and his groups share staff members—with a company whose goal is to educate foreigners about 'the miracles that China has created on the world stage.'"

The *Times* reported that Singham and his allies, including Code Pink, are now "on the front line of what Communist Party officials call a 'smokeless war.'" It's a complex, costly, international web of foreign influence groups and business ties. Under the rulership of Xi Jinping, the *Times* says China has "expanded state media operations, teamed up with overseas outlets and cultivated foreign influencers. The goal is to disguise propaganda as independent content." This includes content published through numerous media and social media sources, from mainstream news publications to YouTube videos and educational courses on college campuses.

They also reportedly "seek to influence real-world politics by meeting with congressional aides, training politicians in Africa, running candidates in South African elections and organizing protests like the one in London that erupted into violence."

This vast Chinese propaganda network has infected important parts of the U.S. and European media, helping China twist narratives globally to accomplish its plans and avert serious crises—you know, crises like being blamed for starting one of the largest global pandemics in human history.

China's Propaganda Virus

In many respects, the COVID-19 pandemic was disastrous for China, but one of the lone bright spots for the communist nation is that its propaganda network and influence-peddling schemes successfully prevented the Chinese government from being widely blamed and punished for the spread of the disease. Despite the facts that COVID-19 originated in China, its existence and danger were covered up by the Chinese government, and the coronavirus killed more than 3.4 million people globally in 2020 alone,[381] it is absolutely astounding that the world didn't call for sweeping punishments of the Chinese Communist Party.[382] It's even more remarkable considering that it's possible—and I would argue highly likely—that the novel coronavirus was cooked up in a Chinese lab controlled by the Communist Party.[383]

Entire books have been written on the COVID-19 pandemic and the Chinese government's strategies for hiding it from the world. I have personally spent hundreds of hours on television and radio talking about the subject, and I covered in great detail the COVID-19 pandemic, its associated lockdowns, and the ways the coronavirus has been used to expand the power of elites in my 2022 book *The Great Reset: Joe Biden and the Rise of Twenty-First-Century Fascism.*[384] So, I am not going to spend the tremendous amount of time needed to cover those topics again in this section of the chapter. However, it is important you have a basic understanding of the propaganda infrastructure that China has put in place around the world, so that when the next crisis comes, you know what to look out for. The coronavirus pandemic provided a great illustration of how that system works and how effective it can be in times of crisis.

In May 2021, the International Federation of Journalists (IFJ) published a detailed report about China's global COVID-19 propaganda strategy. According to the authors, their investigation found that during the pandemic, there was "an activation of the existing media infrastructure China has put in place globally, which includes training programs and sponsored trips for global journalists, content sharing agreements feeding state-sponsored messages into the global news ecosystems, memoranda of understanding with global journalism unions, and increasing ownership of publishing platforms."[385]

"As the pandemic started to spread, Beijing used its media infrastructure globally to seed positive narratives about China in national media, as well as mobilising more novel tactics such as disinformation," the authors also wrote.[386]

China was able to accomplish this feat through a variety of tactics. It increased its "news offerings, providing domestic and international content tailored for each country in non-Anglophone languages."

China also weaponized journalism visas by removing from its country foreign reporters, who were unlikely to toe the Communist Party's line about the pandemic. The vacuum in coverage that was created by this strategy was filled by government-approved journalists and content, which was then "sometimes offered for free" to other countries and foreign news outlets, according to IFJ.[387]

Chinese officials also directly engaged in misinformation and disinformation tactics. For example, China's foreign ministry spokesman, Zhao Lijian, openly promoted China-aligned conspiracy theory websites, "including one that claimed Covid-19 was brought to China by US soldiers attending the Army Games in Wuhan, the city in which the first outbreak was discovered." China then used social media to promote its messages and false news stories by having "an army of Chinese ambassadors and other foreign ministry spokesmen" repeat the same Communist Party talking points. This tactic became known as "Wolf Warrior" diplomacy.[388]

Similar to Russia's Internet Research Agency operation, China also employed a network of paid internet trolls to post propaganda on foreign social media sites, including the most popular platforms in the United States.[389]

According to the IFJ researchers investigating China's propaganda network:

> Beijing has also updated its information control toolkit unleashing both Wolf Warrior diplomats and paid trolls. This much is clear from the action taken by Western social media companies who repeatedly found networks of state-linked Chinese accounts seeding geopolitical narratives favourable to China's Communist Party. In June 2020, Twitter removed 23,750 Chinese accounts at the core of a highly organized network which fed into another 150,000 accounts that amplified this content. The tweets were predominantly in Chinese languages

and spreading geopolitical narratives favourable to the CCP, while spreading disinformation about Hong Kong. This followed a similar move in 2019. In August 2020, Google removed 2,500 fake YouTube accounts linked to China, while in September 2020, Facebook took down around 180 such accounts. These disclosures by tech companies suggest a largescale coordinated attempt to use social media to seed narratives beneficial to the CCP overseas, since these platforms are all banned inside China.

In Italy, one of the earliest victims of the coronavirus pandemic, China was seen as actively propagating disinformation regarding Covid-19. State actors disseminated doctored videos, spread false information suggesting Covid-19 originated from Italy, and seeded the incorrect narrative that handwashing did not succeed in preventing the spread of Covid-19.[390]

China's strategy of using paid trolls to spread misinformation on the internet is not new. It has been utilized by the Chinese Communist Party for at least the past two decades. In 2013, *The Economist* published an extensive investigation about China's misinformation strategies online. According to that report:

A policy toward censoring and manipulating the internet has existed in China since at least 2005 when Mr. Hu, at a internal party speech, spoke of a "smokeless war" being waged by China's enemies and the need to defend the party.

According to Wen Yunchao, a prominent blogger, "the authorities had felt the internet was out of control and they needed to address it immediately. At the end of 2005 they had a meeting in Qingdao to study how to control the internet."

They started to hire online commentators to steer conversations in the right direction, who became known as the "50-Cent Party" because they were paid 50 Chinese cents per post. In

January 2007 Mr Hu gave a speech to the Politburo calling for it to "assert supremacy over online public opinion" and "study the art of online guidance." Controlling the internet was not enough; the party also needed to "use" the internet, said Mr Hu.

The arrival of Twitter-like microblogging services in China, and particularly of Sina Weibo in August 2009, forced the authorities and their web commentators to become more active than ever.[391]

China has not limited its activities to creating and promoting content online. It also spends a significant amount of money influencing so-called independent online journalists, travelers, and social media personalities with large followings.

In 2021, the *New York Times* reported, "State-run news outlets and local governments have organized and funded pro-Beijing influencers' travel, according to government documents and the creators themselves. They have paid or offered to pay the creators. They have generated lucrative traffic for the influencers by sharing videos with millions of followers on YouTube, Twitter and Facebook."[392]

According to the *Times*, "Together, six of the most popular of these influencers have garnered more than 130 million views on YouTube and more than 1.1 million subscribers."

Many of the influencers paid by China are white Westerners from America and Europe. Some have lived in China for a long time and claim that despite the funding they receive from the Chinese Communist government, they are acting independently and without coercion.

But as the *Times* notes, "even if the creators do not see themselves as propaganda tools, Beijing is using them that way. Chinese diplomats and representatives have shown their videos at news conferences and promoted their creations on social media."[393]

"Sympathetic foreign voices are part of Beijing's increasingly ambitious efforts to shape the world conversation about China," the *Times* also reported. "The Communist Party has marshaled diplomats and state news outlets to carry its narratives and drown out criticism, often with the help of armies of shadowy accounts that amplify their posts."[394]

For the Chinese Communist Party, X, Facebook, YouTube, and other platforms have effectively become "propaganda megaphones for the wider world."[395]

One of the influencers who has benefited from the Chinese Communist Party's propaganda efforts is Canadian Kirk Apesland. Apesland publishes a YouTube channel called "Gweilo 60." In Cantonese, *Gweilo* is slang for "foreigner." According to the *Times*, in his videos, Apesland "rejects news of repression in Xinjiang and cites his own happy experiences to contest the idea that China's people are oppressed."[396] Xinjiang is a notorious province in western China where government officials have reportedly detained as many as 1 million Uyghurs, a largely Muslim ethnic minority group, against their will.[397]

Apesland isn't the only influencer downplaying China's human rights violations in Xinjiang. The *Times* also reported:

> Raz Gal-Or started making funny videos when he was a college student in Beijing. Now, the young Israeli brings his millions of subscribers along as he interviews both ordinary people and fellow expatriates about their lives in China.
>
> In a video this spring, Mr. Gal-Or visits cotton fields in Xinjiang to counter allegations of forced labor in the region.
>
> "It's totally normal here," he declares after enjoying kebabs with some workers. "People are nice, doing their job, living their life."[398]

Unsurprisingly, Gal-Or doesn't say anything about the horrible treatment of Uyghurs, the reeducation camps, or the numerous human-rights organizations that have investigated claims against China and found substantial evidence that contradicts the government's narrative. But maybe we should give Gal-Or a break. I mean, there are a lot of great things about China too. Like pork fried rice. And don't forget, "You can't make an omelet without breaking eggs."[399] Wait—haven't we heard that before? I think we have, but I can't remember quite how it came up. Oh, well. I'm sure that regardless of what that whole "omelet" thing was about, it turned out just fine.

Take a moment to think about where the world is today. Fake Twitter accounts and millennial travel vloggers have become some of the favorite weapons of a regime famous for its ruthless brutality. The century-old Chinese Communist Party uses Instagram influencers to strengthen its regime and bolster the party's image with Americans thousands of miles away, all through social media. It sounds so odd, doesn't it? But make no mistake about it; these tactics are potent weapons in history's largest propaganda war, and the stakes couldn't be higher.

In the past, the Chinese Communist Party didn't have the support of the world, in large part because they didn't have direct access to citizens outside its border. It couldn't win public support in countries like the United States because it had no way of reaching Americans. But now, it can transport propaganda directly into your home via the power of the internet.

If China and other tyrannical nations succeed in winning the propaganda wars over the long run, it could transform the future of geopolitics for decades to come, and not for the better. A world in which China is significantly more influential than it is today is not one that you or your children are going to want to live in.

Controlling the Narrative at Home

The Chinese government has undoubtedly spent a lot of time and money spreading misinformation and disinformation, but it's also laser-focused on keeping information from foreigners out of the country as well, or at least limiting what people can see and hear.

Writing for *Foreign Policy* in February 2024, Chinese American scholar Minxin Pei notes that in addition to establishing vast controls on what users can see on the internet, "Beijing's approach to taming the information revolution is unique: It has focused on controlling access to the internet, not just censoring its content. Chinese authorities prioritize knowing who is online—and this allows them to identify, track, intimidate, and punish those who are potential threats." The Chinese government, says Pei, calls this strategy "battlefield control."[400]

How does the Chinese Communist Party keep track of authorized internet users? According to Pei, "the government relies on two bodies for surveillance: the Central Cyberspace Affairs Commission, which is part of the CCP, and police units." Communist Party officials are also involved. They act as censors, choosing what can and cannot be viewed in China.[401]

Pei explains that the Cyberspace Affairs Commission does not have "the workforce and technological capabilities to conduct sophisticated surveillance," so it has focused on promoting disinformation and routine censorship. "For instance, the municipal cyber agency of the city of Longnan, with just under 3 million people, reported that, by the late 2010s, it used big data and cloud computing to monitor online public opinion; in 2019, the agency monitored 515,000 pieces of online information about Longnan, 8,000 of which were deemed to be negative," Pei wrote. Meanwhile, China's cyber police units handle surveillance, enforcement, and monitoring of internet cafés and other public facilities. One cyber police department in the city of Yanan openly acknowledges that its primary goals are "monitoring and controlling harmful information; collecting, analyzing, and reporting developments on the internet; enforcing regulations on internet cafes; and investigating and dealing with cybercrimes."[402]

A Global Crisis

Russia and China are two of the most important players in the global propaganda wars, but they are hardly the only ones. Nearly every large country in the world has adopted disinformation and misinformation strategies, which they use on their own citizens, foreign nations, or both. Advanced technology and personal data have become so affordable and widely available that it's now easier than ever for nations to engage in effective misinformation operations. Even countries with comparatively small intelligence and defense budgets are now getting heavily involved in the ongoing global propaganda war.

For example, in October 2020, less than a month before the presidential election, Democrat voters in several states received a threatening email demanding that they vote for Donald Trump. "You will vote for Trump on Election Day or we will come after you," the message read, according to a report by the *Washington Post*. The message also claimed that the group that sent the email was "in possession of all your information."[403]

The message claimed to come from a group called the Proud Boys, which has openly supported Trump in the past. However, U.S. intelligence officials determined that the emails were actually sent by someone working on behalf of the Iranian government.

John Ratcliffe, who was serving as the director of national intelligence at the time of the incident, said the emails targeted registered voters to "cause confusion, sow chaos, and undermine your confidence in American democracy." Ratcliffe also said the emails were meant to "intimidate voters, incite social unrest, and damage President Trump."[404]

The Iranians were able to gather the voter data used to distribute the emails through publicly available online sources and commercial services that offer voter information to campaigns and some businesses. No hacking or advanced technological infrastructure were required.[405]

That's not to say that countries such as Iran do not have more sophisticated operations as well. They have also in recent years used far more advanced technologies and strategies in their propaganda efforts, as Microsoft outlined in a comprehensive February 2024 report about Iran.

Iran's propaganda network is at least partially composed of a web of online influence operations. These operations, which go by codenames such as Storm-0784, control dozens of online "sockpuppets." According to Microsoft, a sockpuppet is a "false online persona employing fictitious or stolen identities for the purpose of deception." When activated, these operations use social media and the internet to push the agenda of the Iranian government.[406]

For example, in the immediate aftermath of Hamas's barbaric October 7, 2023, attack on innocent Israelis, Iran's Ministry of Intelligence and Security and Islamic Revolutionary Guard Corps waged multiple, technologically advanced propaganda campaigns, both in Iran and abroad. The most complex attack involved an operation called Cotton Sandstorm. According to Microsoft:

> [Iran] made use of new techniques we've not seen from Iranian actors, including using AI as a key component to its messaging. We assess Cotton Sandstorm disrupted streaming television services in the [United Arab Emirates] and elsewhere in December under the guise of a persona called "For Humanity."

For Humanity published videos on Telegram showing the group hacking into three online streaming services and disrupting several news channels with a fake news broadcast featuring an apparently AI generated anchor that claimed to show images of Palestinians injured and killed from Israeli military operations. News outlets and viewers in the [United Arab Emirates], Canada, and the UK reported disruptions in streaming television programming, including BBC, that matched For Humanity's claims.[407]

Iranian-aligned groups also hit Israeli military bases with multiple coordinated "cyber or influence activity" attacks. Additionally, Iran launched propaganda campaigns or cyberattacks in numerous countries perceived to be supportive of Israel. Microsoft said these were likely designed to "undermine international political, military, or economic support for Israel's military operations."[408]

Numerous other countries have launched similar propaganda campaigns and cyberattacks as well. In 2018, one report found that North Korea "operates more than 160 propaganda websites, including news and tourism websites as well as online communities. Regardless of what these sites do, they all share one goal: To promote North Korea and its ideology and turn as many people as they can into North Korean sympathizers."[409] As of 2017, about 7,000 online propaganda agents were working for the North Korean government, according to the Korea Institute of Liberal Democracy, a think tank in neighboring South Korea.[410]

In 2023, the BBC published an article claiming that the government of Venezuela had recruited and paid a large group of citizens to post pro-government content on social media. According to the BBC report:

Rafael is also part of a group of Venezuelans being paid by the state to tweet propaganda.

He spends at least 30 minutes a day posting pro-government content. "The aim is to amplify the information the government puts on Twitter," he explains.

Every day, Venezuela's ministry of communications tweets a "hashtag of the day," which is repeated not only by elected officials' accounts and state sympathisers but also by "digital troops" like Rafael, who are paid to share propaganda. "You have to space it out to avoid being blocked. I do about 100 in the morning and 100 more in the afternoon," he says.

"The idea is to maintain a collective narrative. The fight against the enemy still exists," explains Prof Félix Seijas from the Central University of Venezuela.[411]

In February 2023, Amnesty International published an article about an "alarming crackdown on online expression" in Saudi Arabia. According to the report, Amnesty International "documented the cases of 15 people who were sentenced in 2022 to prison terms of between ten and 45 years simply for peaceful online activities, including the longest sentence believed to ever be imposed on a Saudi woman for peaceful online expression."[412]

The human rights group also claimed that Saudia Arabia's government "is attempting to infiltrate online platforms to control the information that is posted about the Kingdom and its leaders."[413]

The Five Eyes

I suspect most Americans would like to believe that their government, intelligence agencies, and law enforcement officials are more trustworthy when it comes to propaganda than the agencies and governments we've discussed so far. On many issues, I'm sure that's true, but when it comes to propaganda, Americans and other Western governments are just as slimy as the rest—even if their motives are better than those of the leaders of places like Russia and Iran.

In 2013, a former contractor for the U.S. National Security Agency (NSA), Edward Snowden, made headlines when he leaked top-secret documents to journalists, revealing the presence of a vast global surveillance system led, in part, by the United States. Snowden's records showed, as one *Washington Post* article explained, that "secret legal authorities empowered the NSA to sweep in the telephone, Internet and location records of whole populations. One of the leaked presentation slides described the agency's 'collection philosophy' as 'Order one of everything off the menu.'"[414]

One of the most significant revelations that came from Snowden's leaks is something called the "Five Eyes," an important data and intelligence sharing agreement among five nations' national security agencies. The Five Eyes agreement allows intelligence agencies in the United States, the United Kingdom, Canada, Australia, and New Zealand to access each other's data collected from citizens, the vast majority of whom were not being investigated for a crime. Under the deal, Five Eyes members agreed not to spy on each other's citizens, but countries not included in the Five Eyes were fair game. Instead of spying on each other, Five Eyes agencies agreed that they would voluntarily share data, but that the rest of the world would be kept out of the club, unless a situation arose that warranted a necessary exception.[415]

Almost no one's privacy is safe from the Five Eyes, including heads of state. For example, the *Guardian* reported in December 2013, "While revelations that tens of millions of Europeans were having details of their phone calls intercepted created widespread unease, it took the case of one particular German to create a crisis in EU-US relations. Angela Merkel was said to be livid at reports that her mobile phone had been tapped by the NSA, and called Barack Obama to demand an explanation."[416] At the time of the phone tap,

Merkel was serving as chancellor of Germany, the nation's highest political office.

But as troubling as the Five Eyes global surveillance system is, Snowden's leaked documents offered a much more disconcerting revelation. Five Eyes nations were not just spying and collecting data from innocent civilians, including Americans. They were also actively engaging in online misinformation and disinformation campaigns around the world.

The United Kingdom's Joint Threat Research Intelligence Group (JTRIG), for example, was established to engage in psychological and online covert operations. JTRIG's activities include a range of tactics, including cyberattacks, misinformation campaigns, and social media manipulation to influence public opinion or disrupt the activities of adversaries. JTRIG also creates fake online personas, spreads false news and information, disrupts online forums, and exploits vulnerabilities in computer systems.[417]

In 2015, the British Army expanded the United Kingdom's online operations through the creation of the 77th Brigade. This brigade is a "psychological operations unit responsible for 'non-lethal' warfare that reportedly uses social media to 'control the narrative,' as well as disseminating UK government-friendly podcasts and videos. At its creation, the unit announced 1,500 soldiers would take to Facebook and Twitter for this purpose," according to a report by *Wired*.[418]

In 2023, a UK army whistleblower reported that during the COVID-19 lockdowns, the United Kingdom used its 77th Brigade, as well as other government agencies, to monitor its own citizens' social media activity. When the media confronted the government with these accusations, government officials didn't deny the accusation, or even apologize for it.[419]

In January 2023 the *Telegraph* quoted one government spokesman as saying, "Online disinformation is a serious threat to the UK, which is why during the pandemic we brought together expertise from across Government to monitor disinformation about Covid." The spokesman also claimed that the government's spying operation was only used to "assess UK disinformation trends and narratives," not to "target individuals or take any action that could impact anyone's ability to discuss and debate issues freely."[420]

The United States isn't any better. It has a long track record of using online propaganda tactics to manipulate foreign societies and governments. In 2011, for example, the *Guardian* reported:

> The US military is developing software that will let it secretly manipulate social media sites by using fake online personas to influence internet conversations and spread pro-American propaganda.
>
> A Californian corporation has been awarded a contract with United States Central Command (Centcom), which oversees US armed operations in the Middle East and Central Asia, to develop what is described as an "online persona management service" that will allow one US serviceman or woman to control up to 10 separate identities based all over the world.
>
> The project has been likened by web experts to China's attempts to control and restrict free speech on the internet. Critics are likely to complain that it will allow the US military to create a false consensus in online conversations, crowd out unwelcome opinions and smother commentaries or reports that do not correspond with its own objectives.[421]

This propaganda program is just one of many similar online operations run by the U.S. government. Back in 2011, the *Guardian* noted that the online persona program "is thought to have been awarded as part of a programme called Operation Earnest Voice (OEV), which was first developed in Iraq as a psychological warfare weapon against the online presence of al-Qaida supporters and others ranged against coalition forces." At the time of the *Guardian*'s report, Operation Earnest Voice had a budget of $200 million, which it used to carry out information warfare in Afghanistan, Pakistan, and the Middle East.[422]

The U.S. government claims Operation Earnest Voice was designed to "counter extremist ideology and propaganda and to ensure that credible voices in the [Middle Eastern] region are heard." General James Mattis told the U.S. Senate Armed Services Committee that Operation Earnest Voice "supports all activities associated with degrading the enemy narrative, including web engagement and web-based product distribution capabilities."[423]

The American people will likely never know the vast majority of propaganda operations run by U.S. military and intelligence agencies. But considering the government's eagerness to engage in massive data collection efforts, its vast spying operations, and its COVID-19–era collusion with social media companies, it seems clear that Operation Earnest Voice is just the tip of the iceberg.

Surviving the Propaganda Wars

If you have learned anything from this chapter, I hope it's that the internet has become a propaganda battleground. Whenever you go online or open your smartphone, you're entering a warzone.

Social media and other online meeting places are often presented as digital communities that, to varying degrees, reflect what people actually think about almost everything. They allow real people from around the world to interact with one another as though they were sitting in your living room. There is *some* truth to that framing. Facebook and other online websites and applications allow you to share pictures of the baby with grandma, give job updates or look for new employment, or discover a new favorite restaurant. But if you're under the impression that the internet is even remotely close to being a good reflection of reality, then you haven't been paying attention. Stop reading this chapter, go back to the beginning of the book, and start over.

The degree of manipulation that's occurring online is so high and its sources are so powerful that individual citizens have no ability to effectively combat them—at least, not from within the system itself. The only way to truly protect yourself from the Propaganda Wars being waged by foreign powers, big tech companies, news outlets, activists, and others seeking to manipulate your thoughts and feelings is for you to adopt a completely new attitude about what you see, hear, and experience online, including while using your smartphone.

Approach the internet with extreme skepticism. Don't assume anything is true because you read it online, especially on social media. Know that much of what's on the internet is being manipulated by powerful governments and institutions, all of whom have an agenda. Find trusted news websites with well-established backgrounds. If you've never heard of a particular news outlet before, do your homework before believing anything that outlet posts online, because it's entirely possible it's a misinformation website developed by a nefarious actor.

Don't trust videos and audio that have been posted online without first checking trusted sources to see if those videos and audio clips are authentic. And even then, remain skeptical, especially in cases where what you're seeing or hearing supports your preconceived ideological or political beliefs. It's easy to dismiss information that doesn't fit with what you'd like to be true, but it's much harder to be skeptical when you see something online that supports your views. Nefarious actors know this, and they are counting on you to be too eager to share information without taking a hard look to see if it's true.

Keep your kids off social media platforms for as long as possible. Believe me, I know how difficult that can be, but our children are the most susceptible to misinformation and disinformation. They don't have the experience, knowledge, or, in some cases, maturity to approach social media sites with the required caution. As I've shown throughout this book, it's getting harder than ever for all of us to separate fact from fiction, but kids are having the toughest time of us all.

In chapter 3, I outlined several tests that you can use to help you decipher whether a claim is true. If you follow the first component of that guide closely, you will avoid falling for most of the misinformation and disinformation operations used in the global propaganda wars. For example, my Original Source Test would stop nearly all the propaganda operations discussed in this chapter from having a strong effect on your thinking. Never assume that something is true without first checking the original source yourself. If that's not practical because, for example, you don't have the expertise to check the source material, then be patient. Wait for a trusted source to check the material first before drawing any conclusions.

My Crazy Uncle Test is also going to be a critical part of your fact-finding toolbox. If the only place you're hearing about something is on social media, don't believe it. Treat all social media platforms as if they are giant crazy uncles obsessed with conspiracy theories. If you do, you will shield yourself from most of the negative impacts of the propaganda wars.

Propaganda wars are going to continue to rage for the foreseeable future, and there is nothing that we can do about that. What we can do, however, is protect ourselves from their effects to the best of our ability. That cannot happen if we continue living our lives as though social media and other online platforms are safe, reliable, and trustworthy sources of information. They aren't. As I showed in chapter 4 and throughout this chapter, the internet, especially social media, is overrun with bots, fake users, and troll farms. And emerging technologies will make all of those problems worse in the coming years, not better.

You don't need to be another victim of the propaganda wars. You now have the skills and understanding required to avoid future misinformation and disinformation campaigns. It is going to take some practice and time, but we cannot afford to fail. Foreign actors are dividing our nation at an increasingly faster rate. If we, the people, don't learn how to avoid those assaults, then it's just a matter of time before our own ruling class leaders use a propaganda wars crisis as a justification to eliminate Americans' rights, especially when it comes to speech. And without free speech, you cannot have a truly free society.

7

THE TRUTH IS SACRED

On March 6, 1770, one of the most important events in American history occurred. A thirty-four-year-old Boston lawyer from a prominent patriot family destroyed his career. Or at least that's how it seemed to many at the time. His name was John Adams.

Just one night earlier, four colonists had been murdered by a band of bloodthirsty, patriot-hating British soldiers who had reportedly fired indiscriminately into a crowd of unarmed citizens. Seven days later, a fifth victim of the shooting, Patrick Carr, also died from the wounds inflicted by the soldiers. It was an unspeakable crime against innocents. Among the dead were two teenagers and an African American sailor named Crispus Attucks, a man now widely considered to be the American Revolution's first fatality. The deadly attack served as proof that the monstrous English monarchy would stop at nothing to crush the spirit of the Massachusetts colonists.[424]

At least that's how patriot propagandists described it.

On the morning of March 6, city residents could still see the bloodstained snow covering King Street, one of Boston's main thoroughfares. Two days later, on March 8, Samuel Adams, one of the leaders of the Sons of Liberty, an important British-resistance movement in Massachusetts, led a massive funeral procession through Boston's streets.[425] An estimated ten thousand people attended, roughly two-thirds of the city's total population.[426]

Before March's end, Boston merchant and engraver Paul Revere had printed graphic images of British soldiers ruthlessly firing on civilians. The pictures were distributed across Massachusetts and then traveled quickly to other American colonies, sparking outrage everywhere they appeared.[427]

The bloody events of March 5 were branded a "massacre" by the Sons of Liberty, a label largely accepted by Boston's populace.[428] The "Boston Massacre" name was so effective that American historians adopted its use and continue to utilize it today, more than two hundred years later.

In the immediate aftermath of the shooting, the eight British soldiers involved in the massacre—Hugh Montgomery, James Hartigan, William McCauley, Hugh White, William Wemms, Jon Carroll, Matthew Kilroy, and William Warren—along with their captain, Thomas Preston, were arrested at the behest of colonial governor Thomas Hutchinson. Hutchinson was hardly a supporter of the patriot cause, but he had little choice in the matter. A mob of angry Bostonians demanded their arrest shortly after the deaths occurred, and had Hutchinson refused, a full-scale rebellion seemed likely. Boston was already a tinderbox, and the alleged massacre was thought by many to be the spark that could eventually light a long-anticipated revolution.[429]

On March 6, the day after the massacre, attorney John Adams received a loud knock on his door. It was a Tory merchant hoping to persuade Adams to defend the British soldiers, who would soon be charged with murder. The soldiers had claimed they were innocent of all charges, and that they had only acted in self-defense. Incredibly, much to the dismay of his fellow patriots, Adams agreed to defend Captain Preston and his troops, who were prosecuted in two separate trials later in 1770.[430]

John Adams had been convinced that although the Boston Massacre was undoubtedly a horrific tragedy, the soldiers truly had acted in self-defense. The portrait painted by patriots of the soldiers zealously murdering innocent bystanders had been nothing more than propaganda, Adams reasoned.[431] The men deserved a fair trial and a fair defense, a difficult request in colonial Boston, where patriotic ideas and rebellious opinions had flourished for many years before the massacre.

In the months that followed, Adams discovered that contrary to the many claims made by patriots, the soldiers that fired upon the crowd on the night of March 5 were not facing peaceful protesters, but rather an angry mob. Groups of citizens had gathered in several locations throughout the city, "near the Liberty Tree, down Boylston's Alley, near Murray's Barracks, and at Dock Square," in addition to near the Custom House on King Street, the site of the Boston Massacre.[432] In all these confrontations, Bostonians hurled insults at soldiers and argued with them.

Before and during the confrontation on King Street, British soldiers could hear shouting at a distance. Church bells began to ring loudly, which was typically a signal that a fire had broken out.[433] Many Bostonians had rushed out into the street in a panic. The crowd on King Street grew larger and larger. Soon, some began to throw snowballs, ice, and oyster shells at the soldiers.[434] Tensions were rising and would soon boil over.

How, exactly, the shooting began remains a historical mystery. Patriot witnesses claimed to have heard Captain Preston order the soldiers to fire their weapons. Preston and his troops alleged that they had been struck by members of the mob with clubs and that Preston had never ordered them to fire.[435] At trial, witness accounts of the event conflicted wildly, but one thing was clear: the popular notion that the British soldiers were indiscriminately firing on a small crowd of mostly peaceful protesters simply wasn't true. The *massacre* component of the Boston Massacre was, at least to some degree, a myth.

By all accounts, John Adams's performance during the soldiers' trials was masterful and ultimately resulted in highly favorable outcomes for the defendants. The eight soldiers were all found innocent of murder, although two of the soldiers were found guilty of manslaughter. Their punishment was to have the letter *M* branded on their hands—which, while painful, is considerably better than being hanged.[436]

Legal scholars and historians universally agree that the Boston Massacre trials were two of the most influential court cases in America's colonial history, and John Adams himself viewed it as one of the proudest moments of his life, which is really saying something.

In one private journal entry, Adams wrote, "The Part I took in Defence of Cptn. Preston and the Soldiers, procured me Anxiety, and Obloquy enough. It was, however, one of the most gallant, generous, manly, and disinterested Actions of my whole Life, and one of the best Pieces of Service I ever rendered my Country. Judgment of Death against those Soldiers would have been as foul a Stain upon this Country as the Executions of the Quakers or Witches, anciently."[437]

What Adams understood well was that if Americans were serious about building a new society based on individual rights, then it meant defending the liberties of *all citizens*, even when it isn't convenient or when those being protected are viewed as morally deficient. Human rights remain even among those humans we don't like. This is necessary, because all rights, if they are truly rights, must be grounded in eternal, unchanging truths. They don't shift like the sand. They are rooted, stable, and unyielding, or else they are not rights at all. A society that doesn't value or understand the truth cannot be free, because truth and individual freedom are intricately linked.

Shifting Worldviews

All of this begs an important question: How can we know what is an eternal truth? For anything to be considered true, there must be an objective standard by which we can measure it. The reason we know two plus two equals four is because it is objectively, which is to say, universally, true. We know it's universally true because we can measure it and come to the same conclusion no matter how many times we add two and two together. It doesn't matter where you live or in which period you live. Two plus two always equals four because math is grounded in eternal truths about the universe. The same can be said about physics, biology, and many other subjects. We might discover someday a reality about the universe that we didn't know before, but that doesn't mean that truth has changed. It simply means that our understanding of the truth has improved.

The Founding Fathers believed deeply in these ideals, which are reflected in the design of virtually every part of our government and its foundational documents. In the minds of men like Adams— as well as most Americans, up until the present period—eternal human rights were derived primarily from two sources: nature and God. This is what allowed for the idea of individual liberty to flourish in the period of the American Revolution. If God is eternal and all-powerful and is the supreme Source of everything, then no government had the right to take away rights granted by God to individuals. Man could determine which rights were provided to people by examining the Judeo-Christian Scriptures, which were widely believed to contain God's revelation to humankind.

Among those freedom-minded Americans and Europeans in the Founding era who rejected the Bible as authoritative and divinely inspired, there was often an appeal made to natural law and natural rights. The idea was that human beings can discover truths about morality from nature and history. People over thousands of years, in virtually every society, have agreed about certain moral truths, even if their governments didn't always embrace those ideas or live by them.

Even outside of Christendom at the time of the Founding Fathers, there was near-universal acceptance of some kind of objective standard of morality. In societies dominated by Islam, for example, the Quran and other writings were considered to have come directly from God and thus must reflect absolute truth and perfect standards for determining good and evil. In many ancient societies, emperors and kings were considered gods or divinely chosen representatives. Citizens believed they could know the truth because their emperor or king was a god or a reliable arbiter of truth acting on the behalf of a deity or deities.

Everywhere the Founding Fathers looked, they saw societies that believed in objective truths and morality. The debates in their day focused mainly on which claims about objective standards were accurate and which were invented, either innocently or as part of an attempt to amass more power. This was and still is the root of the disagreement between Protestants and Catholics, a conflict that dominated much of the thinking in the days of the Founding Fathers. More specifically, is the Roman Catholic Church's authoritative teaching offices the ultimate authority in theological and moral matters, or are the Christian Scriptures alone the highest source of authority?

What almost no one believed in the Founding era, however, especially in North America, is that truth is subjective and thus that the concepts of right and wrong, good and evil, are social constructs that can change over time. Surely, men like John Adams and Thomas Jefferson believed that people should be able to choose their lawmakers, but they did not believe that lawmakers could rightly or justly impose laws that violated the laws of God and/ or nature. Those laws are greater because they are absolute truths established by a higher authority than an elected or appointed government official.

Over the course of the twentieth century, progressive, socialist, and communist ideological forces have undermined these ideas globally, with varying degrees of success. The dominant religion in North America and Europe today is the idea that good and evil, right and wrong, and fact and fiction can all be determined by popular decree. These ideas are evolving social constructs. In some cases, people believe there really aren't any eternal truths because there are no eternal sources of truth. In other cases, people believe in subjective, ever-changing moral and scientific standards because they've been indoctrinated to think such ideas make sense.

The result of these societal shifts, which have moved people away from believing in well-established, eternally true standards of morality in favor of always-changing subjective standards, has been the development of the Clown World that I outlined in chapter 1. People have become completely untethered from reality because the pursuit of truth has been abandoned by most of our friends, family members, and neighbors. Nearly every concept is subject to change, often without much warning, because change is needed to accomplish some larger goal pursued by ruling-class elites.

Most people on the left didn't just wake up one day and decide, *You know, that whole man-and-woman thing doesn't make sense. We think there are dozens, perhaps even hundreds of genders. And this idea is so important to us that we're going to force the rest of society to accept it.*

No. What really happened is, elites decided that starting a national war over the meaning of "woman" and "man" would help them advance other social and economic goals. And because most people have no way of evaluating transgender ideology, because they don't believe in objective standards of morality and truth, they simply accept whatever elites have told them. In many cases, people rely solely on their emotions to evaluate truth claims, because that's the only thing they feel certain about. But, of course, emotions can be manipulated, and as I showed you in chapter 4, emerging technologies are going to continue to make that problem much worse for many years to come.

John Adams defended eight men with whom he shared very few goals. He did this despite the fact that many of his neighbors and friends opposed him. He also disregarded the reality that the defendants were part of a system that undermined the rights of the men and women of colonial Massachusetts. The reason Adams did this is not because he had a great love for the British Empire. Quite the opposite was true. He did it because it was the moral thing to do. Those soldiers didn't deserve to die. They had rights, and those rights were grounded in eternal truths, which could be clearly seen by Adams from nature and sacred Scripture.

In many parts of our modern Clown World, those British soldiers would not receive such gracious treatment. In fact, in a comparable situation today, they would very likely be punished severely, perhaps even killed. Why? Because Clown World's moral law—if you can even call it that—is determined by the mob, a mob that's guided only by its own passions and the elites who manipulate them.

Don't believe me? Ask the January 6 protesters rotting away in prison. Some surely deserve to be there, but many did nothing more than peacefully trespass on government property. It's worth remembering that many of the same people who want to throw the book at peaceful January 6 protesters are also the folks who want to give amnesty to immigrants who enter America illegally, even those who commit other serious crimes while here. They're also the same people who lauded the 2020 Black Lives Matter protests—which were, in hundreds of cases, actually riots—just weeks after demanding that the government shut down church services and protests against COVID-19 lockdowns.[438] Apparently, pandemic viruses don't work when you're marching for social justice and calling to defund the police.

The lack of an objective standard of morality and truth is also why so many leftists think we should believe claims made by all women who make accusations about sexual assault unless those accusations involve a sufficiently powerful Democrat. Remember that many Democrats, including then senator Kamala Harris, insisted in 2018 during confirmation hearings for Supreme Court Justice Brett Kavanaugh that his accuser *must* be believed.[439] But when similar accusations about sexual assault involving Joe Biden reemerged in 2020, Harris and others ditched their "believe all women" slogan.[440]

Some have suggested that these ideological inconsistences are a symptom of America's slide toward intense political and ideological tribalism. Under this theory, people see whatever it is they want to see, because the "other side" is bad and must be stopped at all costs. While I have no doubt that political and ideological tribalism has become a problem in the United States, I do not believe that it is the root of many of the issues we are experiencing. Rather, I think it is the *effect* of living in a world where most people reject the concept of objective, eternal truths.

Surveys show that many Americans are consciously aware that they do not believe in an objective standard of morality, even though they might not understand why that is dangerous. In April 2023, prominent pollster George Barna released the results of an important national survey called the American Worldview Inventory (AWI). The AWI is published annually by the Cultural Research Center at Arizona Christian University. Barna's survey of two thousand adults found that less than half (46 percent) of Americans agree with the statement, "There are moral absolutes that apply to everyone, all the time."[441]

Barna's poll might not be the biggest headline-grabber I have ever seen, but it could be one of the most important. If only 46 percent of Americans believe that there are moral absolutes that apply to everyone, then that means 54 percent of people think there are literally zero moral absolutes. At best, they aren't sure. Since a human right is a moral absolute, if we take the survey results literally, they suggest most Americans do not believe in the concept of individual liberty.

I have no doubt that if Barna or some other pollster were to ask Americans if they believed in the existence of "human rights" or "freedoms," a lot more than 46 percent of people would say they do, but I don't think it's because they misunderstood Barna's question about moral absolutes. It's because most Americans don't understand what a human right is or where it comes from. For many people, rights have become nothing more than permission slips from the government. To them, a right is only a right if the government says so, and the government should be acting in accordance with the will of voters. So, under this way of thinking, voters are the ultimate arbiters of the meaning of human rights.

That model works well for those who always find themselves agreeing with the majority of voters and as long as government actually does what the voters want. But most people do hold at least one important belief that doesn't conform to the views of the majority in society, and elected and unelected government officials often don't listen to what voters want anyway.

Consider the continued use of daylight savings time. Survey after survey conducted year after year shows that most voters don't want to be required to change their clocks in accordance with the seasons.[442] They want time to stay constant throughout the year.

But despite widespread opposition to the current system, nothing happens. And changing clocks around a couple times a year is about the easiest thing for the government to fix. If government isn't even willing to listen to voters about clocks, why would it listen to them about anything else?

The truth is, half of the American populace doesn't really believe in the concept of eternal rights or absolute truths, just as Barna's survey suggests. And the result is Clown World, where math is racist and "women" with penises are given trophies for overpowering small girls who don't have the testosterone needed to physically compete with them.

Crazy academics and the destruction of women's sports are the least of our troubles, though. They are merely the canaries in the coal mine. We know something is deeply wrong because our society has transformed into Clown World, but Clown World isn't where the story ends. At best, it ends with a technologically powerful authoritarian progressive state that will control virtually everything people say and do. At worst, America will become like Stalin's Soviet Union or Mao's Communist China—except the dictators in charge will have deadlier weapons and better technology to surveil the public. Call me crazy, but neither sounds very appealing to me.

The reason the United States cannot remain a free nation while rejecting the concept of an objective standard of morality is because without well-defined borders for right and wrong and good and evil, even the most well-intentioned nation will resort to liberty-killing utilitarian calculus whenever a significant problem arises. In other words, the question stops being, *How can we fix XYZ without infringing on people's liberties?* Instead, it evolves to, *What's the best way to solve XYZ problem, regardless of whether that solution conflicts with a past or current understanding of rights and liberties?* Or, put another way, if our understanding of rights can evolve—and that's precisely what most people on the left believe today—then you don't really have any rights.

Americans have seen this debate play out repeatedly in recent years. The details may change over time, but the framework remains the same.

The American Left believes racism in public institutions is evil— unless that racism is used to fix some perceived social injustice. In that case, racism can be good.

The Left believes women have the "right to choose"—unless that choice involves injecting vaccines into your body as a condition of keeping employment.

The Left believes in freedom of speech—unless that speech is labeled "misinformation," "disinformation," or "hate speech."

The Left believes girls have the right to the same opportunities as boys in public schools—unless those boys decide they're "girls."

The Left believes in religious freedom—unless that freedom conflicts with a social goal, such as increasing access to contraception and abortion.

In these and many other examples, the "rights" lauded by leftists aren't really rights because they aren't grounded in eternal truths or an objective standard of morality. One minute, freedom of speech can be a good thing. In the next, it's a danger to democracy and needs to be systematically eliminated. That's what happens when a society detaches itself from the concept of eternal truth.

The Soviet Way

The problems that come from attempting to have a free society coupled with one that rejects objective truth is not a uniquely American phenomenon. This is a crisis that applies universally to all humans everywhere.

Perhaps the best illustration of these problems can be seen by examining the history of the Soviet Union. The Soviet government was famous for claiming to support individual rights while at the same time holding its iron-booted foot on the necks of its people. This important example is probably lost on most millennial Americans and especially on even younger generations. They didn't live in the era of the Soviet Union, and they aren't being taught the truth about communism by public schools and colleges. Even those young Americans who know the Soviets were authoritarians typically do not grasp the many similarities between the ideological arguments made by the Soviets in past decades and those made by today's progressives and socialists in the United States.

You might be surprised to learn that Soviet laws established and claimed to protect far more individual rights than what you'll find in the U.S. Constitution. For example, in the Soviet Constitution of 1977, the supreme law for Soviet states and citizens, there is a long list of articles addressing individual rights in the document's seventh chapter alone.[443]

Article 40 guarantees, "Citizens of the USSR have the right to work (that is, to guaranteed employment and pay in accordance with the quantity and quality of their work, and not below the state-established minimum), including the right to choose their trade or profession, type of job and work in accordance with their inclinations, abilities, training and education, with due account of the needs of society. This right is ensured by the socialist economic system, steady growth of the productive forces, free vocational and professional training, improvement of skills, training in new trades or professions, and development of the systems of vocational guidance and job placement."

Article 42 promises, "Citizens of the USSR have the right to health protection. This right is ensured by free, qualified medical care provided by state health institutions; by extension of the network of therapeutic and health-building institutions; by the development and improvement of safety and hygiene in industry; by carrying out broad prophylactic measures; by measures to improve the environment; by special care for the health of the rising generation, including prohibition of child labour, excluding the work done by children as part of the school curriculum; and by developing research to prevent and reduce the incidence of disease and ensure citizens a long and active life."

Article 44 states, "Citizens of the USSR have the rights to housing. This right is ensured by the development and upkeep of state and socially-owned housing; by assistance for co-operative and individual house building; by fair distribution, under public control, of the housing that becomes available through fulfilment of the programme of building well-appointed dwellings, and by low rents and low charges for utility services. Citizens of the USSR shall take good care of the housing allocated to them."

Article 47 promises, "Citizens of the USSR, in accordance with the aims of building communism, are guaranteed freedom of scientific, technical, and artistic work."

Article 50 states, "In accordance with the interests of the people and in order to strengthen and develop the socialist system, citizens of the USSR are guaranteed freedom of speech, of the press, and of assembly, meetings, street processions and demonstrations."

Article 52 declares, "Citizens of the USSR are guaranteed freedom of conscience, that is, the right to profess or not to profess any religion, and to conduct religious worship or atheistic propaganda."

Article 55 says, "Citizens of the USSR are guaranteed inviolability of the home. No one may, without lawful grounds, enter a home against the will of those residing in it."

Article 56 guarantees, "The privacy of citizens, and of their correspondence, telephone conversations, and telegraphic communications is protected by law."

Boy, the Soviet Union sounds great, doesn't it? A right to health care, free press, religious liberty, free speech, housing, a good job, protection against government overreach? Where do I sign up?

Of course, we know that the Soviet Union wasn't a bastion of freedom. In fact, the Soviets were some of the worst violators of human rights in history. They imprisoned dissenters, controlled religious practices, limited travel, murdered innocent civilians, and subjected tens of millions of people to brutal living conditions. In many cases, racial and ethnic minorities faced particularly harsh human rights abuses.[444]

In 1990, scholar Paul Goble, writing for the *Cornell International Law Journal*, noted, "In the Ukraine, for example, Moscow suppressed the Ukrainian Catholic Church because of Moscow's general anti-religious policy, the Church's historical links to Rome, and Uniate identification with Ukrainian national aspirations."[445]

Although Moscow was the source of many of the Soviet Union's brutal tactics, regional Soviet governments also imposed ruthless policies on its people.

For example, Goble noted:

> One particularly good illustration of these violations is the case of Azerbaijani treatment of the Georgian national minority. The Georgians of Azerbaijan have long been subject to harassment that is generically Soviet and specifically Azerbaijani. The Azerbaijanis forced assimilation of Georgians by closing Georgian language schools and restricting Georgian access to higher education. They also refused to issue birth certificates to children with Georgian names and changed the nationality

line in the passports of local Georgians regardless of their own preference. The Azerbaijanis systematically underreported the number of Georgians in the region in order to reduce the amount of community services available to them.[446]

The Soviets didn't just limit basic human rights, either. They also killed tens of millions of people—and that's the conservative figure. Some estimates suggest more than 126 million people died at the hands of the Soviet Communist Party.[447]

Scholar R. J. Rummel was one of the world's leading experts on the human rights abuses imposed by governments in the twentieth century. In his 1990 book titled *Lethal Politics: Soviet Genocide and Mass Murder Since 1917*, Rummel concluded:

In sum, probably somewhere between 28,326,000 and 126,891,000 people were killed by the Communist Party of the Soviet Union from 1917 to 1987; and a most prudent estimate of this number is 61,911,000.

The democide rates over the three generations of Soviet history are shown in the table. Clearly, an infant born in 1917 had a good chance of being killed by the Party sometime in his future. A more precise statement of this is given by the average of the democide rates for each period, weighted by the number of years involved. Focusing on the most-probable mid-risk of .45 percent, throughout Soviet history, including the relatively safe years after the 1950s, the odds of the average citizen being killed by his own government (Party) has been about 45 to 10,000; or to turn this around, 222 to 1 of surviving terror, deportations, the camps, or an intentional famine. As pointed out in the text, this is almost twenty times the risk of an American dying in a vehicular accident.[448]

When confronted with these stunning and horrifying figures, most Americans today often assume that there weren't legal protections for human rights in the Soviet Union. However, as I have already shown, the Soviets included in their constitution numerous protections for individual liberty.

Others assume that the Soviet government simply ignored constitutional protections, but that's not entirely true either. How, then, were Soviet officials able to treat civilians so poorly? How could the Soviet Union kill so many of its own people while operating under a constitution that expressly protected the rights of Soviet citizens? Well, as any good lawyer will tell you, the devil is in the details.

Although it's true that the Soviet Constitution protected freedom of speech, freedom of religion, a free press, and countless other rights, including many not appearing in the U.S. Constitution, it also had numerous provisions that elevated the needs of the collective or state above the rights of the individual. It was these provisions that were often used to undermine freedom by Soviet officials.

For example, in chapter 7 of the Soviet Constitution of 1977, titled, "Basic Rights, Freedoms, and Duties of Citizens of the USSR," article 39 declares that although "citizens of the USSR enjoy in full the social, economic, political and personal rights and freedoms proclaimed and guaranteed by the Constitution of the USSR and by Soviet laws," the "enjoyment by citizens of their rights and freedoms must not be to the detriment of the interests of society or the state, or infringe the rights of other citizens."[449]

In other words, the Soviets, just like many modern American leftists, believed that everyone was entitled to individual liberties, but only if those liberties didn't get in the way of the desires of government officials or the collective.

Other provisions of the Soviet Constitution also advanced this ideological view. For example, in Article 65, the Soviet Constitution declares that citizens must be "uncompromising toward anti-social behaviour" and are to "help maintain public order."[450]

So, Soviet citizens had the right to free speech, but not if that speech could be classified as "anti-social behaviour." Similarly, they were granted the right to organize peacefully, but not if their right to association conflicted with an obligation to "help maintain public order."

In Article 66, parents were given authority over their children, but they also were constitutionally required to "train them for socially useful work, and to raise them as worthy members of socialist society."[451] Thus, parents who raised their children in a way that was considered contrary to socialist values could be punished.

The Soviet view of "rights," "liberties," and "freedom" is virtually indistinguishable from many of the ideas espoused by American progressives and socialists today. These leftists, too, think rights are great, unless they get in the way of "progress."

I have no doubt that the hearts of many American leftists are in the right place and that many of them intend to achieve good for our country. But the road to hell is often paved with good intentions—and make no mistake about it: Americans have never driven faster or more recklessly down the highway to hell than they are right now.

The American Way

How has the United States managed to avoid descending into tyranny? It isn't because of wealth. There have been plenty of periods in America's history when it wasn't the world's richest nation. It isn't because of its natural resources. Russia and China are two of the most resource-rich countries in history, and they are also two of the worst violators of human freedom, both today and historically. It certainly isn't because America's leaders are particularly moral or intelligent. Some of the most dysfunctional, corrupt people on the planet are currently running our government.

The primary reason the United States has become human history's freest, most successful nation is because of its foundational commitment to the belief that every single person is born with human rights and that those rights cannot be taken away by anyone or anything, including a powerful government. Those rights cannot be eliminated because they are tied to eternal truths about people, nature, and God.

We haven't always lived up to those principles, of course. The United States has mistreated many groups throughout its history, in foreign nations and in its own lands. But in every case, those abuses occurred because Americans weren't living up to their own foundational ideals, not because those ideals were defective. Over time, the United States has sought to correct those injustices, and as a result, we are one of the safest, most diverse nations in the world.

Unlike the Soviet Constitution, which promised to its citizens rights while simultaneously undermining them, America's founding legal documents specifically declare that many individual rights cannot be taken away by government, no matter what the collective, the military, or the government wants.

In the opening paragraph of the Declaration of Independence, which was authored primarily by Thomas Jefferson, the American Founders declared, "When in the Course of human events, it becomes necessary for one people to dissolve the political bands which have connected them with another, and to assume among the powers of the earth, the separate and equal station to which the Laws of Nature and of Nature's God entitle them, a decent respect to the opinions of mankind requires that they should declare the causes which impel them to the separation."[452]

Note that here, in the Declaration of Independence's first sentence, the Founders evoked the "Laws of Nature and of Nature's God" as a justification for rejecting the authority of the British monarchy. They didn't stop there, either. The next sentence of the Declaration asserts that the Founders and the people of the United States "hold these truths to be self-evident, that all men are created equal, that they are endowed by their Creator with certain unalienable Rights, that among these are Life, Liberty and the pursuit of Happiness."

The term "unalienable Rights" means rights that cannot be transferred or eliminated. These rights were, in the minds of the Founders, "self-evident," meaning apparent or obvious. And the reason they were obvious is because they could be seen in nature and were in accordance with established religious ideas.

Or, stated differently, Americans believed they had the authority to declare independence from the British Crown because they had eternal rights that come from nature and God, and those rights cannot be taken away by any government authority, regardless of what most people in society want. That's an extremely stark contrast from the Soviet Constitution and the views of many modern American progressives and socialists, who contend that rights are limited by government and the needs of the collective.

The leftist notion that the ends can justify the means was completely foreign to the Founding Fathers. In fact, their beliefs were based on a radically different ideology. To America's founders, the ends *never* justify the means if the means involve depriving people of their rights.

Following the conclusion of the Revolutionary War, Americans slowly worked to develop a permanent, legally binding document, a constitution, that could forever unite the states. Before the passage of the U.S. Constitution, which was formally ratified by states in 1788, states operated under a deeply flawed framework called the Articles of Confederation. Although many Americans don't realize it, many of the Founding Fathers opposed early drafts of the U.S. Constitution. Although the reasons for their opposition varied, one of the major themes was a great concern that the Constitution would give too much power to the federal government.

To ensure passage of the Constitution, supporters of the Constitution, called *federalists*, agreed to adopt a series of amendments called the Bill of Rights. The purpose of the Bill of Rights was to protect individual liberties from the national government. Each state had its own constitution or was developing a constitution to protect individual rights at the state level.

Among other things, the Bill of Rights protects Americans' rights to a free press, religious liberty, free speech, and peaceful assemblies.[453]

It also guarantees they have the authority to "keep and bear Arms" and establishes a prohibition on the quartering of soldiers in citizens' homes.[454]

The Bill of Rights further guarantees the national government cannot conduct "unreasonable searches and seizures," prosecute a person for the same crime multiple times, or deprive its citizens of "life, liberty, or property, without due process of law."[455]

Trials must also be "speedy" and public, juries composed of impartial local residents, and defendants given access to legal counsel.[456]

Defendants in common law cases must be given access to a jury trial, and excessive bail and punishments are prohibited.[457]

Further, the Bill of Rights explicitly states, "The enumeration in the Constitution, of certain rights, shall not be construed to deny or disparage others retained by the people."[458]

Put differently, the Bill of Rights contains essential liberties, but not necessarily all rights belonging to the people.

Finally, the Bill of Rights commands, "The powers not delegated to the United States by the Constitution, nor prohibited by it to the States, are reserved to the States respectively, or to the people."[459] This final amendment expressly limits the federal government's authority again, this time by stating that powers not given to the national government by the Constitution belong to the states or to the people.

All of this brings another question to mind: Why would the Bill of Rights be necessary in a nation governed by a democratic republic? That's what many of our left-wing friends would say today. The answer is, because the Founders understood that without constitutional protections in place that affirm that some rights are permanent and not subject to change, a majority of voters could and almost certainly would eventually eliminate the rights of their neighbors.

The Bill of Rights is grounded in the beliefs that there are eternal truths and an objective standard of morality, and that the democratic desires of the people do not supersede those rights. If the king of England didn't have the authority to restrict essential freedoms, then neither would voters or their elected government officials.

The Truth Is Sacred

With everything going on in our Clown World today, why spend time writing a book about understanding the truth? Undoubtedly, there are other topics that would more effectively inflame people's outrage and are likely to sell more books as a result. I've got plenty of other book ideas, and I hope I eventually get to all of them. But if I don't, I'll sleep well at night knowing that at the very least, I tried to warn and equip you about this vital topic. Talking about

THE TRUTH IS SACRED   237

the truth may not be the best form of clickbait, but it is what this country desperately needs.

The men and women who created America were steeped in works from ancient Roman and Greek authors, giants of the Enlightenment era, and, of course, the Bible. Some of their favorite authors were Adam Smith, David Hume, Marcus Aurelius, John Locke, Cicero, and Montesquieu.[460] They knew their Bibles, even those that were not believers, and they were shaped by a strong faith in God—even if they disagreed with one another about various other religious issues. The Founders understood the importance of first principles and the role those principles play in building virtuous, honorable, faithful, democratic societies.

However, most modern Americans have little understanding of these ideas. They have never heard of John Locke or Adam Smith, never mind having read their work. They care very little about pursuing the truth, and who can blame them? Half the country doesn't believe that universal moral principles exist, so why would they waste their time trying to understand those principles?[461]

We live in a culture that is flooded with lies—lies about when life begins, about basic human biology, about the fundamentals of economics, about the meaning of racism, and about a billion other things too. It's overwhelming, and it can be depressing for those of us who care about these issues.

But as difficult as our modern truth crisis is, if we truly care about saving our country, our local communities, and our churches, we need to prioritize discovering and protecting the truth. We need to guard against lies at all costs. We need to become people deserving of others' trust. We need to uncover the sources of lies and work to dismantle their influence on our lives and the lives of our children. That won't be easy, but it is the only way to escape the endless cycle of propaganda wars that plagues this nation daily.

For those of you who believe in God and thus that there is a higher lawgiver than government, this task should be more than merely a worthwhile venture or wise political tactic. As a believer, especially if you are Christian, you have a sacred duty to uphold the truth and to never give in to the lies of this age. It may cost you your wealth. It may cost you your job. It may end up hurting your family life or your friendships. I know I have experienced great suffering at times because of my desire to always seek the truth, no matter where it leads, so I don't tell you these things lightly. But as Jesus said, "What will it profit a man if he gains the whole world and forfeits his soul?" (Matthew 16:26).

Further, in 2 Timothy, the apostle Paul wrote, "All Scripture is breathed out by God and profitable for teaching, for reproof, for correction, and for training in righteousness, that the man of God may be complete, equipped for every good work" (3:16–17). If you really believe that—and if you don't, then you're not a Christian— then you must not, to the best of your ability to prevent it, allow your family, your community, and your country to continue to be ruled by falsehoods that contradict the truths of Scripture. Lies, even small ones, are nothing less than rebellion against God.

The ninth commandment handed down by Moses to the Israelites demands, "You shall not bear false witness against your neighbor," a clear prohibition against lying (Exodus 20:16).

Leviticus 19:11 says in part, "You shall not deal falsely; you shall not lie to one another."

Colossians 3:9–10 instructs Christians, "Do not lie to one another, seeing that you have put off the old self with its practices and have put on the new self, which is being renewed in knowledge after the image of its creator."

God couldn't possibly be clearer—you, as a believer, are not to lie, and that includes participating in the lies of others. Every time you participate in a lie, no matter how small, you sin, and as the late theologian R.C. Sproul rightly noted, "Sin is cosmic treason."[462] It's a direct defiance against your God.

But the situation is even more dire than that. God isn't merely the perfect Arbiter of truth and one who hates lies. *God is truth*, and truth is the opposite of a lie. Jesus told His disciples, "I am the way, and the truth, and the life" (John 14:6). That means you cannot reject the concepts of objective morality and objective standards of truth without directly rejecting Jesus. And if God is truth and God is perfectly holy, then the rejection of truth isn't just morally wrong; it's evil.

I know how easy it is to just go along with the lies of our Clown World. Standing for the truth is a dangerous business. But that's what the people of God are called to do.

Whether you believe the story of Adam and Eve recorded in the book of Genesis is a historically accurate narrative or an allegorical story meant to convey eternal truths, there are so many important things the church today can learn from it.

Genesis 3:1–13 reads:

> Now the serpent was more crafty than any other beast of the field that the LORD God had made.
>
> He said to the woman, "Did God actually say, 'You shall not eat of any tree in the garden'?" And the woman said to the serpent, "We may eat of the fruit of the trees in the garden, but God said, 'You shall not eat of the fruit of the tree that is in the midst of the garden, neither shall you touch it, lest you die.'" But the serpent said to the woman, "You will not surely die. For God knows that when you eat of it your eyes will be opened, and you will be like God, knowing good and evil." So when the woman saw that the tree was good for food, and that it was a delight to the eyes, and that the tree was to be desired to make one wise, she took of its fruit and ate, and she also

gave some to her husband who was with her, and he ate. Then the eyes of both were opened, and they knew that they were naked. And they sewed fig leaves together and made themselves loincloths.

And they heard the sound of the LORD God walking in the garden in the cool of the day, and the man and his wife hid themselves from the presence of the LORD God among the trees of the garden. But the LORD God called to the man and said to him, "Where are you?" And he said, "I heard the sound of you in the garden, and I was afraid, because I was naked, and I hid myself." He said, "Who told you that you were naked? Have you eaten of the tree of which I commanded you not to eat?" The man said, "The woman whom you gave to be with me, she gave me fruit of the tree, and I ate." Then the LORD God said to the woman, "What is this that you have done?" The woman said, "The serpent deceived me, and I ate."

In the remainder of Adam and Eve's story, we learn that God punished all of humanity for its rebellion against His simple command not to eat a piece of fruit from a specific tree: He removed Adam and Eve and all of their descendants—including you and me—from the garden of Eden. As a result of humanity's rejection of God's law, death entered the world—the exact opposite of what the serpent, whom scholars widely consider to be Satan, had promised to Eve (see Romans 5:12–14). In other words, the destruction of the relationship between God and humankind and the emergence of death on earth were the direct results of a single lie: "You will not surely die" (Genesis 3:4).

In many respects, America is collectively walking through the garden of Eden once again. God has told His people what they must do to live. And now, the world is telling them something very different. "Don't be one of those religious zealots," it says. "Don't be a bigot. Don't be selfish. Don't be self-righteous. Just give in a little. What could possibly go wrong? Sure, God says 'the wages of sin is death,' but He doesn't really mean it" (Romans 6:23).

You know, it's funny. Humans are the most intelligent creatures on earth, but even after thousands of years, many of us still haven't learned the most foundational lesson of life: God is holy and we are not, at least, not without an absolute reliance on Him. Most Americans used to understand this, but not any longer.

Our Choice

From September 5 to October 26, 1774, representatives from twelve of the thirteen British colonies gathered at Carpenters' Hall in Philadelphia for the First Continental Congress. Many of the colonies' most important political leaders attended, including George Washington and John Adams. The representatives were tasked with an immense challenge: developing a plan to combat the increasingly hostile treatment of the colonial citizens by the British Crown.[463]

On September 7, at one of the earliest meetings of the representatives, the Continental Congress asked Rev. Jacob Duche, the rector of nearby Christ Church in Philadelphia, to pray for the attendees.[464] Duche, an Anglican minister who would soon become the Continental Congress's first chaplain, read Psalm 35 and then delivered a passionate prayer.[465] According to attendees, both Duche's reading of the psalm and his prayer, which he delivered without preparation, had an immense impact on the members of the Continental Congress. In a letter sent one week later by John Adams to his wife, Abigail, John wrote, "I must confess I never heard a better Prayer or one, so well pronounced," later adding, "It has had an excellent Effect upon every Body here."[466]

The Continental Congress recorded Duche's prayer, which continues to be displayed by the Office of the Chaplain at the U.S. House of Representatives—although, for how much longer, who knows.

In his inspiring prayer, Duche asks "our Heavenly Father, high and mighty King of kings, and Lord of lords" to "look down in mercy ... on these our American States, who have fled to Thee from the rod of the oppressor and thrown themselves on Thy gracious protection, desiring to be henceforth dependent only on Thee."

Later, Duche asks the "God of wisdom" to be present with the Continental Congress and "that order, harmony and peace may be effectually restored, and truth and justice, religion and piety, prevail and flourish amongst the people."[467]

This is the prayer we need in our day, for we, too, desperately require the restoration of "order, harmony and peace," as well as "religion and piety" and, as I've discussed throughout this book, "truth and justice."

I am not sure I will live to see our country return to those principles. Perhaps you won't either. This era of propaganda wars is only just beginning. Our greatest challenges still lie ahead. But it doesn't matter if we ourselves live long enough to see America's restoration. We do not determine the times in which we live, only how we live in the time that we've been given. I know how I will spend the remainder of my life—with "a firm reliance on the protection of divine Providence";[468] with a passion and a commitment to the truth and rights of *all* people, just like John Adams in the wake of the Boston Massacre; and most important, with the faith that the God of Abraham, Isaac, and Jacob hasn't yet given up on the United States of America.

What you must decide now is, will *you?*

NOTES

1. Welcome to Clown World

1 The quotes attributed to Anne DeLessio-Parson in this chapter come from a television interview conducted in October 2019 on *Watters' World* on the Fox News Channel. The quotes from the producers and thoughts by DeLessio-Parson written in this chapter are fictitious. See Jeremy Barr, "Critical Race Theory Is the Hottest Topic on Fox News. And It's Only Getting Hotter," *Washington Post*, June 24, 2021, https://www.washingtonpost.com/media/2021/06/24/critical-race-theory-fox-news.

2 The technician's and the producer's quotes in this scene are fictitious but are similar to comments regularly made by television producers before a remote interview begins.

3 Jesse Watters's interview with Anne DeLessio-Parson, *Watters' World*, Fox News Channel, October 2019 (incomplete date available).

4 Watters, interview with DeLessio-Parson.

5 Watters, interview with DeLessio-Parson.

6 Watters, interview with DeLessio-Parson.

7 Rachel Crowell, "Modern Mathematics Confronts Its White, Patriarchal Past," *Scientific American*, August 12, 2021, https://www.scientificamerican.com/article/modern-mathematics-confronts-its-white-patriarchal-past/.

8 Theodore Kim, "Racism in Our Curriculums Isn't Limited to History. It's in Math, Too," *Washington Post*, December 8, 2021, https://www.washingtonpost.com/outlook/2021/12/08/racism-our-curriculums-isnt-limited-history-its-math-too.

9 Monica Miles et al., "Cultivating Racial Solidarity among Mathematics Education Scholars of Color to Resist White Supremacy," *International Journal of Critical Pedagogy* 10, no. 2 (2019): 99, https://libjournal.uncg.edu/ijcp/article/view/1901/1376, citing T. C. Howard and O. Navarro, "Critical race theory 20 Years Later: Where Do We Go from Here?," *Urban Education* 51, no. 3 (2016), 255.

10 Miles et al., 100.

11 Elise Takahama, "Is math racist? New Course Outlines Prompt Conversations about Identity, Race in Seattle Classrooms," *Seattle Times*, October 8, 2019,

https://www.seattletimes.com/education-lab/new-course-outlines-prompt-conversations-about-identity-race-in-seattle-classrooms-even-in-math.

12 Takahama, "Is Math Racist?"

13 Takahama, "Is Math Racist?"

14 See Sarah Mervosh, "Math Scores Dropped Globally, but the U.S. Still Trails Other Countries," *New York Times*, December 5, 2023, https://www.nytimes.com/2023/12/05/us/math-scores-pandemic-pisa.html

15 See Dave Roos, "Human Sacrifice: Why the Aztecs Practiced This Gory Ritual," History, updated July 11, 2023, https://www.history.com/news/aztec-human-sacrifice-religion.

16 See Takahama, "Is Math Racist?"

17 The following story and quotations are taken from Linda Jacobson, "Can Right Answers Be Wrong? Latest Clash over 'White Supremacy Culture' Unfolds in Unlikely Arena: Math Class," The 74, June 21, 2021, https://www.the74million.org/article/can-right-answers-be-wrong-latest-clash-over-white-supremacy-culture-unfolds-in-unlikely-arena-math-class.

18 See Jacobson, "Can Right Answers Be Wrong?"

19 "Fact Check: Biden Brags about Deficit Reduction While Adding Nearly $10 Trillion in New Spending," House Budget Committee, September 12, 2022, https://budget.house.gov/press-release/fact-check-biden-brags-about-deficit-reduction-while-adding-nearly-10-trillion-in-new-spending.

20 Rachel Sharp, "Joe Biden Confuses His Wife with His Sister during His Super Tuesday Victory Speech before a Vegan Protester Shouting 'Let Dairy Die' Storms the Stage and Lunges at him," *Daily Mail*, March 4, 2020, https://www.dailymail.co.uk/news/article-8072813/Protesters-storm-stage-Bidens-Super-Tuesday-speech-dragged-away-WIFE.html.

21 "Biden, 81, Confuses Cabinet Secretaries: Joe Mixes Up Alejandro Mayorkas and Xavier Becerra—Moments after Karine Jean-Pierre Said There's Nothing Wrong His Mental Stamina," *Daily Mail.com*, January 22, 2024, https://www.dailymail.co.uk/news/article-12993755/Biden-81-confuses-cabinet-secretaries-Joe-mixes-Alejandro-Mayorkas-Xavier-Becerra-moments-Karine-Jean-Pierre-said-theres-wrong-mental-stamina.html.

22 Josh Christenson, "Biden Can't Recall Recent Ireland Visit, Seems to Forget Hunter's Love Child during Q&A with Kids," *New York Post*, updated April 28, 2023, https://nypost.com/2023/04/27/biden-cant-recall-visit-to-ireland-he-took-two-weeks-ago.

23 Kevin Breuninger, "Mitch McConnell Freezes, Struggles to Speak in Second Incident This Summer," CNBC, August 30, 2023, https://www.cnbc.com/2023/08/30/mitch-mcconnell-freezes-struggles-to-speak-in-second-incident-this-summer.html.

24 John Bonifield, "Sen. John Fetterman's Hospitalization for Depression after His Stroke Raises Questions about the Connection. Here's What We Know," CNN, February 20, 2023, https://www.cnn.com/2023/02/20/health/john-fetterman-depression-hospitalization/index.html.

25 Miranda Nazzaro, "Senate Passes Formal Dress Code after Backlash," *The Hill*, September 27, 2023, https://thehill.com/homenews/senate/4226915-senate-

passes-formal-dress-code-after-backlash.

26 Bethany Allen-Ebrahimian and Zach Dorfman, "Exclusive: Suspected Chinese Spy Targeted California Politicians," Axios, December 8, 2020, https://www.axios.com/2020/12/08/china-spy-california-politicians.

27 See Oriana Gonzalez, "Eric Swalwell Says He Was 'Shocked' When FBI Alerted Him to Suspected Chinese Spy," Axios, December 9, 2020, https://www.axios.com/2020/12/09/eric-swalwell-china-spy-investigation-california.

28 The remainder of this story is from Allen-Ebrahimian and Dorfman, "Exclusive."

29 Tucker Carlson, "Tucker Carlson: Why Is Eric Swalwell Still on House Intel Committee after Chinese Spy Revelations?" foxnews.com, December 8, 2020, https://www.foxnews.com/opinion/tucker-carlson-eric-swalwell-chinese-spy-house-intelligence-committee.

30 Yaron Steinbuch and Mark Moore, "Swalwell Mum on Sex with China Spy, but Family Remains Facebook Friends with Honeytrap," New York Post, December 9, 2020, https://nypost.com/2020/12/09/rep-swalwell-wont-say-if-he-had-sex-with-chinese-spy.

31 Allen-Ebrahimian and Dorfman, "Exclusive."

32 See Glenn Beck, "Ilhan Omar: All In The Family," BlazeTV, YouTube, July 26, 2019, https://youtu.be/y34621LVK-E.

33 Amy Forliti, "Rep. Omar Filed Joint Tax Returns before She Married Husband," Associated Press, June 12, 2019, https://apnews.com/article/b49ee5604ec2435a90945820b7c973eb.

34 Forliti, "Rep. Omar Filed Joint Tax Returns before She Married Husband."

35 Forliti, "Rep. Omar Filed Joint Tax Returns before She Married Husband."

36 Victor Nava, "Non-Binary Biden Nuclear Official Sam Brinton Fired after Multiple Luggage Theft Charges: Reports," New York Post, December 12, 2022, https://nypost.com/2022/12/12/non-binary-biden-nuclear-official-sam-brinton-fired-after-multiple-luggage-theft-charges-reports.

37 Nava, "Non-Binary Biden Nuclear Official Sam Brinton Fired after Multiple Luggage Theft Chargess."

38 Gabriel Hays, "Rachel Levine Ripped for Demanding Censorship of 'Misinformation' on 'Gender-Affirming Care' for Kids," Fox News Channel, December 26, 2022, https://www.foxnews.com/media/rachel-levine-ripped-demanding-censorship-misinformation-gender-affirming-care-kids.

39 Elizabeth Napolitano, "Anheuser-Busch Exec Steps Down after Bud Light Sales Slump Following Dylan Mulvaney Controversy," CBS MoneyWatch, November 16, 2023, https://www.cbsnews.com/news/bud-light-anheuser-busch-marketing-chief-steps-down-boycott-dylan-mulvaney.

40 Kristopher Brooks, "Bud Light Is No Longer America's Best-Selling Beer. Here's Why," CBS MoneyWatch, June 15, 2023, https://www.cbsnews.com/news/bud-light-no-longer-best-selling-beer-boycott-sales.

41 Lisa Fickenscher, "Beer Sales Plunge to Lowest Levels in 24 Years—Thanks to Bud Light's Disastrous Dylan Mulvaney Campaign," New York Post, December 27, 2023, https://nypost.com/2023/12/27/business/beer-sales-plummeting-to-lowest-level-in-24-years-amid-dylan-mulvaney-fiasco.

42 Dale Fox, "Dylan Mulvaney Reacts to Attitude Woman of the Year Award:

'The Queer Community Sees Me for My Truth,'" *Attitude*, October 11, 2023, https://www.attitude.co.uk/culture/dylan-mulvaney-attitude-awards-2023-speech-449471/.

43 Samuel Forey, "Hamas Attack: October 7, a Day of Hell on Earth in Israel," *Le Monde*, October 30, 2023, https://www.lemonde.fr/en/international/article/2023/10/30/hamas-attack-october-7-a-day-of-hell-on-earth-in-israel_6213560_4.html.

44 See, for example, Sally Tamarkin, "Why Queer Solidarity with Palestine Is Not 'Chickens for KFC,'" *Them*, November 22, 2023, https://www.them.us/story/lgbtq-solidarity-palestine-saed-atshan; and Brendan O'Neill, "'Queers for Palestine' Must Have a Death Wish," *Telegraph* (UK), November 9, 2023, https://www.telegraph.co.uk/news/2023/11/09/queers-for-palestine-must-have-a-death-wish.

45 "Statue of Abraham Lincoln with Kneeling Slave Removed in Boston," Associated Press, reposted by Fox News, December 29, 2020, https://www.foxnews.com/us/statue-of-abraham-lincoln-with-slave-kneeling-removed-in-boston.

46 Nicole Chavez and Justin Gamble, "San Francisco Reparations Committee Proposes a $5 Million Payment to Each Black Resident," CNN, January 19, 2023, https://www.cnn.com/2023/01/19/us/san-francisco-reparations-proposal-reaj/index.html.

47 Chavez and Gamble, "San Francisco Reparations Committee Proposes a $5 Million Payment to Each Black Resident."

48 Joe Biden, "Remarks by President Biden on the Third Anniversary of the January 6th Attack and Defending the Sacred Cause of American Democracy," delivered in Blue Bell, Pennsylvania, on January 5, 2024, whitehouse.gov, https://www.whitehouse.gov/briefing-room/speeches-remarks/2024/01/05/remarks-by-president-biden-on-the-third-anniversary-of-the-january-6th-attack-and-defending-the-sacred-cause-of-american-democracy-blue-bell-pa/#:~:text=The%20defense%2C%20protection%2C%20and%20preservation,freedom%20is%20on%20the%20ballot.

49 Marshall Cohen, "Colorado's Secretary of State Urges Supreme Court to Keep Trump off Ballot," CNN, January 31, 2024, https://www.cnn.com/2024/01/31/politics/colorado-secretary-of-state-tells-supreme-court-to-keep-trump-off-ballot/index.html.

50 Brittany Bernstein, "Over 80 Percent of Democrats Believe States Should Disqualify Trump from 2024 Ballot: Poll," *National Review*, January 7, 2024, https://www.nationalreview.com/news/over-80-percernt-of-democrats-believe-states-should-disqualify-trump-from-2024-ballots-poll.

51 "Vice President Kamala Harris Launches Reproductive Freedoms Tour," whitehouse.gov, December 19, 2023, https://www.whitehouse.gov/briefing-room/statements-releases/2023/12/19/vice-president-kamala-harris-launches-reproductive-freedoms-tour.

52 See Ted Johnson, "Disney Takes Heat over Public Stance on Florida's "Don't Say Gay" Law, but NBCUniversal and Other Studios Keep Away the Fray," *Deadline*, April 6, 2022, https://deadline.com/2022/04/disney-florida-dont-say-gay-backlash-impact-hollywood-studios-1234994109.

53 Mere Abrams, "68 Terms That Describe Gender Identity and Expression," Health-

line, January 26, 2024, https://www.healthline.com/health/different-genders.

54 Amy Norton, "Suicide Rates among U.S. Adolescents Doubled in 10 Years," HealthDay, reposted by *U.S. News and World Report*, May 1, 2023, https://www. usnews.com/news/health-news/articles/2023-05-01/suicide-rates-among-u-s-adolescents-doubled-in-10-years.

55 "Thomas Jefferson, Extract from Thomas Jefferson to Peter Carr," August 10, 1787, The Jefferson Monticello, https://tjrs.monticello.org/letter/1297.

56 Ida Auken, "Welcome to 2030. I Own Nothing, Have No Privacy, and Life Has Never Been Better," World Economic Forum, weforum.org, November 11, 2016, made available by archive.org, accessed February 1, 2024, https://web.archive. org/web/20200919081413/https://www.weforum.org/agenda/2016/11/ shopping-i-can-t-really-remember-what-that-is?utm_content=buffer60978&utm_ medium=social&utm_source=twitter.com&utm_campaign=buffer.

2. The Propaganda Industrial Complex

57 The facts and quotations in this section are taken from "Tabletop Exercise: Event 201," Center for Health Security, Johns Hopkins Bloomberg School of Public Health, accessed July 11, 2024, https://centerforhealthsecurity.org/our-work/ tabletop-exercises/event-201-pandemic-tabletop-exercise#about.

58 "New York Times Statement about 1932 Pulitzer Prize Awarded to Walter Duranty," New York Times Company, nytco.com, accessed July 11, 2024, https:// www.nytco.com/company/prizes-awards/new-york-times-statement-about-1932-pulitzer-prize-awarded-to-walter-duranty.

59 "New York Times Statement."

60 See "Today It's Global Warming; In the '70s It Was the Coming Ice Age," Washington Policy Center, April 22, 2009, https://www.washingtonpolicy.org/ publications/detail/today-its-global-warming-in-the-70s-it-was-the-coming-ice-age.

61 "What Is the Kyoto Protocol?" United Nations Framework Convention on Climate Change, UNFCCC, accessed July 11, 2024, https://unfccc.int/kyoto_proto-col#:~:text=In%20short%2C%20the%20Kyoto%20Protocol,accordance%20 with%20agreed%20individual%20targets.

62 "Clean Energy and Climate Change," Council on Environmental Quality, George W. Bush administration, White House Archives, accessed July 11, 2024, https:// georgewbush-whitehouse.archives.gov/ceq/clean-energy.html.

63 "FACT SHEET: Overview of the Clean Power Plan," U.S. Environmental Protec-tion Agency, archive.epa.gov, accessed July 11, 2024, https://archive.epa.gov/epa/ cleanpowerplan/fact-sheet-overview-clean-power-plan.html.

64 "The Paris Agreement," United Nations Framework Convention on Climate Change, UNFCCC, accessed July 11, 2024, https://unfccc.int/process-and-meetings/the-paris-agreement

65 "FACT SHEET: Overview of the Clean Power Plan."

66 See Douglas Holtz-Eakin et al., "The Green New Deal: Scope, Scale, and Implica-tions," American Action Forum, February 25, 2019, https://www.americanaction-forum.org/research/the-green-new-deal-scope-scale-and-implications.

67 See Dan Lashof, "Tracking Progress: Climate Action under the Biden Administra-

tion," World Resources Institute, January 29, 2024, https://www.wri.org/insights/biden-administration-tracking-climate-action-progress.

68 See Francesca Paris et al., "A Detailed Picture of What's in the Democrats' Climate and Health Bill," *New York Times*, updated August 16, 2022, https://www.nytimes.com/interactive/2022/08/13/upshot/whats-in-the-democrats-climate-health-bill.html.

69 See Lashof, "Tracking Progress"; and Hannah Fry and Tony Briscoe, "Biden Administration Revs Up Plans to Transition from Gas-Powered Vehicles to EVs," *Los Angeles Times*, March 20, 2024, https://www.latimes.com/environment/story/2024-03-20/biden-administration-speeds-transition-to-electric-vehicles.

70 Justin Haskins, "Are Financial Institutions Using ESG Social Credit Scores to Coerce Individuals, Small Businesses?" The Heartland Institute, February 27, 2022, https://heartland.org/publications/financial-institutions-are-expanding-esg-social-credit-scores-to-target-individuals-small-businesses.

71 "Key Global Trends in Sustainability Reporting," KPMG, accessed July 11, 2024, https://kpmg.com/xx/en/home/insights/2022/09/survey-of-sustainability-reporting-2022/global-trends.html.

72 Joseph Bast and Roy Spencer, "The Myth of the Climate Change '97%,'" *Wall Street Journal*, May 26, 2014, https://www.wsj.com/articles/joseph-bast-and-roy-spencer-the-myth-of-the-climate-change-97-1401145980.

73 "David Legates," The Heritage Foundation, accessed July 9, 2024, https://www.heritage.org/staff/david-legates.

74 "About Dr. Roy Spencer," drroyspencer.com, accessed July 9, 2024, https://www.drroyspencer.com/about.

75 Nongovernmental International Panel on Climate Change, "Chapter Contributing Authors," accessed September 19, 2019, http://climatechangereconsidered.org/nipcc-scientists.

76 Scott Waldman, "Adviser Who Applauded Rise in CO2 to Leave Administration," *E&E News*, September 11, 2019, https://www.eenews.net/stories/1061113085; Office of the Faculty, "William Happer," Princeton University, accessed September 19, 2019, https://dof.princeton.edu/about/clerk-faculty/emeritus/william-happer, no longer accessible.

77 "John R. Christy, PhD," University of Alabama in Huntsville, accessed July 9, 2024, https://www.uah.edu/science/departments/atmospheric-earth-science/faculty-staff/dr-john-christy.

78 See Roger Pielke, "How Academic 'Blacklists' Impede Serious Work on Climate Science," *Forbes*, February 9, 2020, https://www.forbes.com/sites/rogerpielke/2020/02/09/a-climate-blacklist-that-works-it-should-make-her-unhirable-in-academia/?sh=587e43066368.

79 See Jessica Guynn, "Science vs. Social Media: Why Climate Change Denial Still Thrives Online," *USA Today*, January 19, 2024, https://www.usatoday.com/story/tech/news/2024/01/19/climate-change-denial-spreading-social-media/72257689007.

80 See David B. Rivkin Jr. and Andrew M. Grossman, "Punishing Climate-Change Skeptics," Cato Institute, March 23, 2016, https://www.cato.org/commentary/punishing-climate-change-skeptics.

81 The Heartland Institute, "Hurricanes," Climate at a Glance, accessed March 6, 2024, https://climateataglance.com/climate-at-a-glance-hurricanes.

82 The Heartland Institute, "Tornadoes," Climate at a Glance, accessed March 6, 2024, https://climateataglance.com/climate-at-a-glance-tornadoes.

83 The Heartland Institute, "U.S. Heatwaves," Climate at a Glance, accessed March 6, 2024, https://climateataglance.com/climate-at-a-glance-u-s-heatwaves.

84 The Heartland Institute, "Temperature Related Deaths," Climate at a Glance, accessed March 6, 2024, https://climateataglance.com/climate-at-a-glance-temperature-related-deaths.

85 The Heartland Institute, "Crop Production," Climate at a Glance, accessed March 6, 2024, https://climateataglance.com/crop-production.

86 Heartland Institute, "Crop Production."

87 Bob Woods, "Recycling 'end-of-life' solar panels, wind turbines, is about to be climate tech's big waste business," CNBC, last updated November 27, 2023, https://www.cnbc.com/2023/05/13/recycling-end-of-life-solar-panel-wind-turbine-is-big-waste-business.html.

88 Russell Gold, "Thousands of Old Wind Turbine Blades Pile Up in West Texas," *Texas Monthly*, August 24, 2023, https://www.texasmonthly.com/news-politics/sweetwater-wind-turbine-blades-dump.

89 See Tim Benson, "Mining Expansion Necessary for Green New Deal Would Devastate the Global Environment," The Heartland Institute, April 14, 2020, https://heartland.org/opinion/mining-expansion-necessary-for-green-new-deal-would-devastate-the-global-environment.

90 See Benson, "Mining Expansion Necessary for Green New Deal Would Devastate the Global Environment"; Lee Miller and David Keith, "Climatic Impacts of Wind Power," *Joule* 2, no. 12, https://www.sciencedirect.com/science/article/pii/S254243511830446X.

91 *Planet of the Humans*, directed by Jeff Gibbs (Toronto: Rumble Media, 2020), film.

92 See the official *Planet of the Humans* website, accessed July 11, 2024, https://planetofthehumans.com.

93 Justin Haskins, "Rasmussen/Heartland Poll: Viewers of Conservative Media More Likely to Get the Facts Right on Police Shootings," The Heartland Institute, May 14, 2021, https://heartland.org/opinion/rasmussenheartland-poll-police-shootings.

94 Haskins, "Rasmussen/Heartland Poll."

95 "1,135 People Have Been Shot and Killed by Police in the Past 12 Months," *Washington Post*, updated July 2, 2024, https://www.washingtonpost.com/graphics/investigations/police-shootings-database.

96 See Haskins, "Rasmussen/Heartland Poll."

97 Bret Stephens, "The Mask Mandates Did Nothing. Will Any Lessons Be Learned?" *New York Times*, February 21, 2023, https://www.nytimes.com/2023/02/21/opinion/do-mask-mandates-work.html.

98 Bret Stephens, "The Mask Mandates Did Nothing. Will Any Lessons Be Learned?," *New York Times*, Opinion, February 21, 2023, https://www.nytimes.com/2023/02/21/opinion/do-mask-mandates-work.html.

99 Chloe Taylor, "Coronavirus Crisis Presents a 'Golden Opportunity' to Reboot

the Economy, Prince Charles Says," CNBC, June 3, 2020, https://www.cnbc.com/2020/06/03/prince-charles-covid-19-a-golden-opportunity-to-reboot-the-economy.html.

100 "Tabletop Exercise: Atlantic Storm," Center for Health Security, Johns Hopkins Bloomberg School of Public Health, accessed July 11, 2024, https://centerforhealthsecurity.org/our-work/tabletop-exercises/atlantic-storm-a-tabletop-exercise.

101 "Atlantic Storm: Scenario Players," Center for Health Security, Johns Hopkins Bloomberg School of Public Health, accessed July 11, 2024, https://centerforhealthsecurity.org/sites/default/files/2022-11/players0900.pdf.

102 "Tabletop Exercise: Atlantic Storm."

103 "Tabletop Exercise: Dark Winter," Center for Health Security, Johns Hopkins Bloomberg School of Public Health, accessed March 8, 2024, https://centerforhealthsecurity.org/our-work/tabletop-exercises/dark-winter-a-training-tabletop-exercise.

104 "Tabletop Exercise: Clade X," Center for Health Security, Johns Hopkins Bloomberg School of Public Health, accessed March 8, 2024, https://centerforhealthsecurity.org/our-work/tabletop-exercises/clade-x-tabletop-exercise.

105 "About Cyber Polygon," Cyber Polygon 2020, accessed March 8, 2024, https://2020.cyberpolygon.com/#:~:text=Cyber%20Polygon&text=An%20international%20capacity%20building%20initiative,of%20intersectoral%20cooperation%20against%20cyberthreats.

106 Kendra Nichols, "Prepping for a Cyber Pandemic: Worldwide Drill Underway," ABC27 WHTM, updated July 15, 2021, https://www.abc27.com/investigators/prepping-for-a-cyber-pandemic-worldwide-drill-underway.

107 "Live Stream Agenda," Cyber Polygon 2020, accessed March 8, 2024, https://2020.cyberpolygon.com/agenda.

108 See, for example, "Klaus Schwab Urges New Mechanisms to Boost International Cooperation in a Multipower World," World Governments Summit, February 14, 2023, https://www.worldgovernmentsummit.org/press/releases/klaus-schwab-urges-new-mechanisms-to-boost-international-cooperation-in-a-multipower-world.

109 "World Government Summit 2023: Agenda," World Governments Summit, accessed March 11, 2024, https://www.worldgovernmentsummit.org/events/2023/agenda.

110 "Are We Ready for a New World Order?" World Governments Summit 2022, March 29, 2022, https://www.worldgovernmentsummit.org/events/2022/session-detail/a0f3z0are-we-ready-for-a-new-world-order-.

111 "The Great Narrative: Overview," World Economic Forum, accessed March 11, 2024, https://www.weforum.org/events/the-great-narrative-2021/about.

112 See "Conference of the Parties (COP)," United Nations Framework Convention on Climate Change, accessed March 11, 2024, https://unfccc.int/process/bodies/supreme-bodies/conference-of-the-parties-cop#:~:text=The%20COP%20meets%20every%20year%2C%20unless%20the%20Parties%20decide%20otherwise.

113   Remy Melina, "Are Elephants Really Afraid of Mice?," Live Science, June 1, 2016, https://www.livescience.com/33261-elephants-afraid-of-mice-.html.

3. A Politically Incorrect Guide to Discovering and Uncovering the Truth

114   Glenn Beck and Justin Haskins, *Dark Future: Uncovering the Great Reset's Terrifying Next Phase* (Nashville: Mercury Ink, 2023).

115   See "Hearing Wrap Up: The World Health Organization's Flawed Framework Must Be Reformed," Committee on Oversight and Accountability, U.S. House of Representatives, December 14, 2023, https://oversight.house.gov/release/hearing-wrap-up-the-world-health-organizations-flawed-framework-must-be-reformed.

116   See "Hearing Wrap Up: The World Health Organization's Flawed Framework Must Be Reformed," Committee on Oversight and Accountability.

117   Alastair Talbot, "LA Times Columnist Sparks Outrage after Saying Black Republican Larry Elder Is Pushing 'White Supremacist Worldview' and Poses 'Real Threat to Communities of Color' with His Run for California Governor," *DailyMail.com*, September 13, 2021, https://www.dailymail.co.uk/news/article-9985749/LA-Times-columnist-sparks-outrage-describing-Larry-Elder-white-supremacist.html.

118   Emma Colton, "Larry Elder Egged by Woman in Gorilla Mask in 'Racist' Attack in California," Fox News, September 9, 2021, https://www.foxnews.com/politics/critics-gorilla-mask-threw-egg-larry-elder-los-angeles.

119   Katie Robertson, "After Hospital Blast, Headlines Shift with Changing Claims," *New York Times*, October 18, 2023, https://www.nytimes.com/2023/10/18/business/media/hospital-blast-gaza-reports.html.

120   Daniel Byman, "Hamas's October 7 Attack: Visualizing the Data," Center for Strategic and International Studies, December 19, 2023, https://www.csis.org/analysis/hamass-october-7-attack-visualizing-data.

121   Robertson, "After Hospital Blast, Headlines Shift with Changing Claims."

122   Robertson, "After Hospital Blast, Headlines Shift With Changing Claims."

123   Oren Oppenheim, "Rep. Rashida Tlaib Draws Fire for Not Apologizing for Saying Israel Caused Gaza Hospital Blast," ABC News, October 18, 2023, https://abcnews.go.com/Politics/tlaib-refuses-apologize-blaming-israel-gaza-hospital-blast/story?id=104085727.

124   The following story and quotations are taken from David Zweig, "Did the Entire Media Industry Misquote a Hamas Spokesperson?," *Silent Lunch*, October 28, 2023, https://www.silentlunch.net/p/did-the-entire-media-industry-misquote.

125   "Benjamin Franklin's Last Great Quote and the Constitution," National Constitution Center blog, November 13, 2023, https://constitutioncenter.org/blog/benjamin-franklins-last-great-quote-and-the-constitution#:~:text=%E2%80%9COur%20new%20Constitution%20is%20now,and%20taxes%2C%E2%80%9D%20Franklin%20said.

126   See the World Economic Forum's website at https://www.weforum.org.

127   You can watch more videos at "World Economic Forum Annual Meeting," World Economic Forum, accessed March 7, 2024, https://www.weforum.org/events/world-economic-forum-annual-meeting-2024.

128 See "Events," World Economic Forum, https://www.weforum.org/events.

129 "World Governments Summit 2024," World Governments Summit, accessed March 11, 2024, https://www.worldgovernmentsummit.org/events/2024.

130 See, for example, *ESG Today*, accessed March 11, 2024, https://www.esgtoday.com.

131 See, for example, *American Banker*, accessed March 11, 2024, https://www.americanbanker.com/magazine.

132 See "Center for Health Security," Johns Hopkins Bloomberg School of Public Health, accessed March 11, 2024, https://centerforhealthsecurity.org.

133 See *Governing Magazine*, accessed March 11, 2024, https://www.governing.com; and *Heartland Daily News*, The Heartland Institute, accessed March 11, 2024, https://heartlanddailynews.com.

134 *UN Chronicle*, United Nations, accessed March 11, 2024, https://www.un.org/en/chronicle.

135 See "About the PRI," Principles for Responsible Investment, accessed March 11, 2024, https://www.unpri.org/about-us/about-the-pri.

136 BlackRock is the largest asset manager in the United States and another global leader of the ESG movement. See, for example, "Weekly market commentary," BlackRock, accessed March 11, 2024, https://www.blackrock.com/us/individual/insights/blackrock-investment-institute/weekly-commentary.

137 "Press Releases," U.S. Department of State, accessed July 17, 2024, https://www.state.gov/press-releases; "Remarks and Highlights," U.S. Mission to the United Nations, accessed July 17, 2024, https://usun.usmission.gov/category/remarks-and-highlights.

138 "Central Bank Digital Currency Tracker," Atlantic Council, accessed March 11, 2024, https://www.atlanticcouncil.org/cbdctracker.

139 "The 17 Goals," Department of Economic and Social Affairs, United Nations, accessed March 11, 2024, https://sdgs.un.org/goals.

140 See Glenn Beck and Justin Haskins, *The Great Reset: Joe Biden and the Rise of Twenty-First-Century Fascism* (Nashville: Mercury Ink, 2021).

141 See "Now Is the Time to Press the Reset Button on Capitalism," World Economic Forum, accessed March 11, 2024, https://www.weforum.org/videos/now-is-the-time-to-press-the-reset-button-on-capitalism-b7c64e853b; Klaus Schwab, "Now Is the Time for a 'Great Reset,'" World Economic Forum, June 3, 2020, https://www.weforum.org/agenda/2020/06/now-is-the-time-for-a-great-reset.

142 Schwab, "Now Is the Time for a 'Great Reset.'"

143 Schwab, "Now Is the Time for a 'Great Reset.'"

144 Lia Eustachewich, "Coca-Cola Slammed for Diversity Training That Urged Workers to Be 'Less White,'" *New York Post*, February 23, 2024, https://nypost.com/2021/02/23/coca-cola-diversity-training-urged-workers-to-be-less-white.

145 Charles Apple, "In Control," *Spokesman-Review*, accessed March 13, 2024, https://www.spokesman.com/stories/2020/jun/25/control-house-and-senate-1900.

146 Thomas DiLorenzo, "A New Deal for the World," *The Free Market* 17, no. 1 (January 1999), https://mises.org/free-market/new-deal-world.

147 Henry Hazlitt, "The Fallacies of the NRA," Mises Institute, June 30, 2003, https://mises.org/mises-daily/fallacies-nra.
148 DiLorenzo, "A New Deal for the World."
149 The editors of Encyclopedia Britannica, "Japanese American internment," *Encyclopaedia Britannica*, britannica.com, updated May 31, 2024, https://www.britannica.com/event/Japanese-American-internment.

4. You Can't Believe Your Eyes: How Emerging Technologies Are Manipulating You and Your Children

150 See Charles R. Kesler, "America's Cold Civil War," *Imprimis* 47, no. 10 (October 2018), https://imprimis.hillsdale.edu/americas-cold-civil-war.
151 "ANES History," American National Election Studies, accessed April 8, 2024, https://electionstudies.org/about-us/history.
152 "Affective Polarization of Parties: Own-Party and Rival-Party Feelings," American National Election Studies, accessed April 8, 2024, https://electionstudies.org/data-tools/anes-guide/anes-guide.html?chart=affective_polarization_parties.
153 "Affective Polarization of Parties."
154 "Strength of Partisanship," American National Election Studies, accessed April 8, 2024, https://electionstudies.org/data-tools/anes-guide/anes-guide.html?chart=strength_of_pid.
155 Amy McCaig, "Are American Voters Really as Polarized as They Seem? Rice Research Suggests Yes," Rice University, *Rice News*, February 19, 2024, https://news.rice.edu/news/2024/are-american-voters-really-polarized-they-seem-rice-research-suggests-yes.
156 "The Shift in the American Public's Political Values," Pew Research Center, October 20, 2017, https://www.pewresearch.org/politics/interactives/political-polarization-1994-2017.
157 "The Shift in the American Public's Political Values."
158 See Karen Yuan and Matt Peterson, "The History of 'Fake News' in America," *Atlantic*, January 9, 2018, https://www.theatlantic.com/membership/archive/2018/01/the-history-of-fake-news-in-america/550103; Jacob Soll, "The Long and Brutal History of Fake News," *Politico*, December 18, 2016, https://www.politico.com/magazine/story/2016/12/fake-news-history-long-violent-214535.
159 Randy Skretvedt and Christopher H. Sterling, "American Radio Goes to War," *Encyclopaedia Britannica*, August 18, 2023, https://www.britannica.com/topic/radio/American-radio-goes-to-war.
160 "Golden Age of Radio in the US," Digital Public Library of America, accessed July 12, 2024, https://dp.la/exhibitions/radio-golden-age/radio-broadcast-news.
161 Richard Galant, "The Most Trusted Man in America," CNN, June 5, 2012, https://www.cnn.com/2012/06/05/opinion/brinkley-walter-cronkite/index.html.
162 Jeremy Hobson, "How Ted Turner's Vision for CNN Sparked the 24-Hour News Cycle," WBUR, May 12, 2020, https://www.wbur.org/hereandnow/2020/05/12/cnn-ted-turner-lisa-napoli.
163 See Tricia Escobedo, "When a National Disaster Unfolded Live in 1986," CNN, March 31, 2016, https://www.cnn.com/2016/03/31/us/80s-cnn-challenger-

coverage/index.html.

164   See Liane Hansen and David Folkenflik, "The Power of the 24-Hour News Cycle," NPR, May 29, 2005, https://www.npr.org/2005/05/29/4671485/the-power-of-the-24-hour-news-cycle.

165   "What Is an Echo Chamber?" GCF Global, accessed April 8, 2024, https://edu.gcfglobal.org/en/digital-media-literacy/what-is-an-echo-chamber/1/.

166   Felix Richter, "Facebook Keeps on Growing," Statista, February 4, 2021, https://www.statista.com/chart/amp/10047/facebooks-monthly-active-users/?fbclid=-IwAR3jreSsQpn1D4YC_V9gkjWPnkk-qiN-nkDCNxs-yBF4L8G7wADdvH-B3ZaQ.

167   Rohit Shewale, "Facebook Users Statistics 2024 (Worldwide Data)," Demand Sage, April 5, 2024 https://www.demandsage.com/facebook-statistics.

168   Brian Dean, "How Many People Use YouTube? [New Data]," *Backlinko* (blog), February 8, 2024, https://backlinko.com/youtube-users.

169   Brian Dean, "Instagram Statistics: Key Demographic and User Numbers," *Backlinko* (blog), March 25, 2024, https://backlinko.com/instagram-users.

170   Brian Dean, "X (Twitter) Statistics: How Many People Use X?," *Backlinko* (blog), last updated April 10, 2024, https://backlinko.com/twitter-users.

171   "Social Media and News Fact Sheet," Pew Research Center, November 15, 2024, https://www.pewresearch.org/journalism/fact-sheet/social-media-and-news-fact-sheet.

172   See BER staff, "Paying Attention: The Attention Economy," *Berkeley Economic Review*, March 31, 2020, https://econreview.studentorg.berkeley.edu/paying-attention-the-attention-economy.

173   See Michael H. Goldhaber, "Attention Shoppers!" *Wired*, December 1, 1997, https://www.wired.com/1997/12/es-attention/.

174   "Social Network Advertising Spending in the United States from 2021 to 2025," Statista, accessed July 12, 2024, https://www.statista.com/statistics/736971/social-media-ad-spend-usa.

175   See "About Addiction Center," Addiction Center, accessed April 8, 2024, https://www.addictioncenter.com/about.

176   "Social Media Addiction," Addiction Center, accessed April 8, 2024, https://www.addictioncenter.com/drugs/social-media-addiction.

177   "Social Media Addiction."

178   Matt Richtel, "Is Social Media Addictive? Here's What the Science Says," *New York Times*, October 25, 2023, https://www.nytimes.com/2023/10/25/health/social-media-addiction.html.

179   Richtel, "Is Social Media Addictive?"

180   "Social Media Addiction."

181   Emily A. Vogels, Risa Gelles-Watnick, and Navid Massarat, "Teens, Social Media and Technology 2022," Pew Research Center, August 10, 2022, https://www.pewresearch.org/internet/2022/08/10/teens-social-media-and-technology-2022.

182   Richtel, "Is Social Media Addictive?"

183   Katie Wiseman, "Indiana's attorney general once sued Meta; now they're coming to Jeffersonville," *Indy Star*, January 26, 2024, https://www.indystar.com/story/

news/2024/01/26/indiana-ag-todd-rokita-sued-facebooks-parent-company-meta-jeffersonville-louisville-kentucky/72355829007.

184   See Kira E. Riehm et al., "Associations Between Time Spent using Social Media and Internalizing and Externalizing Problems among US Youth," *JAMA Psychiatry* 76, no. 12 (September 11, 2019): 1266–73, https://doi.org/10.1001/jamapsychiatry.2019.2325.

185   Caryl M. Stern, "Generation Z Is Waging a Battle against Depression, Addiction and Hopelessness," Walton Family Foundation, September 8, 2022, https://www.waltonfamilyfoundation.org/stories/foundation/generation-z-is-waging-a-battle-against-depression-addiction-and-hopelessness.

186   "Is TikTok Causing Tics in Teen Girls? What Parents Need to Know," Cleveland Clinic: Health Essentials, November 9, 2021, https://health.clevelandclinic.org/tiktok-causing-tics-in-teen-girls.

187   "Is TikTok Causing Tics in Teen Girls?"

188   See Peter Simons, "For Teen Girls, Rare Psychiatric Disorders Spread Like Viruses on Social Media," Mad in America, November 12, 2023, https://www.madinamerica.com/2023/11/for-teen-girls-rare-psychiatric-disorders-spread-like-viruses-on-social-media.

189   See "Surgeon General Issues New Advisory about Effects Social Media Use Has on Youth Mental Health," U.S. Department of Health and Human Services, May 23, 2023, https://www.hhs.gov/about/news/2023/05/23/surgeon-general-issues-new-advisory-about-effects-social-media-use-has-youth-mental-health.html.

190   Office of the Surgeon General, *Social Media and Youth Mental Health: The U.S. Surgeon General's Advisory 2023*, p. 13, https://www.hhs.gov/sites/default/files/sg-youth-mental-health-social-media-advisory.pdf.

191   Kari Paul, "Zuckerberg Tells Parents of Social Media Victims at Senate Hearing: 'I'm Sorry for Everything You've Been Through,'" *Guardian* (UK), January 31, 2024, https://www.theguardian.com/us-news/2024/jan/31/tiktok-meta-x-congress-hearing-child-sexual-exploitation.

192   See Congress.gov, "S. 1291—118t Congress (2023–24): Protecting Kids on Social Media," April 26, 2023, https://www.congress.gov/bill/118th-congress/senate-bill/1291.

193   "Florida's DeSantis Signs Law Restricting Social Media for People under 16," Reuters, March 25, 2024, https://www.reuters.com/world/us/floridas-desantis-signs-law-restricting-social-media-people-under-16-2024-03-25.

194   Elle Hunt, "Facebook to Change Trending Topics after Investigation into Bias Claims," *Guardian* (UK), May 23, 2016, https://www.theguardian.com/technology/2016/may/24/facebook-changes-trending-topics-anti-conservative-bias.

195   Joe Mullin, "PragerU Sues YouTube, Says It Censors Conservative Videos," *Ars Technica*, November 25, 2017, https://arstechnica.com/tech-policy/2017/10/prageru-sues-youtube-says-it-censors-conservative-videos.

196   Kalhan Rosenblatt, "Facebook, YouTube and Apple Remove Alex Jones and Infowars from Their Platforms," NBC News, August 6, 2018, https://www.nbcnews.com/tech/tech-news/facebook-removes-four-pages-belonging-infowars-alex-jones-n897861.

197 Michael Nunez, "Former Facebook Workers: We Routinely Suppressed Conservative News," *Gizmodo*, May 9, 2016, https://gizmodo.com/former-facebook-workers-we-routinely-suppressed-conser-1775461006.

198 Kate Conger and Lauren Hirsch, "Elon Musk Completes $44 Billion Deal to Own Twitter," *New York Times*, October 27, 2022, https://www.nytimes.com/2022/10/27/technology/elon-musk-twitter-deal-complete.html.

199 Jared Gans, "Musk Says Files on 'Free Speech Suppression' Will Be Published on Twitter," *The Hill*, November 29, 2022, https://thehill.com/policy/technology/3755038-musk-says-files-on-free-speech-suppression-will-be-published-on-twitter.

200 Matt Taibbi [@mtaibbi], "1. Thread: THE TWITTER FILES," X, December 2, 2022, https://twitter.com/mtaibbi/status/1598822959866683394.

201 Bari Weiss [@bariweiss], "THREAD: THE TWITTER FILES PART TWO. TWITTER'S SECRET BLACKLISTS," X, December 8, 2022, https://twitter.com/bariweiss/status/1601007575633305600.

202 Weiss, "THREAD: THE TWITTER FILES PART TWO."

203 Matt Taibbi [@mtaibbi], "THE REMOVAL OF DONALD TRUMP: Part One: October 2020–January 6th," X, December 9, 2022, https://twitter.com/mtaibbi/status/1601352083617505281.

204 Taibbi, "1. Thread: THE TWITTER FILES."

205 Matt Taibbi [@mtaibbi], "1. THREAD: The Twitter Files, Part Six TWITTER, THE FBI SUBSIDIARY," X, December 16, 2022, https://twitter.com/mtaibbi/status/1603857534737072128.

206 Taibbi, 1. THREAD: The Twitter Files, Part Six."

207 Michael Shellenberger [@shellenberger], "1. TWITTER FILES: PART 7," X, December 19, 2022, https://twitter.com/shellenberger/status/1604871630613753856.

208 See Thomas Barrabi, "Mark Zuckerberg Tells Joe Rogan Facebook Was Wrong to Ban the [New York] Post's Hunter Biden Laptop Story," *New York Post*, August 25, 2022, https://nypost.com/2022/08/25/mark-zuckerberg-criticizes-twitters-handling-of-the-posts-hunter-biden-laptop-story.

209 Emma-Jo and Gabrielle Fonrouge, "Smoking-Gun Email Reveals How Hunter Biden Introduced Ukrainian Businessman to VP Dad," *New York Post*, October 14, 2020, https://nypost.com/2020/10/14/email-reveals-how-hunter-biden-introduced-ukrainian-biz-man-to-dad.

210 See Kari Paul, "Facebook and Twitter Restrict Controversial New York Post Story on Joe Biden," *Guardian* (UK), October 14, 2020, https://www.theguardian.com/technology/2020/oct/14/facebook-twitter-new-york-post-hunter-biden.

211 See Taibbi "1. Thread: THE TWITTER FILES."

212 See Noah Manskar, "Twitter, Facebook Censor Post over Hunter Biden Expose," *New York Post*, October 14, 2020, https://nypost.com/2020/10/14/facebook-twitter-block-the-post-from-posting/.

213 See Taibbi "1. Thread: THE TWITTER FILES."

214 Taibbi "1. Thread: THE TWITTER FILES."

215 Tim Murtaugh, "Media's Suppression of Hunter Biden's Laptop Was Election

Interference," *Washington Times*, March 24, 2022, https://www.washingtontimes.com/news/2022/mar/24/medias-suppression-of-hunter-laptop-was-election-i.

216   Ella Lee, "State Department Cancels Facebook Meetings after Court Order: Report," *The Hill*, July 6, 2023, https://thehill.com/regulation/court-battles/4083426-state-department-cancels-facebook-meetings-after-court-order-report.

217   Andrew Chapados, "Secret Reports Show Homeland Security Worked with Universities to 'Censor Americans' Online Speech' before 2020 Election," Blaze Media, November 7, 2023, https://www.theblaze.com/news/dhs-stanford-disinformation-campaign-bigtech.

218   Victor Nava, "Amazon 'Censored' COVID-19 Vaccine Books after 'Feeling Pressure' from Biden White House: Docs," *New York Post*, February 5, 2024, https://nypost.com/2024/02/05/news/amazon-censored-covid-19-vaccine-books-after-feeling-pressure-from-biden-white-house-docs.

219   Nava, "Amazon 'Censored' COVID-19 Vaccine Books."

220   Tristan Harris, "How a Handful of Tech Companies Control Billions of Minds Every Day," user @TED, YouTube, July 28, 2017, https://www.youtube.com/watch?v=C74amJRp730.

221   Harris, "How a Handful of Tech Companies Control Billions of Minds Every Day."

222   Tristan Harris, testimony before the Subcommittee on Consumer Protection and Commerce of the Committee on Energy and Commerce, U.S. House of Representatives, January 8, 2020, available on YouTube, https://www.youtube.com/watch?v=gDL9z_lof3Q.

223   Harris, "How a Handful of Tech Companies Control Billions of Minds Every Day."

224   Shirin Ali, "Facebook's Formula Prioritized Anger and Ended Up Spreading Misinformation," *The Hill*, October 27, 2021, https://thehill.com/changing-america/enrichment/arts-culture/578724-5-points-for-anger-1-for-a-like-how-facebooks.

225   See Ari Levy, "The Most Liberal and Conservative Tech Companies, Ranked by Employees' Political Donations," CNBC, July 2, 2020, https://www.cnbc.com/2020/07/02/most-liberal-tech-companies-ranked-by-employee-donations.html.

226   See Jacqueline Zote, "How the Facebook Algorithm Works and Ways Our Brand Can Outsmart It," Sprout Social, November 9, 2022, https://sproutsocial.com/insights/facebook-algorithm.

227   See Alexander S. Gillis, "Algorithm," Tech Target, accessed July 12, 2024, https://www.techtarget.com/whatis/definition/algorithm.

228   See Brian Dean, "TikTok Statistics You Need to Know," BackLinko, February 15, 2024, https://backlinko.com/tiktok-users.

229   See Deborah D'Souza, "TikTok: What It Is, How It Works, and Why It's Popular," *Investopedia*, February 15, 2024, https://www.investopedia.com/what-is-tiktok-4588933.

230   WSJ Staff, "Inside TikTok's Algorithm: A WSJ Video Investigation," *Wall Street Journal*, July 21, 2021, https://www.wsj.com/articles/tiktok-algorithm-video-

investigation-11626877477.

231 See WSJ Staff. "Inside TikTok's Algorithm."

232 Sapna Masheshwari, "Videos about Bin Laden's Criticism of U.S. Surge in Popularity on TikTok," *New York Times*, November 16, 2023, https://www.nytimes.com/2023/11/16/technology/videos-bin-laden-letter-tiktok.html.

233 See "The World's Most Valuable Resource Is No Longer Oil, but Data," *Economist*, May 6, 2017, https://www.economist.com/leaders/2017/05/06/the-worlds-most-valuable-resource-is-no-longer-oil-but-data.

234 See WSJ Staff, "Inside TikTok's Algorithm."

235 "U.S. Spy Chief 'Cannot Rule Out' That China Would Use TikTok to Influence U.S. elections," CNBC, March 12, 2024, https://www.cnbc.com/2024/03/13/us-spy-chief-cannot-rule-out-that-china-would-use-tiktok-to-influence-us-elections.html.

236 "Privacy Policy," TikTok, accessed April 8, 2024, https://www.tiktok.com/legal/page/us/privacy-policy/en.

237 Zen Soo, "Former ByteDance Executive Says Chinese Communist Party Tracked Hong Kong Protestors Via Data," AP News, June 7, 2023, https://apnews.com/article/tiktok-china-bytedance-user-data-d257d98125f69ac80f983e6067a84911.

238 Brian Fung, "Analysis: There Is Now Some Public Evidence That China Viewed TikTok Data," CNN, June 8, 2023, https://www.cnn.com/2023/06/08/tech/tiktok-data-china/index.html.

239 Fung, "Analysis."

240 See Haleluya Hadero, "Why TikTok Is Being Banned on Gov't Phones in US and Beyond," AP News, February 28, 2023, https://apnews.com/article/why-is-tiktok-being-banned-7d2de01d3ac5ab2b8ec2239dc7f2b20d.

241 Michelle Gallardo, "TikTok Ban Update: Bill in Senate Could Affect Local Businesses Promoting on Social Media," ABC 7 News (Chicago), March 26, 2024, https://abc7chicago.com/tiktok-ban-update-shop-xo-marshmallow-account/14573843.

242 Glenn Beck and Justin Haskins, *Dark Future: Uncovering the Great Reset's Terrifying Next Phase* (Nashville: Mercury Ink, 2023).

243 See "Yuval Noah Harari," World Economic Forum, last accessed July 12, 2024, https://www.weforum.org/people/yuval-noah-harari.

244 Nate Hopper, "How Humankind Could Become Totally Useless," *Time*, February 16, 2017, https://time.com/4672373/yuval-noah-harari-homo-deus-interview.

245 See "Audience Ad Targeting," Facebook, last accessed July 12, 2024, https://www.facebook.com/business/ads/ad-targeting.

246 See Stacey McLachlan, "85+ Important Social Media Advertising Statistics to Know," *Hootsuite* (blog), April 6, 2023, https://blog.hootsuite.com/social-media-advertising-stats.

247 See Charlie Campbell, "How China Is Using 'Social Credit Scores' to Reward and Punish Its Citizens," *Time*, https://time.com/collection/davos-2019/5502592/china-social-credit-score/.

248 "The Global Risks Report 2019," World Economic Forum, https://www3.weforum.org/docs/WEF_Global_Risks_Report_2019.pdf.

249   See "Introducing ChatGPT," OpenAI, November 30, 2022, https://openai.com/blog/chatgpt.

250   Amanda Hetler, "ChatGPT," *Tech Target*, last accessed April 8, 2024, https://www.techtarget.com/whatis/definition/ChatGPT.

251   See Tobias Knecht, "A Brief History of Bots and How They've Shaped the Internet Today," Abusix, May 4, 2021, https://abusix.com/blog/uncategorised/a-brief-history-of-bots-and-how-theyve-shaped-the-internet-today.

252   See "Musk Countersuit Accuses Twitter of Fraud over 'Bot' Count," AP News, August 5, 2022, https://apnews.com/article/elon-musk-twitter-inc-technology-933f52cf58fea145e71f1112563951d4.

253   Assaf Dar, "We Checked Elon Musk's Claims about Twitter Bots; Here's What We Found," *CPO Magazine*, December 7, 2022, https://www.cpomagazine.com/cyber-security/we-checked-elon-musks-claims-about-twitter-bots-heres-what-we-found.

254   Dar, "We Checked Elon Musk's Claims."

255   Marek N. Posard, "Elon Musk May Have a Point about Bots on Twitter," RAND, September 23, 2022, https://www.rand.org/pubs/commentary/2022/09/elon-musk-may-have-a-point-about-bots-on-twitter.html.

256   "2023 Imperva Bad Bot Report," Imperva, last accessed April 8, 2024, https://www.imperva.com/resources/resource-library/reports/2023-imperva-bad-bot-report/.

257   Anthony Cuthbertson, "Nearly Half of All Internet Traffic Is Now Bots, Study Reveals," *Independent* (UK), May 15, 2023, https://www.independent.co.uk/tech/internet-bots-web-traffic-imperva-b2339153.html.

258   Tushar Richabadas, "Threat Spotlight: How Bad Bot Traffic Is Changing," Barracuda, October 18, 2023, https://blog.barracuda.com/2023/10/18/threat-spotlight-bad-bot-traffic-changing.

259   Dani Di Placido, "The Dead Internet Theory, Explained," *Forbes*, January 16, 2024, https://www.forbes.com/sites/danidiplacido/2024/01/16/the-dead-internet-theory-explained/?sh=2d8096b057c2.

260   Yoshija Walter, "Artificial Influencers and the Dead Internet Theory," Springer Link, February 5, 2024, https://link.springer.com/article/10.1007/s00146-023-01857-0.

261   Walter, "Artificial Influencers and the Dead Internet Theory."

262   David Bauder, "Sports Illustrated Found Publishing AI Generated Stories, Photos and Authors," *PBS News Hour*, November 29, 2023, https://www.pbs.org/newshour/economy/sports-illustrated-found-publishing-ai-generated-stories-photos-and-authors.

263   Bill McCarthy and Anuj Chopra, "Proliferating 'News' Sites Spew AI-Generated Fakes Stories," Yahoo News, March 10, 2024, https://www.yahoo.com/news/proliferating-news-sites-spew-ai-012349209.html.

264   McKenzie Sadeghi et al., "Tracking AI-Enabled Misinformation: 794 'Unreliable AI-Generated News' Websites (and Counting), Plus the Top False Narratives Generated by Artificial Intelligence Tools," NewsGuard, last updated July 12, 2024, https://www.newsguardtech.com/special-reports/ai-tracking-center.

265   See Sabrina Ortiz, "The best AI Image Generators to Try Right Now," ZDNet,

February 5, 2024, https://www.zdnet.com/article/best-ai-image-generator.

266 Miles Klee and Nikki MCann Ramirez, "AI Has Made the Israel-Hamas Misinformation Epidemic Much, Much Worse," *Rolling Stone*, October 27, 2023, https://www.rollingstone.com/politics/politics-features/israel-hamas-misinformation-fueled-ai-images-1234863586.

267 David Klepper, "Fake Babies, Real Horror: Deepfakes from the Gaza War Increase Fears about AI's Power to Mislead," AP News, November 28, 2023, https://apnews.com/article/artificial-intelligence-hamas-israel-misinformation-ai-gaza-a1bb303b637ffbbb9cbc3aa1e000db47.

268 See "Creating Video from Text," OpenAI, last accessed April 8, 2024, https://openai.com/sora.

269 Justinas Vainilavicius, "YouTube Scam Features Fake Jennifer Aniston," *Cyber News*, January 25, 2024, https://cybernews.com/news/youtube-scam-features-fake-jennifer-aniston.

270 See Charles Bethea, "The Terrifying A.I. Scam That Ues Your Loved One's Voice," *New Yorker*, newyorker.com, March 7, 2024, https://www.newyorker.com/science/annals-of-artificial-intelligence/the-terrifying-ai-scam-that-uses-your-loved-ones-voice.

271 Chris Stokel-Walker, "TV Channels Are Using AI-Generated Presenters to Read the News. The Question Is, Will We Trust Them?" BBC, January 26, 2024, https://www.bbc.com/future/article/20240126-ai-news-anchors-why-audiences-might-find-digitally-generated-tv-presenters-hard-to-trust.

5. The ~~Will~~ Control of the People: Elections in the Era of Misinformation

272 Kenneth Vogel and David Stern, "Ukrainian Efforts to Sabotage Trump Backfire," *Politico*, January 11, 2017, https://www.politico.com/story/2017/01/ukraine-sabotage-trump-backfire-233446.

273 Vogel and Stern, "Ukrainian Efforts to Sabotage Trump Backfire."

274 Vogel and Stern, "Ukrainian Efforts to Sabotage Trump Backfire."

275 Vogel and Stern, "Ukrainian Efforts to Sabotage Trump Backfire."

276 Vogel and Stern, "Ukrainian Efforts to Sabotage Trump Backfire."

277 Vogel and Stern, "Ukrainian Efforts to Sabotage Trump Backfire."

278 See Aaron Blake, Philip Bump, and Irfan Uraizee, "The Full Trump-Ukraine Impeachment Timeline," *Washington Post*, last updated January 27, 2020, https://www.washingtonpost.com/graphics/2019/politics/trump-impeachment-timeline.

279 See Natasha Bertrand, "Senate Panel Look into Ukraine Interference Comes Up Short," *Politico*, December 2, 2019, https://www.politico.com/news/2019/12/02/senate-panel-ukraine-election-interference-074796.

280 Bertrand, "Senate Panel Look into Ukraine Interference Comes Up Short."

281 For a good quick summary of the alleged corruption of the Biden family, see Tristan Justice, "There Is More Evidence to Impeach Biden over Ukraine Than There Ever Was for Trump," *Federalist*, July 24, 2023, https://thefederalist.com/2023/07/24/there-is-more-evidence-to-impeach-biden-over-ukraine-than-there-ever-was-for-trump.

282 Greg Palast, "Florida's 'Disappeared Voters': Disfranchised by the GOP," *The*

Nation, February 5, 2001, https://www.thenation.com/article/archive/floridas-disappeared-voters-disfranchised-gop.

283   See "Democrats Challenge Certification of Florida Bush-Gore Election Results," CNN, November 16, 2000, https://www.cnn.com/2000/LAW/11/16/certification.update.02.pol/index.html.

284   Vincent Bugliosi, "None Dare Call It Treason," *The Nation*, January 18, 2001, https://www.thenation.com/article/archive/none-dare-call-it-treason.

285   Colby Itkowitz, "Hillary Clinton: Trump Is an 'Illegitimate President,'" *Washington Post*, September 26, 2019, https://www.washingtonpost.com/politics/hillary-clinton-trump-is-an-illegitimate-president/2019/09/26/29195d5a-e099-11e9-b199-f638bf2c340f_story.html.

286   Itkowitz, "Hillary Clinton."

287   Jordan Boyd, "Election Watchdog Fines Clinton Campaign for Lying about Steele Dossier in Finance Filings," *Federalist*, March 30, 2022, https://thefederalist.com/2022/03/30/election-watchdog-fines-clinton-campaign-for-lying-about-steele-dossier-in-finance-filings.

288   See Tristan Justice, "Newly Declassified Documents Reinforce Corruption of Steele Dossier, FISA Warrants," *Federalist*, July 18, 2020, https://thefederalist.com/2020/07/18/newly-declassified-documents-reinforce-corruption-of-steele-dossier-fisa-warrants.

289   Boyd, "Election Watchdog Fines Clinton Campaign for Lying about Steele Dossier in Finance Filings."

290   See Elaine Kamarck et al., "Voting by Mail in a Pandemic: A state-by-state Scorecard," Brookings Institute, last updated November 3, 2020, https://www.brookings.edu/articles/voting-by-mail-in-a-pandemic-a-state-by-state-scorecard.

291   Axel Hufford, "Ballot Drop Boxes in the 2020 Elections," Healthy Elections Project, Standord University-MIT, March 10, 2021, https://web.mit.edu/healthyelections/www/final-reports/ballot-drop-boxes.html.

292   Beth LeBlanc, "Judge Rules Benson's Ballot Signature Verification Guidance 'Invalid,'" *Detroit News*, March 15, 2021, https://www.detroitnews.com/story/news/politics/2021/03/15/judge-rules-secretary-state-bensons-ballot-signature-verification-guidance-invalid/4699927001.

293   Hannah Hartig, "Republican Gains in 2022 Midterms Driven Mostly by Turnout Advantage," Pew Research Center, July 12, 2023, https://www.pewresearch.org/politics/2023/07/12/voter-turnout-2018-2022.

294   Sophie Lewis, "Joe Biden Breaks Obama's Record for Most Votes Ever Cast for a U.S. presidential candidate," CBS News, last updated December 7, 2020, https://www.cbsnews.com/news/joe-biden-popular-vote-record-barack-obama-us-presidential-election-donald-trump.

295   "Presidential Election Results: Biden Wins," *New York Times*, November 3, 2020, https://www.nytimes.com/interactive/2020/11/03/us/elections/results-president.html.

296   I use the word "likely" here because there would have been a tie in the Electoral College under this scenario. That means state delegations in the U.S. House of Representatives would have decided the outcome of the race. Because Republicans controlled a strong majority of state delegations, it's "likely" that Trump, a

Republican, would have been named president under this scenario.

297   "Presidential Election Results: Biden Wins."

298   See, for example, Stefan Becket et al., "2020 Election 'Most Secure in History,'
       Security Officials Say," CBS News, updated November 13, 2020, https://www.
       cbsnews.com/live-updates/2020-election-most-secure-history-dhs.

299   Becket "2020 Election 'Most Secure in History,' Security Officials Say."

300   Jen Kirby, "Trump's Own Officials Say 2020 Was America's Most
       Secure Election in History," Vox, November 13, 2020, https://www.vox.
       com/2020/11/13/21563825/2020-elections-most-secure-dhs-cisa-krebs.

301   Alyza Sebenius and Bloomberg, "The 2020 Election Was the 'Most Secure
       in American History,'" Fortune, November 13, 2020, https://fortune.
       com/2020/11/13/the-2020-election-was-the-most-secure-in-american-history.

302   Paul LeBlanc and Alex Marquardt, "Election Officials, Including Federal Govern-
       ment, Contradict Trump's Voter-Fraud Conspiracy Theories," CNN, updated
       November 13, 2020, https://www.cnn.com/2020/11/12/politics/2020-
       election-trump-voter-conspiracies/index.html.

303   "Joint Statement from Elections Infrastructure Government Coordinating
       Council & the Election Infrastructure Sector Coordinating Executive Commit-
       tees," Cybersecurity and Infrastructure Security Agency, U.S. Department of
       Homeland Security, November 12, 2020, https://www.cisa.gov/news-events/
       news/joint-statement-elections-infrastructure-government-coordinating-
       council-election.

304   "Joint Statement from Elections Infrastructure Government Coordinating
       Council & the Election Infrastructure Sector Coordinating Executive Commit-
       tees."

305   See Jack McPherrin et al., Who Really Won the 2020 Election?: Measuring the
       Effect of Mail-in Ballot Fraud in the Trump-Biden Race for the White House,
       Heartland Institute, February 24, 2024, https://heartland.org/wp-content/
       uploads/2024/02/Feb-24-2020-Election-Analysis-vWeb_Final.pdf.

306   Justin Haskins, "Mail-in Voter Fraud Was Rampant in 2020: Here's How to
       Stop It in Future Elections," Heartland Institute, February 9, 2024, https://
       heartland.org/publications/mail-in-voter-fraud-was-rampant-in-2020-heres-
       how-to-stop-it-in-future-elections.

307   Haskins, "Mail-in Voter Fraud Was Rampant in 2020."

308   McPherrin et al., Who Really Won the 2020 Election?

309   McPherrin et al., Who Really Won the 2020 Election?

310   McPherrin et al., Who Really Won the 2020 Election?

311   McPherrin et al., Who Really Won the 2020 Election?

312   See Miranda Devine, Laptop from Hell: Hunter Biden, Big Tech, and the Dirty
       Secrets the President Tried to Hide (New York: Post Hill, 2021).

313   "Election Integrity: 54% Say Not Enough Done to Prevent Cheating,"
       Rasmussen Reports, February 23, 2024, https://www.rasmussenreports.com/
       public_content/politics/biden_administration/election_integrity_54_say_not_
       enough_done_to_prevent_cheating.

314   Alex Seitz-Wald and Mike Memoli, "Fake Joe Biden Robocall Tells New
       Hampshire Democrats Not to Vote Tuesday," NBC News, January 22, 2024,

https://www.nbcnews.com/politics/2024-election/fake-joe-biden-robocall-tells-new-hampshire-democrats-not-vote-tuesday-rcna134984.

315 Seitz-Wald and Memoli, "Fake Joe Biden Robocall Tells New Hampshire Democrats Not to Vote Tuesday."

316 Seitz-Wald and Memoli, "Fake Joe Biden Robocall Tells New Hampshire Democrats Not to Vote Tuesday."

317 Brendan Rascius, "2024 New Hampshire Primary Has a Twist—It Doesn't Matter for Democrats. Wait, What?," *Miami Herald*, https://www.miamiherald.com/news/nation-world/national/article284290148.html#storylink=cpy.

318 "Presidential Election Results: Biden Wins."

319 Megan Hickey, "Vallas Campaign Condemns Deepfake Video Posted to Twitter," CBS Chicago, February 27, 2023, https://www.cbsnews.com/chicago/news/vallas-campaign-deepfake-video.

320 Hickey, "Vallas Campaign Condemns Deepfake Video Posted to Twitter."

321 Hickey, "Vallas Campaign Condemns Deepfake Video Posted to Twitter."

322 Hickey, "Vallas Campaign Condemns Deepfake Video Posted to Twitter."

323 "Mayoral Election in Chicago, Illinois (2023)," Ballotpedia, accessed March 20, 2024, https://ballotpedia.org/Mayoral_election_in_Chicago,_Illinois_(2023).

324 Morgan Meaker, "Slovakia's Election Deepfakes Show AI Is a Danger to Democracy," *Wired*, October 3, 2023, https://www.wired.com/story/slovakias-election-deepfakes-show-ai-is-a-danger-to-democracy.

325 Ali Swenson and Kelvin Chan, "Election Disinformation Takes a Big Leap with AI Being Used to Deceive Worldwide," Associated Press, updated March 14, 2024, https://apnews.com/article/artificial-intelligence-elections-disinformation-chatgpt-bc283e7426402f0b4baa7df280a4c3fd.

326 Swenson and Chan, "Election Disinformation Takes a Big Leap."

327 Robert McMillan, Alexa Corse, and Dustin Volz, "New Era of AI Deepfakes Complicates 2024 Elections," *Wall Street Journal*, updated February 15, 2024, https://www.wsj.com/tech/ai/new-era-of-ai-deepfakes-complicates-2024-elections-aa529b9e.

328 Isaac Stanley-Becker and Naomi Nix, "Fake Images of Trump Arrest Show 'Giant Step' for AI's Disruptive Power," *Washington Post*, March 22, 2023, https://www.washingtonpost.com/politics/2023/03/22/trump-arrest-deepfakes.

329 The following story on Yoon and its quotations are taken from Timothy Martin, "These Campaigns Hope 'Deepfake' Candidates Help Get Out the Vote," *Wall Street Journal*, March 8, 2022, https://www.wsj.com/articles/these-campaigns-hope-deepfake-candidates-help-get-out-the-vote-11646756345.

330 See Jack Holmes, "Joe Biden Talking about Kids Touching His Hairy Legs in a Swimming Pool Is Not Great Viewing," *Esquire*, December 2, 2019, https://www.esquire.com/news-politics/a30077381/joe-biden-hairy-legs-swimming-pool-story.

331 The following story is taken from "Imran Khan: Pakistan Ex-PM Used Artificial Intelligence to Campaign from Jail," BBC, December 18, 2023, https://www.bbc.com/news/world-asia-67752610.

332 Swenson and Chan, "Election Disinformation Takes a Big Leap with AI Being Used to Deceive Worldwide."

333 Taylor Penley, "Mark Ruffalo Blasts Musk's X for Allowing 'Disinformation' after Sharing AI fakes of Trump on Epstein Flight," Fox News, January
9, 2024, https://www.foxnews.com/media/mark-ruffalo-musk-x-allowing-
disinformation-sharing-ai-fakes-trump-epstein-flight.
334 Penley, "Mark Ruffalo Blasts Musk's X for Allowing 'Disinformation.'"
335 Penley, "Mark Ruffalo Blasts Musk's X for Allowing 'Disinformation.'"
336 Penley, "Mark Ruffalo Blasts Musk's X for Allowing 'Disinformation.'"
337 Steve Contorno and Donie O'Sullivan, "DeSantis Campaign Posts Fake Images
of Trump Hugging Fauci in Social Media Video," CNN, updated June 8, 2023,
https://www.cnn.com/2023/06/08/politics/desantis-campaign-video-fake-ai-
image/index.html.
338 Contorno and O'Sullivan, "DeSantis Campaign Posts Fake Images."
339 Stanley-Becker and Nix, "Fake Images of Trump Arrest Show 'Giant Step' for
AI's Disruptive Power."
340 See @EliotHiggins post, originally posted March 20, 2023, last viewed March 21,
2024, https://www.washingtonpost.com/politics/2023/03/22/trump-arrest-
deepfakes.
341 The following story and quotations are taken from Dan De Luce and Kevin
Collier, "Experts War-Gamed What Might Happen If Deepfakes Disrupt the
2024 Election. Things Went Sideways Fast," NBC News, March 16, 2024,
https://www.nbcnews.com/politics/2024-election/war-game-deepfakes-
disrupt-2024-election-rcna143038.
342 Miles Taylor, "I Am Part of the Resistance Inside the Trump Administration,"
New York Times, September 5, 2018, https://www.nytimes.com/2018/09/05/
opinion/trump-white-house-anonymous-resistance.html.
343 Taylor, "I Am Part of the Resistance Inside the Trump Administration."
344 De Luce and Collier, "Experts War-Gamed What Might Happen If Deepfakes
Disrupt the 2024 Election."
345 "About Us: Issue One Is the Leading Crosspartisan Political Reform Group in
Washington, D.C.," Issue One, accessed March 21, 2024, https://issueone.org/
about-us.
346 De Luce and Collier, "Experts War-Gamed What Might Happen If Deepfakes
Disrupt the 2024 Election."
347 De Luce and Collier.
348 De Luce and Collier.
349 The information and quotations in the remainder of this chapter are taken from
Ellissa Cavaciuti-Wishart et al., "Global Risks Report 2024," World Economic
Forum, January 2024, https://www3.weforum.org/docs/WEF_The_Global_
Risks_Report_2024.pdf.

6. Propaganda Wars: Protecting America from Foreign Manipulation

350 "The Deadly Virus: The Influenza Epidemic of 1918," U.S. National Archives
and Records Administration, accessed March 25, 2024, https://www.archives.
gov/exhibits/influenza-epidemic.
351 "Research Starters: Worldwide Deaths in World War II," National World War
II Museum, last accessed March 25, 2024, https://www.nationalww2museum.

org/students-teachers/student-resources/research-starters/research-starters-worldwide-deaths-world-war.

352 Katherine Waite, "Airborne Propaganda: The Battle for Hearts and Minds," British Online Archives, January 20, 2022, https://microform.digital/boa/posts/category/articles/436/airborne-propaganda-the-battle-for-hearts-and-minds.

353 "Airborne Leaflet Propaganda," Naval Air Station Fort Lauderdale Museum, September 20, 2012, http://blog.nasflmuseum.com/events-blog/airborne-leaflet-propaganda; Waite, "Airborne Propaganda.

354 James Erdmann, "The Monroe Leaflet Bomb: Its Evolution and Significance," *Air Power Historian* 8, no, 2 (April 1962), https://www.jstor.org/stable/44512713.

355 *Russian Active Measures Campaigns and Interference in the 2016 U.S. Election, vol. 2:37, Russia's Use of Social Media with Additional Views* report of the U.S. Senate Select Committee on Intelligence, 116th Congress, October 8, 2019, https://www.intelligence.senate.gov/sites/default/files/documents/Report_Volume2.pdf; "Inside Russia's Notorious 'Internet Research Agency' Troll Farm," Spyscape Museum, accessed March 25, 2024, https://spyscape.com/article/inside-the-troll-factory-russias-internet-research-agency.

356 Adrian Chen, "The Agency," *New York Times Magazine*, June 2, 2015, https://www.nytimes.com/2015/06/07/magazine/the-agency.html.

357 Max Seddon, "Documents Show How Russia's Troll Army Hit America," *BuzzFeed News*, June 2, 2014, https://www.buzzfeednews.com/article/maxseddon/documents-show-how-russias-troll-army-hit-america.

358 *Russian Active Measures Campaigns and Interference*, 2:03.

359 *Russian Active Measures Campaigns and Interference*, 2:03.

360 *Russian Active Measures Campaigns and Interference*, 2:53.

361 *Russian Active Measures Campaigns and Interference*, 2:06.

362 Seddon, "Documents Show How Russia's Troll Army Hit America."

363 *Russian Active Measures Campaigns and Interference*.

364 Chen, "The Agency."

365 *Russian Active Measures Campaigns and Interference*.

366 *Russian Active Measures Campaigns and Interference*.

367 See Andy Greenberg and Andrew Couts, "Security News This Week: Russia's Notorious Troll Farm Disbands," *Wired*, July 8, 2023, https://www.wired.com/story/russia-internet-research-agency-disbands.

368 The following information on Yevgeny Prigozhin is from the Associated Press, "Wagner Mercenary Leader, Russian Mutineer, 'Putin's Chef': The Many Sides of Yevgeny Prigozhin," AP World News, August 23, 2023, https://apnews.com/article/russia-wagner-prigozhin-jet-crash-05cf962c8a218a685434b2f8a83297cd.

369 Greenberg and Couts, "Security News This Week."

370 Steven Myers, "Spate of Mock News Sites with Russian Ties Pop Up in U.S.," *New York Times*, March 7, 2024, https://www.nytimes.com/2024/03/07/business/media/russia-us-news-sites.html.

371 Myers, "Spate of Mock News Sites with Russian Ties Pop Up in U.S."

372 Myers, "Spate of Mock News Sites with Russian Ties Pop Up in U.S."

373 Myers, "Spate of Mock News Sites with Russian Ties Pop Up in U.S."

374 Chen, "The Agency."

375 Mara Hvistendahl et al., "A Global Web of Chinese Propaganda Leads to a
     U.S. Tech Mogul," *New York Times*, last updated August 10, 2023, https://
     www.nytimes.com/2023/08/05/world/europe/neville-roy-singham-china-
     propaganda.html.

376 See February 19, 2021, post on Jodie Evans's Facebook page, https://www.
     facebook.com/MsJodieEvans/posts/d41d8cd9/3896379447088392.

377 Hvistendahl et al., "A Global Web of Chinese Propaganda Leads to a U.S. Tech
     Mogul."

378 See Daniel Libit, "Code PINK CHANGES ITS HUE," *Politico*, April 2, 2009,
     https://www.politico.com/story/2009/04/code-pink-changes-its-hue-020774.

379 See Francesca Block, "Meet the American Millionaire Marxists Funding
     Anti-Israel Rallies," *New York Post*, November 16, 2023, https://nypost.
     com/2023/11/16/opinion/meet-the-american-millionaire-marxists-funding-
     anti-israel-rallies.

380 The remainder of the information and quotations in this subsection are taken
     from Hvistendahl et al., "A Global Web of Chinese Propaganda Leads to a U.S.
     Tech Mogul."

381 "The True Death Toll of COVID-19," World Health Organization, accessed
     March 28, 2024, https://www.who.int/data/stories/the-true-death-toll-of-
     covid-19-estimating-global-excess-mortality.

382 For sources about China's COVID-19 cover-up, see the numerous sources
     available at "The Chinese Communist Party's Coronavirus Cover-up," U.S. House
     Foreign Affairs Committee Republicans, last accessed March 28, 2024, https://
     foreignaffairs.house.gov/chinas-coronavirus-cover-up/#. See also *The Origins
     of the COVID-19 Global Pandemic, Including the Roles of the Chinese Communist
     Party and the World Health Organization*, U.S. House Foreign Affairs Committee
     minority staff report, September 21, 2020, https://foreignaffairs.house.gov/
     wp-content/uploads/2020/09/159a63d0-fc6f-11ea-9a73-a0369f35f6fa.
     pdf; Warren Strobel, "Chinese Lab Mapped Deadly Coronavirus Two Weeks
     Before Beijing Told the World, Documents Show," *Wall Street Journal*, updated
     January 17, 2024, https://www.wsj.com/world/china/chinese-lab-mapped-
     deadly-coronavirus-two-weeks-before-beijing-told-the-world-documents-show-
     9bca8865/.

383 See Paul Sacca, "Esteemed Molecular Biologist Warns of 'Smoking Gun'
     Evidence COVID-19 Was Engineered by Researchers at Chinese Lab," Blaze
     Media, March 3, 2024, https://www.theblaze.com/news/covid-engineered-
     researchers-chinese-lab-wuhan.

384 Glenn Beck and Justin Haskins, *The Great Reset: Joe Biden and the Rise of Twenty-
     First-Century Fascism* (Nashville: Mercury Ink, 2022).

385 Louisa Lim, Julia Bergin, and Johan Lidberg, "The COVID-19 Story: Unmasking
     China's Global Strategy," International Federation of Journalists, May 2021,
     https://www.ifj.org/fileadmin/user_upload/IFJ_-_The_Covid_Story_Report.pdf.

386 Lim, Bergin, and Lidberg, "The COVID-19 Story."

387 Lim, Bergin, and Lidberg, "The COVID-19 Story."

388 Lim, Bergin, and Lidberg, "The COVID-19 Story."

389 Lim, Bergin, and Lidberg, "The COVID-19 Story."

390   Lim, Bergin, and Lidberg, "The COVID-19 Story."

391   "Cat Mouse: How China Makes Sure Its Internet Abides by the Rules," *Economist*, April 6, 2013, https://www.economist.com/special-report/2013/04/06/cat-and-mouse.

392   Paul Mozur et al., "How Beijing Influences the Influencers," *New York Times*, December 13, 2021, https://www.nytimes.com/interactive/2021/12/13/technology/china-propaganda-youtube-influencers.html.

393   Mozur et al., "How Beijing Influences the Influencers."

394   Mozur et al., "How Beijing Influences the Influencers."

395   Mozur et al., "How Beijing Influences the Influencers."

396   Mozur et al., "How Beijing Influences the Influencers."

397   "Who Are the Uyghurs and Why Is China Being Accused of Genocide?" BBC News, May 24, 2022, https://www.bbc.com/news/world-asia-china-22278037.

398   Mozur et al., "How Beijing Influences the Influencers."

399   See "New York Times Statement about 1932 Pulitzer Prize Awarded to Walter Duranty," New York Times Company, accessed March 6, 2024, https://www.nytco.com/company/prizes-awards/new-york-times-statement-about-1932-pulitzer-prize-awarded-to-walter-duranty.

400   Minxin Pei, "China's Secret to Controlling the Internet," *Foreign Policy*, February 18, 2024, https://foreignpolicy.com/2024/02/18/china-internet-control-ccp-technology-cyber-surveillance-policy-sentinel-state.

401   Pei, "China's Secret to Controlling the Internet."

402   Pei, "China's Secret to Controlling the Internet."

403   Ellen Nakashima et al., "U.S. Government Concludes Iran Was Behind Threatening Emails Sent to Democrats," *Washington Post*, October 22, 2020, https://www.washingtonpost.com/technology/2020/10/20/proud-boys-emails-florida.

404   Nakashima et al., "U.S. Government Concludes Iran Was Behind Threatening Emails Sent to Democrats."

405   Nakashima et al., "U.S. government Concludes Iran Was Behind Threatening Emails Sent to Democrats."

406   Microsoft Threat Intelligence, "Iran Surges Cyber-Enabled Influence Operations in Support of Hamas," Microsoft, February 7, 2024, https://www.microsoft.com/en-us/security/business/security-insider/reports/iran-surges-cyber-enabled-influence-operations-in-support-of-hamas.

407   Microsoft Threat Intelligence, "Iran Surges Cyber-Enabled Influence Operations in Support of Hamas."

408   Microsoft Threat Intelligence, "Iran Surges Cyber-Enabled Influence Operations in Support of Hamas."

409   Tae-jun Kang, "North Korea's Influence Operations, Revealed," *Diplomat*, July 25, 2018, https://thediplomat.com/2018/07/north-koreas-influence-operations-revealed.

410   Kang, "North Korea's Influence Operations, Revealed."

411   Reha Kansara and Rachelle Krygier, "Venezuela: 'I'm paid to tweet state propaganda,'" BBC, May 25, 2023, https://www.bbc.com/news/blogs-trending-65622685.

412   "Saudi Arabia: Alarming Crackdown on Online Expression," Amnesty Interna-

tional, February 14, 2023, https://www.amnesty.org/en/latest/news/2023/02/saudi-arabia-alarming-crackdown-on-online-expression.

413 "Saudi Arabia: Alarming Crackdown on Online Expression."

414 Barton Gellman, "Edward Snowden, after Months of NSA Revelations, Says His Mission's Accomplished," *Washington Post*, December 23, 2013, https://www.washingtonpost.com/world/national-security/edward-snowden-after-months-of-nsa-revelations-says-his-missions-accomplished/2013/12/23/49fc36de-6c1c-11e3-a523-fe73f0ff6b8d_story.html.

415 Julian Borger, "NSA Files: What's a Little Spying between Old Friends?" *Guardian* (UK), December 2, 2013, https://www.theguardian.com/world/2013/dec/02/nsa-files-spying-allies-enemies-five-eyes-g8.

416 Borger, "NSA Files."

417 Liat Clark, "Take a Look Inside GCHQ's Manipulation Toolkit," *Wired*, July 15, 2014, https://www.wired.com/story/gchq-social-media-tools; see also Glenn Greenwald and Andrew Fishman, "Controversial GCHQ Unit Engaged in Domestic Law Enforcement, Online Propaganda, Psychology Research," The Intercept, June 22, 2015, https://theintercept.com/2015/06/22/controversial-gchq-unit-domestic-law-enforcement-propaganda.

418 Laurie Clarke, "Twitter Needs to Start Exposing the UK's Murky Online Propaganda," October 8, 2019, *Wired*, https://www.wired.com/story/uk-disinformation-twitter-facebook.

419 Telegraph Reporters, "Army's 'Information Warfare' Unit Monitored Covid Lockdown Critics," *Telegraph* (UK), January 29, 2023, https://www.Telegraph.co.uk/news/2023/01/29/armys-information-warfare-unit-monitored-covid-lockdown-critics.

420 Telegraph Reporters, "Army's 'Information Warfare' Unit Monitored Covid Lockdown Critics."

421 Nick Fielding and Ian Cobain, "Revealed: US Spy Operation That Manipulates Social Media," *Guardian* (UK), March 17, 2011, https://www.theguardian.com/technology/2011/mar/17/us-spy-operation-social-networks.

422 Fielding and Cobain, "Revealed."

423 Fielding and Cobain, "Revealed."

7. The Truth Is Sacred

424 See "Boston Massacre," U.S. National Park Service, accessed April 1, 2024, https://www.nps.gov/articles/000/boston-massacre.htm#:~:text=Boston%20National%20Historical%20Park,and%20angering%20an%20entire%20colony.

425 See "Who Were the Sons of Liberty?" American Battlefield Trust, accessed April 1, 2024, https://www.battlefields.org/learn/articles/who-were-sons-liberty.

426 "Boston Massacre."

427 See "Perspectives on the Boston Massacre," Massachusetts Historical Society, accessed April 1, 2024, https://www.masshist.org/features/massacre/visual.

428 "Boston Massacre."

429 "Boston Massacre."

430 "John Adams and the Boston Massacre Trials," *BRIA* (*Bill of Rights in Action*) 16, no. 1 (Winter 1999), Teach Democracy, https://teachdemocracy.org/bill-of-

rights-in-action/bria-16-1-a-john-adams-and-the-boston-massacre-trials.

431   See Christopher Klein, "Why John Adams Defended British Soldiers in the Boston Massacre Trials," History Channel, https://www.history.com/news/boston-massacre-trial-john-adams-dan-abrams.

432   "Boston Massacre."

433   "What Happened at the Boston Massacre?" Jamestown Settlement Museum and American Revolution Museum at Yorktown, accessed April 1, 2024, https://www.jyfmuseums.org/learn/teacher-resources-programs/classroom-resources/the-boston-massacre.

434   "John Adams and the Boston Massacre Trials."

435   "What Happened at the Boston Massacre?"

436   NCC Staff, "On This Day, the Boston Massacre Lights the Fuse of Revolution," National Constitution Center, March 5, 2024, https://constitutioncenter.org/blog/on-this-day-the-boston-massacre-lights-the-fuse-of-revolution.

437   From the diary of John Adams, written on the three-year anniversary of the Boston Massacre, "1773. March 5th. Fryday.," *Founders Online*, National Archives, https://founders.archives.gov/documents/Adams/01-02-02-0003-0002-0002. (Original source: *The Adams Papers: Diary and Autobiography of John Adams, vol. 2, 1771–1781*, ed. L. H. Butterfield [Cambridge, MA: Harvard University Press, 1961], 79.)

438   For example, see Michael Graham, "Pro-BLM Politicians Struggle to Explain Pandemic Protest Hypocrisy," InsideSources, June 9, 2020, https://insidesources.com/pro-blm-politicians-struggle-to-explain-pandemic-protest-hypocrisy.

439   See Stephanie Kirchgaessner, "Revealed: Senate Investigation into Brett Kavanaugh Assault Claims Contained Serious Omissions," *Guardian* (UK), April 28, 2023, https://www.theguardian.com/us-news/2023/apr/28/brett-kavanaugh-investigation-omissions-senate-sexual-assault-claims; Rebecca Morin, "Kamala Harris on Kavanaugh Accuser: 'I Believe Her,'" *Politico*, September 18, 2018, https://www.politico.com/story/2018/09/18/kamala-harris-kavanaugh-accuser-827907.

440   See Seth McLaughlin, "Tara Reade, Joe Biden Accuser, Reinforces 'Creeper' Image," *Washington Times*, April 28, 2020, https://www.washingtontimes.com/news/2020/apr/28/tara-reade-joe-biden-accuser-reinforces-creeper-im.

441   George Barna, "American Worldview Inventory 2023: Release #3: How the Faith of Americans Has Shifted Since the Start of the Pandemic," Cultural Research Center at Arizona Christian University, April 20, 2023, https://www.arizonachristian.edu/wp-content/uploads/2023/04/CRC_AWVI2023_Release_03.pdf.

442   See, for example, "Daylight Saving Time vs Standard Time," AP-NORC at the University of Chicago, apnorc.org, poll conducted October 24–28, 2019, https://apnorc.org/projects/daylight-saving-time-vs-standard-time/?doing_wp_cron=1712171029.4792270660400390625000.

443   The articles that follow are taken from the Constitution of the Soviet Union (1977, Unamended), Government of the former Soviet Union, approved October 7, 1977, translated by the Novosti Press Agency, made available on Wikisource.org, https://en.wikisource.org/wiki/Constitution_of_the_Soviet_Union_(1977,_Unamended).

444   See, for example, Paul A. Goble, "Federalism and Human Rights in the Soviet
       Union," *Cornell International Law Journal* 23, no. 2, Article 10 (1990), https://
       core.ac.uk/download/pdf/80563151.pdf#:~:text=Violations%20found%20
       throughout%20the%20USSR%20through%20the,did%20not%20have%20
       to%20contend%20with%20Western.
445   Goble, "Federalism and Human Rights in the Soviet Union," 402–3.
446   Goble, 403.
447   R. J. Rummel, *Lethal Politics: Soviet Genocide and Mass Murder Since 1917*
       (Piscataway, NJ: Transaction, 1990), "Chapter 1: 61,911,000 Victims: Utopi-
       anism Empowered," Appendix 1.1, made available online by the University of
       Hawaii, accessed April 4, 2024, https://www.hawaii.edu/powerkills/USSR.
       *CHAP.1.HTM#:~:text=In%20sum%2C%20probably%20somewhere%20
       between,of%20this%20number%20is%2061%2C911%2C000.*
448   Rummel, *Lethal Politics*, appendix 1.1.
449   Constitution of the Soviet Union (1977).
450   Constitution of the Soviet Union.
451   Constitution of the Soviet Union, art. 66.
452   U.S. Declaration of Independence.
453   U.S. Const. amend. I.
454   U.S. Constitution, amends. II and III.
455   U.S. Constitution, amends. IV and V.
456   U.S. Constitution, amend. VI.
457   U.S. Constitution, amends. VII and VIII.
458   U.S. Constitution, amend. IX.
459   U.S. Constitution, amend. X.
460   See Michael Vaccari, "Review: Who Inspired the Founders of the United States?"
       America Magazine, americamagazine.com, August 20, 2021, https://www.
       americamagazine.org/arts-culture/2021/08/20/ricks-greeks-romans-founding-
       fathers-241223, citing Thomas E. Ricks, *First Principles: What America's Founders
       Learned from the Greeks and Romans and How That Shaped Our Country* (Harper
       Collins, 2020).
461   See George Barna, "American Worldview Inventory 2023: Release #3."
462   R. C. Sproul, "Cosmic Treason," Ligonier Ministries, May 1, 2008, https://www.
       ligonier.org/learn/articles/cosmic-treason.
463   See "First Continental Congress," George Washington Presidential Library at
       Mount Vernon, accessed July 15, 2024, https://www.mountvernon.org/library/
       digitalhistory/digital-encyclopedia/article/first-continental-congress/#:~:tex-
       t=The%20First%20Continental%20Congress%20convened,future%20under%20
       growing%20British%20aggression.
464   See "First Prayer of the Continental Congress, 1774," Office of the Chaplain, U.S.
       House of Representatives, accessed July 15, 2024, https://chaplain.house.gov/
       archive/continental.html#:~:text=Take%20them%2C%20therefore%2C%20
       Heavenly%20Father,unerring%20justice%2C%20sounding%20in%20their.
465   See "John Adams to Abigail Adams, 16 September, 1774," Founders Online,
       National Archives, https://founders.archives.gov/documents/Adams/04-01-02-
       0101; quoting *The Adams Papers, Adams Family Correspondence, vol. 1, December*

1761–May 1776, ed. Lyman H. Butterfield (Cambridge, MA: Harvard University Press, 1963), 156–57. Kevin Dellape, *America's First Chaplain: The Life and Times of the Reverend Jacob Duché* (Bethlehem, PA: Lehigh University Press, 2013).

466 "John Adams to Abigail Adams, 16 September, 1774."
467 "First Prayer of the Continental Congress, 1774," Office of the Chaplain, U.S. House of Representatives.
468 U.S. Declaration of Independence.